Incivility

Has anyone ever pushed in front of you in a queue? Stolen your parking space? Talked on their mobile phone during a film at the cinema? In our everyday lives we all encounter rude and inconsiderate people. This unique book provides the first ever systematic investigation of typical encounters with rudeness. Through a meticulous analysis of over 500 events, it maps out what people experience as rude, where and when this happens and what takes place in the exchange between the participants. The inquiry further charts the emotional and social consequences of rudeness and victimization, with the results challenging the widespread assumption that bad behaviour is toxic to community life. In conclusion the study draws upon its findings and surveys a range of strategies for reducing the level of incivility in everyday life, identifying some simple and innovative solutions. *Incivility* will appeal to criminologists, sociologists and scholars of urban studies.

PHILIP SMITH is Professor in the Department of Sociology, and Co-Director of the Yale Center for Cultural Sociology at Yale University.

TIMOTHY L. PHILLIPS is Senior Lecturer in the Department of Sociology at the University of Tasmania.

RYAN D. KING is Associate Professor in the Department of Sociology at the University at Albany, SUNY.

D1530126

Incivility

The Rude Stranger in Everyday Life

PHILIP SMITH

TIMOTHY L. PHILLIPS

RYAN D. KING

CAMBRIDGE UNIVERSITY PRESS
Cambridge, New York, Melbourne, Madrid, Cape Town, Singapore,
São Paulo, Delhi, Dubai, Tokyo, Mexico City

Cambridge University Press
The Edinburgh Building, Cambridge CB2 8RU, UK

Published in the United States of America by Cambridge University Press, New York

www.cambridge.org
Information on this title: www.cambridge.org/9780521719803

First published 2010
Reprinted 2011

Printed in the United Kingdom at the University Press, Cambridge

A catalogue record for this publication is available from the British Library

Library of Congress Cataloguing in Publication data
Smith, Philip (Philip Daniel), 1964–
  Incivility : the rude stranger in everyday life / Philip Smith,
  Timothy L. Phillips, Ryan D. King.
    p. cm.
  Includes bibliographical references and index.
  ISBN 978-0-521-89551-4 – ISBN 978-0-521-71980-3 (pbk.)
  1. Courtesy. I. Phillips, Timothy L. II. King, Ryan D. III. Title.
  HF5389.3.U6S65 2010
  177′.1–dc22
  2010011225

ISBN 978-0-521-89551-4 Hardback
ISBN 978-0-521-71980-3 Paperback

This book is dedicated to the memory of Raymond Smith and Donald Phillips. Always happy to talk to strangers, both were believers in the virtue of civility.

Contents

Figures and tables

Figures

Tables

Preface and acknowledgements

This book is the product of several years of collaborative activity by the three authors in various combinations. Describing this division of labour is somewhat complex, but might be helpful to readers should they wish to direct questions to the team. The original grant proposals, focus group pilot work, survey instrument design and administration, conceptual thinking about the new area and the book proposal were the work of Timothy Phillips and Philip Smith. The former was particularly responsible for figuring out how to capture something commonplace yet elusive using survey methods. Smith is the chief author of Chapters 1, 8 and 9, although contributions from the other two team members were also made. Chapters 2, 3 and 4 were initially written by Smith and Phillips, then revised by Ryan King as the book developed. Chapters 5, 6 and 7 were equally authored by King and Smith. Some material from Phillips appears at the start of the last of these.

Along the way this book has had the benefit of support from the many institutions that sheltered its authors at one point or another in the research or writing process. In Australia we thank the University of Tasmania, the University of Queensland and the Australian National University. In the United States we express gratitude to Yale University and the University at Albany. In Europe we were hosted by Trinity College Dublin and the Kulturwissenschaftliches Kolleg, Universität Konstanz. We thank the professional research teams who took the project to the field. In Albany, Lauren Porter provided research assistance as the book neared completion. This book would never have happened without the substantial financial support of the Australian Research Council – their generous Discovery Grant enabled us to field the survey. In an era when research funding is increasingly tied to demonstrating some visible and concrete social or economic benefit, it has been gratifying to know that basic research with no immediate financial or policy payoff still has its supporters.

Along the way various colleagues have provided clues and insights into how to think about our findings and which questions to ask, often just in casual conversation or e-mail exchange. Some paragraphs were more directly inspired by the lateral thinking of our peers. In alphabetical order we thank: Jeffrey Alexander, Scott Boorman, Mike Emmison, David Garland, Bernhard Giesen, Bob Holton, Jim McKay, Joachim Savelsberg, Barry Schwartz, Jonathan Simon. Randall Collins is especially acknowledged for providing detailed written feedback on some of our findings. Carlo Tognato brought to our attention the interesting policies of Antanas Mockus. Although this book contains completely new written material, we worked our way towards it with four basic journal publications, the first three of which were based on the somewhat provisional focus group data only. These appeared in the *Australian Journal of Social Issues*, the *Journal of Sociology*, the *Sociological Review* and in *Urban Studies* (Phillips 2006; Phillips and Smith 2003, 2006a; Smith and Phillips 2004). For good ideas we thank the anonymous reviewers for these journals as well as the referees of our Cambridge proposal and manuscript. Our thanks also go to the Glasgow University Urban Studies group for diffuse intellectual support and for looking to build upon our research in the UK context. Finally, we must mention the team at Cambridge. Notably John Haslam was an early supporter of this project and Carrie Parkinson kept an eye on progress. Both were infinitely patient and understanding as various personal and professional complications delayed the arrival of the typescript.

1 | *Redirecting incivility research*

The theme of growing incivility is both a commonplace and a universal of human life. Through the ages and across civilizations there has always been talk of poor public behaviour, of increasingly unruly streets and of the decline and fall of good manners. It is a current journalistic staple to document troublesome youth, identify emergent forms of disorder from 'road rage' to 'cell phone rage', and to conduct simple experiments or cheap stunts to demonstrate that common courtesies are no longer to be found in the urban jungle (Safe 2000). Books on freefalling manners have long replaced those about etiquette on bestseller lists (Truss 2005). In a related trend, each decade sees an academic leader denounce the triumph of anti-civic individualism whether in the form of the 'lonely crowd', 'narcissism', the end of 'public man' or 'bowling alone'. What makes our age distinctive is not the presence of such a complaint about the demise of an interpersonally civil society, but rather the intensity and form of the anxiety. A 'crisis' of civility has been identified with greater virulence and enthusiasm than ever before. Working in a sometimes uneasy, sometimes convenient, alliance, the media, politicians and academics have come together over the past dozen or so years and located profound dangers which call for desperate remedies. This activity has taken an unhelpful turn. Inspired by a criminological imagination it has come to look telescopically rather than broadly, imagines and investigates incivility in restrictive and extreme ways and stigmatizes the marginalized prematurely. In this book we propose and deploy a new approach. It is one that could radically change the understanding of incivility in our time.

The tyranny of the stereotype

We can begin to substantiate and illustrate our case with an exhibit, the so-called 'Respect Agenda' launched with much ballyhoo in January

2006 by then British Prime Minister, Tony Blair. This initiative framed anti-social behaviour as both symptom and cause of a wider and more insidious malaise in which selfishness and individualism have come to replace civic-mindedness, thus threatening the organic roots of community life. Quoting the social and moral critic R. H. Tawney, Blair claimed in his speech that 'what we are witnessing is the breakdown of societies on the basis of rights divorced from obligations'. On the one hand, this had given rise to escalating incivility, and on the other hand, to a toothless legal system. There seemed to be little that the police or courts could do to deal with vandalism, graffiti or the youth 'spitting at an old lady on her way to the shops'. Such unruly behaviour, Blair told us drawing on the work of urban historian Richard Sennett, is 'more common in poor areas' and in those with low social capital. It was also associated with 'families who are out of control and in crisis' whose 'children are roaming the streets and disrupting the classrooms'. This sub-proletarian anarchy can lead to a 'tyranny of a minority' that generates 'fear and intimidation' of the decent majority. What was needed the Prime Minister said was his Respect Action Plan. This would protect the liberty of the worthy and deserving through more efficient enforcement, through new powers that would prevent the antisocial deviant from hiding behind the law, and through social programmes to support constructive activities for young people (Blair 2006).

If somewhat constrained by the pressures of political correctness from pointing the finger directly at those in shell suits and hoodies, Tony Blair's treatment nevertheless managed to situate antisocial behaviour in a subtle matrix of explicit and implicit cues. These mobilize common sense to imagine the problem in a particular way. His is a representation that makes possible what critics have called a policy of the 'criminalization of everyday incivility' (Cohen 2004). Nasty people, it would seem, are encountered in so-called sink estates where satellite TV dishes spring from the walls and cars without licence plates quietly rust away on blocks. These are poverty-ridden neighbourhoods where unruly youths loiter in gangs and the neighbours have a pit bull called Tyson. The consequences are more serious than just an affront to our bourgeois aesthetic. There follow crime, constrained behaviour, fear, drawn curtains and a spiral of decline.[1] Such

---

[1] Our reconstruction of the connotations behind Blair's speech was validated by a series of BBC online reports consequent upon the launch of the Respect

a vision, which amplifies perceptions of low-level deviance by tying it to disreputable classes, exaggerates its consequences through indexing to urban poverty and then looks down the social hierarchy to allocate blame is hardly novel. As the literature on moral panics and moral crusades has long made clear, stories with innocents and victims often draw upon the tacit repertoires of class-based disorder.

It is easy and somewhat cheap to point the finger at politicians. It would be a rare leader who could resist the lure of populism, especially in the context of the law-and-order debate. More troubling is the way that this cultural pattern has filtered into academic production. It is to be found at the heart of the influential 'broken windows' criminology that has somewhat unfortunately set the agenda for thinking about incivility on our campuses and in our think tanks.

As is now perhaps well known, 'broken windows' was courageously announced in an *Atlantic Monthly* article nearly thirty years ago. The authors, political scientist James Q. Wilson and criminologist George Kelling (1982), ingeniously claimed that small acts of incivility, if left unchecked in an area, would eventually lead to major crime. Squeegee bandits, graffiti writers, winos, card sharks and peddlers seem capable of only low-level harm. However, we need to be mindful that they send out a signal that an area is going out of control. The law-abiding feel hassled and threatened. As their quality of life starts to drop, those who can afford to do so abandon ship. They move out, thus removing those watchful guardians of the street who deter crime. Petty vice escalates unchecked. Perceiving that nobody cares, more serious criminal elements move in. The result is a feedback cycle of signs and behaviours that leads to neighbourhood decline, much as one broken window left unfixed is an invitation to smash the next. What is called for, Wilson and Kelling suggest, is a rigorous clampdown on low-level incivilities before things get out of control. This is an intuitively appealing hypothesis. Further, it has the great theoretical merit of suggesting that situated interpretation by real social actors can play a role in mediating the impact of structural inequality. There is space here for agency and culture. Practical implications are

Agenda. These documented the lives of ordinary people who were prisoners in their own homes or who had been terrorized by bad neighbours in poor housing estates.

also to be found. The broken windows paradigm has led, albeit in indirect and much debated ways, to experiments with 'zero tolerance policing' and to a renewed interest in incivility research among criminologists and urban planners. However, the theory has not always held its ground in empirical tests.

Studies have shown that real and perceived incivilities map onto the reported crime rates that make up official statistics. They also map onto residents' perceptions of crime in the neighbourhood. We further know that areas with low social and economic status are indeed characterized by higher levels of incivility – at least as conventionally measured. All this is pretty much as predicted. The problem is that the independent causal influence of incivility on crime and decline has been less often investigated (e.g., Harcourt 2001). For the most part, research suggests that both crime and incivility have been generated by underlying structural disadvantage (Sampson, Morenoff and Gannon-Rowley 2002; Sampson and Raudenbush 1999; Taylor 2000). Or in common-sense terms, a bad area is a bad area – one that gives rise to both more trivial and more serious offending. Although much money has been spent and much ink spilled in this effort at evaluation, to our thinking the success or failure of the 'broken windows' hypothesis should not be the main game in town. What has been missed is the distorting effect – perhaps unintended – that 'broken windows' has had on our thinking about incivility. As a paradigm it defines such activity as the province of marginal populations. In one short paragraph Wilson and Kelling conjure up the image of streets full of teenagers, drinkers, fighters and panhandlers (1982, p. 32). The activity of such types is understood to generate fear and to take place in grim inner city settings. Finally, incivility is perceived as falling almost entirely within the purview of criminology and inner-urban sociology – it is something we should study with respect to crime and renewal rather than open up to a more general sociological investigation. This is a narrow understanding that has pushed theory and research in a particular direction. It has produced a new common sense about where incivility 'naturally' takes place, one that we argue can be seen tacitly shaping Tony Blair's 'Respect Agenda'. In the very process of testing 'broken windows' academic research has been unwittingly complicit in a process that has closed down broader and more creative thinking. Let's explore this problematic legacy more closely.

A relentless focus on the deprived inner city area means we know quite a lot about underclass environments. However, scholars have excluded from intensive research the experiences of the middle and working classes who live in more typical neighbourhoods, those who are affluent or simply not welfare dependent. This restrictive focus helps to perpetuate the moral binary that separates the unruly from the socially respectable, and propagates the myth that incivility is a problem only in certain parts of the city. There is selection afoot whereby the places that are scrutinized seemingly correspond to the urban iconography of video games such as 'Grand Theft Auto' with associated lurkers, drug dealers and thugs. It would seem as if there is no incivility in Surbiton, Surrey or Fairfield, Connecticut. Stigma aside, all this information on the inner city is limited in its scientific value as there has been precious little effort at benchmarking against such 'respectable' places. The microscopic attention given to the urban underclass environment creates real problems for generalizing knowledge. These are atypical environments in which the nature and interpretation of incivility is hard to disentangle from the effects of race, crime, place and poverty. Might it not make more sense to first explore incivility in settings that could be variously described as more neutral, simple or typical? For instance, what about incivilities transpiring in supermarkets, car parks or leafy suburbs?

It is not only the focus on one part of the city that is problematic about the criminological agenda. By emphasizing the distinctive incivility patterns of the spatially fixed ghetto and failed housing project the 'broken windows' legacy understands where people sleep as the defining feature of our urban experience. Even the best research has this 'neighbourhood' quality. The British Crime Survey, for example, provides a list of rude behaviours and incivilities ('noisy neighbours', 'rubbish or litter lying around', 'people using or dealing drugs') and asks respondents how much of a problem these are in their local area, this being defined as within a 15-minute walk from the respondent's home (Home Office 2006). Yet residential areas are just part of the total matrix of life. During the daily round we move to and from work, visit shops and consumption zones, make use of cars and public transport, go to watch live sporting events or sit in a bar. These are the little understood public environments in which many people are perhaps most likely to encounter incivility, especially those living in single-family dwellings in the dormitory suburbs. In

their path-breaking paper, Wilson and Kelling themselves open up
this possibility for a more mobile, non-residential understanding of
the city. For example:

One of us (Kelling) spent many hours walking with Newark foot-patrol
officers to see how they defined 'order' and what they did to maintain it.
One beat was typical: a busy but dilapidated area in the heart of Newark,
with many abandoned buildings, marginal shops (several of which prom-
inently displayed knives and straight-edged razors in their windows), *one
large department store*, and, most important, *a train station* and *several
major bus stops*. Though the area was run-down, its streets were filled
with people, because it was *a major transportation centre*. The good order
of this area was important not only to those who lived and worked there
but also *to many others, who had to move through it on their way home,
to supermarkets, or to factories.* (Wilson and Kelling 1982, p. 30, italics
added)

Asking survey questions about incivility in 'your local area' or
'where you live' will miss this fluid experience of social mixing completely. The understanding of the city that is at play in current research
is remarkably static. Methodological convenience has led to studies
that try to merge census data with crime reports and household surveys. It ties incivility to place, not to activity in any profound way.
It is an approach that comes nowhere near understanding urban life
as a surface of movements, and incivilities as the product of chance
encounters. The possibility for such a rethinking was indicated long
ago in the work of the German aesthete and philosopher, Walter
Benjamin. For Benjamin (1983) the city even in Victorian times was
all about circulations of anonymous publics through civic and consumption spaces. It was the anxious surging of the crowd and the
strolling of the indolent flâneur that were truly constitutive features
of urban modernity, not the 'hood' or the council estate.

The ghetto/crime context that conditions thinking about incivility
has generated a body of academic research that almost exclusively
focuses on fear as the emotion of interest and aversion as the focal
behavioural response. To interrogate this relationship researchers
have made use of survey modules from the criminological tradition.
These typically ask about fear without offering alternative emotional
responses. This is partly a methodological convenience and partly
a function of a narrowly defined research agenda. With just a little

creative thinking we might reasonably hypothesize several different scenarios.[2] The French sociologist Emile Durkheim (1980 [1893]) suggested that norm breaking generated intense anger and the desire for vengeance. The Berlin-dwelling Georg Simmel (1997) spoke of the blasé attitude which we must develop in order to survive the psychic shocks of modern life. For the thinker Norbert Elias (1978 [1939]) rude behaviour could generate disgust. It was a crude or 'uncivilized' activity, often involving failures to control the body. Outside of the deprived inner city and the street gang encounter we might reasonably expect these emotional possibilities to appear with some frequency.

Finally, we note that incivilities are measured in the existing research agenda in a narrow way. Early theoretical treatments within the 'broken windows' tradition made mention of tricky interpersonal confrontations, 'hey-honey' hassles, the degradation of solicitation, the intimidating presence of the squeegee bandit and so forth. Indeed, the original Wilson and Kelling article speaks almost exclusively of badly behaved individuals – drunks, panhandlers and intimidating youth – as generating a sense of fear and disorder. One feels that the catchy metaphor of the 'broken window' was taken all too literally by subsequent researchers who started to fixate on built and visible forms of disorder. To be fair, capturing the verbal and embodied has proven to be too difficult so far (although we believe we have started to crack the problem). Current observational research has taken the methodologically convenient path of measuring what can be counted by the passing observer. In practice this has entailed looking for graffiti, burnt-out cars, empty lots, boarded up buildings, drug needles and so forth. These can be coded by researchers on their clipboards as they tour blighted neighbourhoods.[3] The resulting information can then be correlated with census data or crime data. The problem here is that researchers are counting things, not exploring the interactions that we – and we

[2] To its credit the British Crime Survey does offer a range of emotional reactions to respondents. Commonly reported were annoyance, frustration, anger and worry.

[3] Sampson and Raudenbush (1999) attempted to code behaviours as well as spaces in a systematic block coding exercise involving the videotaping of streetscapes from an anonymous cruising SUV. Although good data were collected for the urban fabric, unruly interpersonal activity was elusive. Aside from loitering, other antisocial behaviours were observed so rarely as to have little value for statistical purposes. It would seem that low-level incivility is too subtle and infrequent to be amenable to observational sociology.

think Wilson and Kelling – feel are at the heart of incivility. Survey research does somewhat better. The British Crime Survey, for example, asks not only about 'vandalism and graffiti' and 'abandoned cars', but also about 'being insulted, pestered or intimidated', 'racial attacks and harassment' and 'people being drunk or rowdy' in the respondent's area (Home Office 2006). These turn out to be quite common in everyday life, but are not investigated in depth as personally experienced incidents. Rather respondents make blanket statements about whether such and such an activity goes on 'in general'. Whether we are counting things or asking about general modes of incivil interaction, it is deeply problematic that many of these indicators are of decay (abandoned buildings and cars) and others are quite simply crimes (drug needles, racial attacks). So the tie of incivility to more serious social breakdown is implicit in both the weltanschauung and methodology of such research. Minor breaches of social norms are off the radar. Whether in block coding or in survey research there has been no real effort to investigate fleeting, micro-level interactions. Videotapes and surveys cannot capture rude gestures, foul talk, poor body management and the dirty look. These are the little bits of grit which that most brilliant and eclectic observer of social life, Erving Goffman (1971), suggested were central to social interaction and the management of relations in public. Found wherever there are people, these are a universal irritant.

Another kind of incivility

In order to understand just how far the criminological gaze has taken us from the everyday experience of the majority, consider the following examples of routine incivility. The first two are taken from internet help pages, bulletin boards and blogs, these being a growing and convenient source of discussion and advice on matters of practical ethics.

First up a BabyCenter.com mom-to-be says:

> When I'm out in public, whether I'm grocery shopping or waiting in line at the post office, people ask personal questions about my pregnancy and sometimes even put their hand on my belly. How can I tell them to mind their business without being rude? (Anon. 2001)

Notice that here the routinely experienced incivility takes place in a 'safe' environment. It is to be found inside respectable commercial establishments, not on the street. Unlike spraying graffiti, burning-out a car or dealing drugs, talking to or touching a pregnant woman is unlikely to be regarded as a crime. The victim of the incivility feels frustration and anger at the intrusion into her personal space and privacy, but it seems not fear. She will probably go back to the post office again.

Here is another example, this time a response to the question 'Have you ever had an experience with an extremely rude stranger?' from a discussion thread at 'Yahoo Answers?' The context is that the writer has lost her cell phone in the cinema and has gone back in with the usher to try to find it:

> The usher was trying to get under the seat with his flashlight to look for my phone and still the lady would not move. He said 'excuse me' but she was like, 'No I'm not moving'. She was making the situation very difficult. The usher was getting annoyed as she wouldn't move and she was in his way. After a few minutes he found my phone and gave it to me. He got up and I thanked him, then the lady said 'I can't believe the rudeness of that, trying to watch a movie and he's looking for a stupid phone!' While the movie hadn't even started! (Anon. 2008)

Here we have another non-violent, non-threatening situation in a regular public space. Both the phone's owner and the lady in the seat feel they have certain rights and hold reasonable expectations about public behaviour. Drugs, drink, panhandling and violence are conspicuously absent.

How about the great outdoors? Puget Sound is in the Pacific Northwest, joining Washington State in the United States with British Columbia, Canada. This is a beautiful area of sheltered water, surrounded by mountains and dotted with picturesque islands linked by cute boats. Tourists can go whale watching and retired folk from Seattle might enjoy the water views from their log cabin style homes. We could not be further from the inner city ghetto, yet even in this watery temperate paradise we find incivility afoot. In April 2007 the *New York Times* (Yardley 2007) reported on the growing problem of people cutting into line at the sometimes lengthy queues for the car ferry. Brad Collins, the supervisor at one terminal, reported that there were 'two kinds of line cutters – the person who knows what they are doing and the person who doesn't know what they are doing'. The

laid back locals were sometimes being disadvantaged by tourists who
were unfamiliar with local customs and conventions about where to
queue. Other, more aggressive newcomers had imported city norms.
These were 'me centred' people with 'Darwinian driving inclinations'
who simply exploited the courtesy of the locals. For example, they
might slip into a spot that had been left clear in front of someone's
driveway. Frustration could boil over. When a car pushed in front of
89-year-old Jack Welden he bumped it with his own until the arriviste
got the message and took off. Reports the *Times*: 'the civility prac-
ticed with such reason and rigor in parts of the Pacific Northwest has
not necessarily expanded with the population'. Legislation was now
being mooted in the state assembly that would criminalize automotive
queue jumping with a $101 fine and help to maintain 'politeness' and
'sensitivity' in the region. What are the issues here? Not fear, not poverty and urban decay, not violent crime. Rather the relevant themes
we might investigate are time scarcity, space competition, a sense of
fairness, local knowledge, selfishness and ignorance, the distribution
of community norms and the availability of low-level interpersonal
sanction.

These three examples suggest a very different social and experiential universe from the one opened up by criminological inquiry
into incivility. It is a more general and encompassing arena, yet para-
doxically one about which we know far less. Where do such low-
key unpleasant events take place and how can we predict them? Just
how do people feel about rude and inconsiderate behaviour? Who is
at risk? Why do some events escalate and result in retaliation when
others get quietly dropped? These are just some of the questions we
set out to answer in our study.

Researching everyday incivility: a new approach

So far we have established that existing research has severe limita-
tions. It looks for the most part at problem neighbourhoods and not
at a representative sample of spaces and communities; it has a geo-
static approach that does not fully come to terms with the movements
central to urban and rural experiences and lifestyles; it imposes closed
researcher-led definitions of incivility, these replicating the political
orthodoxy by tapping into more serious or even criminal behaviours;
it misses out on low-level rudeness and fleeting encounters. In this

book we suggest an alternative approach, one that opens up new territory rather than tramping over the same old ground. We look at the broader incidence of incivility. Radically, we insist our rethinking must penetrate through to questions of methodology, even if we insist on the need for measurement. We see the need for a post-positivist and somewhat democratic turn which places experience and interpretation at the heart of the data collection strategy. Research should not prejudge the 'problem' in terms of an urban renewal or social policy agenda imposed by outside experts, but rather explore the wider distribution of incivil experiences in our society and take those experiences as the thing to be investigated. Pivotal to this move is the somewhat counter-intuitive realization that *incivility is a subjective reality.* Our position here follows Hamlet's dictum that 'Nothing is good or bad but thinking makes it so'. Incivility is whatever is taken as offensive, impolite or crude because human subjects impose meanings on actions. It makes no sense to try to determine how much rude behaviour is taking place by counting something we researchers might think is rude – such as coding the use of a particular swear word or 'the finger' on a videotape of a high street. Diverse social groups have varying definitions and boundaries for rudeness and meaning can often be heavily context-bound (Millie 2008). Apparent insults, for example, can be ironic or affectionate or ritualistic. Swearing might be acceptable in a bar, but not the play park. The N-word can be used between African-American buddies but not by whites. Returning to an example given above, looking for a cell phone in a cinema might be rude to some. Not helping look for it might be rude to others. So we should be asking where, when and how people experience something that they interpret as rude, for it is the act of interpretation that makes the rudeness.

Our position here comes out of Max Weber's insistence on verstehen or 'interpretative understanding', the ethnomethodologist Harold Garfinkel's demand that we take members' categories seriously, Jean-Paul Sartre's focus on the radical contingency of subjectivity such that the agent determines the meaning of an act, and labelling theory's observation that deviance is an attribution given to an act or individual. It can be clarified with some analogies. Imagine a project trying to map the incidence and distribution of hot sex, wonderful ice cream or truly great coffee in a city. Although there might be strong correlations between subjective readings and objective factors that we can count such as duration of genital contact, real vanilla pods or the percentage of Arabica beans, contextual and interpretative environments play a powerful role in determining how any particular instantiation becomes socially relevant. Coffee is a drink, but a really great coffee is a matter of opinion and circumstance. Counting and pricing pods, beans and orgasms will only get us so far as we are interested in an experience with qualities or in understanding a noun that has an adjective attached. Eye contact is a physiological process, but a dirty look is an interpretation of that gaze. Some feel that writing graffiti is an affront and others that it is a creative act. To explore the distribution of incivility we really need to investigate the distribution of experiences of incivility, to count that which is taken as incivil by ordinary people in their daily lives. Many years ago the sociologists William I. Thomas and Florian Znaniecki remarked that the definition of the situation is real because it has real consequences for human action. Incivility exists in our heads, but has its origins and implications in the realm of concrete human interaction. It is this curious dual reality that we must take as the starting point for inquiry.[4]

To develop an alternative approach that emerged from the personal experiences of ordinary people and that opened up the question

---

[4] From childhood the idea that rudeness exists 'out there' and can be defined objectively in a catalogue of bad behaviours has been deeply ingrained. It can be hard to shake off this ontological certainty, and it is no surprise that during seminars and presentations to general audiences we have sometimes encountered objections to our approach and methodology along the lines of the following questions: 'What about acts *that are rude* that nobody notices? How do you propose to capture these? They are not in your data set' [under-count]; 'Don't individuals have different understandings of what is rude, so some people might interpret something as rude that *was not really* rude? Your data might be contaminated by mistaken attribution' [over-count]; 'What is rude might vary by social class or other social location. Doesn't your work simply capture what your respondents in different social groups think is rude rather than generate a benchmark of how much rudeness is *really* going around?' [systematic and socially distributed perceptual error]; 'Your respondents identified themselves as victims. How do we know they are not *really responsible* for the rude encounter?' [faulty event narrative]. These are interesting questions, but we feel irrelevant to the task at hand. To our reading these kinds of questions betray an objectivist fallacy, a theme we have highlighted with the italicized words above. The questioner believes that rudeness is something that can exist outside of its interpretation. Our response is that rudeness comes into existence only when it is detected. It has behavioural and psychological consequences because it is perceived or remembered by a human subject. Whether or not this detection within

of incivility to all social groups with their diverse definitions and understandings, we turned first to the focus group method. Participants from various demographics in Melbourne, Australia were prompted by us in the early 2000s to talk in an open-ended way about their experiences of everyday rudeness. The results were astonishing. Conditioned by the iconography of the existing academic literature, we had been expecting tales of fear, youth perpetrators, threatening signs and bad areas to be central to the narratives. In truth the converse was apparent. Most episodes were trivial, people seemed angry or indifferent, encounters took place in remarkably ordinary places like supermarkets, and the perpetrators were generally older and looked respectable. We had started to uncover the forgotten world of what we came to call 'everyday incivility' (see Phillips 2006; Phillips and Smith 2003; Smith and Phillips 2004).

Forgotten? Well perhaps not. When we discussed our work with both colleagues and non-academic friends we noted a high level of interest and emotional energy. People had opinions and wanted to tell us their own stories. When we gave seminars on this topic they invariably generated a much better turnout than those in the weeks immediately before and after. Clearly the experience of everyday incivility was common and strangely compelling. Within the lifeworld this was not a forgotten issue. Yet somehow prior social research had never investigated this in a systematic way. We have already told the story of how criminology, policy and politics switched investigations away from everyday incivility in favour of 'worst case scenario' incivility. Qualitative inquiry, however, had come close. In his pioneering discussions from the 1960s and 1970s, Erving Goffman correctly noted the importance of due deference and demeanour on the streets for everyone and flagged the role of civil inattention in public

---

the lifeworld and its subsequent memory trace is 'accurate' or is consistent with some abstract universal standard is another matter altogether. For our part, we do not believe a naturalistic methodology exists that could yield a workable sample of non-observed but still rude events. Nor do we see it as possible, practical, ethical or even useful at this stage in the field to judge what is 'really rude' and to identify errors in interpretation by our respondents. To make this case is not to suggest that rude experiences are purely scattered and ideographic and so not amenable to an objectifying social scientific inquiry. To the contrary, our entire project will demonstrate that these are structured as a social fact. There are patterns to experiences and to the social situations that generate these.

space. He also observed brilliantly the strategies that people use to avoid stigma and build the dignity of the self. Crucially, his work understood the encounter as the atom of social life, and so he tried to develop analytic techniques and typologies for unpacking such episodes where individuals come together. For Goffman (1963, 1967, 1971) it was coordinated action within the encounter that formed the basis of civil relations in public. Yet as his work progressed it took on a somewhat dark tone, with the street increasingly seen as something to be scanned for threats, and the individual working to maintain a defensible space. Later studies in his tradition pushed this agenda. When Lyn Lofland (1973) paid attention to the subjective experience of the stranger she noted the interaction techniques which people deployed in the city to head off potentially incivil encounters. They might, for example, fake activity like reading to avoid having to talk to a stranger or try to look confident when waiting at night at the bus stop. Other ethnographies similarly couched the study of encounters with strangers in terms of fear and the management of risk (Merry 1981). Incivility was tied once again to stranger danger.

The slide towards urban paranoia and the view from a broken window was regrettable, but it was not the only problem. In symbolic interactionist work there was a focus on developing concepts and identifying ideal types of behaviour, working impressionistically outwards from the researcher's own intuitions and research settings. This method, which situates the intellectual as the privileged reader of the street, gives rise to real problems of validity in interpretation. Feminist critics, for example, suggested that Goffman's readings of public interaction, body management and eye contact were falsely universal projections of the male perspective. Women's relations in public, they insisted, were all about avoiding sexual harassment. Further, questions of generalizability remained. Despite their limited focus on the inner city 'problem', criminologists managed to look at the matter of prevalence and were able to document how much of a certain kind of thing was going on. Their positivistic methodology allowed inferences to be made about causes and consequences and comparative risks, albeit for a limited pool of incivil artefacts and behaviours. This useful stab at measuring reality was really not on the agenda of the symbolic interactionists, who instead wished to document and celebrate the creativity of the agent and fathom the complex process through which we accomplish the social order.

Table 1.1 *Criminological and interactionist approaches to incivility*

	Criminology	Interactionism
Tries to get at:	Prevalence **	Process*
The objective of research is:	Prediction and social control*	Interpretation and understanding*
The basic unit of interest is:	The 'block'; the neighbourhood	The interaction, the situation*
Looks at:	Visible signs of disorder like graffiti and youths hanging out	The embodied micro-order of gaze, the body, language**
Method:	Quantitative*	Qualitative
Incivility is of interest in:	Bad areas where there are social problems	Everywhere as this is a universal aspect of social life**
Current research tends to be about:	Causes and consequences of social disorder*	Accomplishment of civility, politeness and normal appearances
Incivility exists:	Objectively. We researchers can define what it is using common sense.	Subjectively. It is an experience arising from interpretation.**

* Indicates that our project attempts to connect with this aspect.
** Indicates a strong tie with our project.

We suggest that what is needed at this point is some effort to bridge the two literatures and to take what is best from each of them. Table 1.1 indicates the properties of criminological and interactionist work. We try to find a middle ground and engage with both traditions. This book makes use of quantitative methodology in order to identify aggregate patterns, regularities and the drivers of everyday incivilities. At the same time we are interested in situations, interpersonal dynamics, emotions and perceptions. Importantly, as we have already noted, the incivility in our study was identified as such by the respondent. In effect we will be looking at felt experiences of incivility, but treat these as the starting point for a positivistic inquiry. In the table we have placed an asterisk where we feel our project connects with the agenda of a particular cell, two asterisks where we feel a strong tie.

It is with this focus on low-level, interpersonal, member-defined incivility in mind that we designed the Everyday Life Incivility in Australia Survey (ELIAS).[5] Australia can be considered a representative multicultural, economically developed nation. It has a high level of urban concentration and of overseas-born population. When we look to international comparative data on crime, social attitudes or lifestyles it is generally in the middle of the pack for OECD nations.

The ELIAS Survey was a cross-sectional study collecting information on everyday encounters with the rude stranger. It adapted many basic tools from the longstanding tradition of the crime victimization survey. From June to August 2005 the survey was administered to 1,621 adults living in Australia using telephone interviewing and random sampling from the electronic residential white pages. The sample was stratified such that quotas were met on age, gender and state of residence matching parameters taken from the census. Prior to the telephone interview a letter had been sent to the selected households about the project, announcing the possibility of a future telephone call and asking for participation. We requested in the letter that the recipient try to remember any incivil events that might happen to them over the next few weeks. The response rate, defined as the number who agreed to participate as a proportion of all who were contacted was 30 per cent. This was similar to that achieved by the Australian Bureau of Statistics in its own research on various topics.[6] Cross-checks with

[5] The ELIAS Survey was generously supported by a Discovery Grant from the Australian Research Council. We also note that the ELIAS acronym is simply convenient. It does not indicate support for the views of the noted theorist of a 'civilizing process' Norbert Elias nor represent a systematic effort to test or operationalize his ideas. For the record, the authors of this book have a longstanding interest in neo-Durkheimian sociology.

[6] Over recent years response rates for telephone survey work have been declining. A culture has emerged in which there is suspicion of unsolicited calls. This has arisen thanks to the growth of irritating telemarketing and the availability of call filtering technologies such as voice messaging and caller number display. It is emblematic that the author Bret Easton Ellis has stated a preference for an 'unlisted outgoing-only phone line' (2005). With respect to the ELIAS Survey, we also note that our response rate of 30 per cent compares well with other telephone-based surveys. For instance, the Council on Market and Opinion Research in the United States continuously tracks response rates and finds an average response rate of about 10 per cent. The response rate is also comparable with surveys of approximately the same length and number of respondents (e.g., the American Mosaic Survey in the United States had a response rate of about 36 per cent).

findings from other surveys (see Bean 2005; Johnson 2005; Public Agenda 2002; this book Chapters 5 and 7) enabled us to confirm the validity and reliability of our data. The interviews lasted on average 29 minutes, although some were over in as little as 15 minutes and others took as long as 45 minutes. The length of the call depended on response paths triggered by various filter questions and in particular whether the respondent had an incivil event of any complexity to report.

As we have explained, although we wished to focus on the forgotten world of embodied, interpersonal incivilities we did not prejudge what these might be. Instead of imposing our own categories by asking respondents whether or not certain things had happened to them, the interviewer simply provided a cue that would allow them to define what they had personally experienced as rude:

Now, can you think of an occasion within *the past month* when you *came across a rude stranger*? Can you recall such an event? We're looking in particular at events that occurred in Australia, that involved another person you'd never seen or met before, just another member of the general public (rather than someone at their work), someone you came across in the course of simply going about your everyday life activities (rather than connected with your work).

Notice first how this statement allowed us to eliminate those incivil events that did not involve a personal encounter with a rude stranger. It excludes, for example, anything the respondent might have seen on television, something their neighbours had experienced and told them about, and also took out of the frame any incivil objects they might have witnessed, such as a burning car seen from the window of a bus. Further, the preamble contains several criteria which could be used to establish a data set of closely comparable events. If the respondent answered 'Yes' to the general prompt they were then taken through these one by one. We turn to these briefly and provide a rationale.

1. I'd like to ask you about the most recent occasion you came across a rude stranger. How long ago did this event happen?

Events that took place over one month before the phone call were rejected. We anticipated that incivil events take place with greater frequency than criminal acts. However, as some of these are trivial they are probably less memorable than crime victimizations. Although crime victim surveys typically work with a 12-month recall period, we reduced this so as to improve data reliability (see Cantor and Lynch 2000). We were further concerned that a longer time frame might lead to an over-representation of more spectacular rude stranger encounters. Research in 1950s America on experiences of racism discovered that events over a year prior that were reported tended to feature only overt physical and verbal abuse. Those reported that were more recent also included things like non-explicit verbal rudeness (e.g., sneers), nasty looks or being ignored by a sales clerk (Hindman 1953). Because our interest was in every act of rudeness, no matter how trivial or inconsequential, a very narrow time window was stipulated.

2. Did this event happen in Australia?

For purposes of comparability we needed to ensure that there was a broadly shared social and cultural context to the events. We were especially worried that some of the rude encounters reported might have reflected travel in the Asia-Pacific region. For example, a respondent might have been offended by a beggar while on a beach holiday in Bali.

3. Was the rude stranger completely unfamiliar to you, that is a person you had never seen or met before?

We were in search of the pure stranger who is consistent with the archetype of anonymous public life in modernity. We anticipated confounding effects where the person could be thought of as a 'familiar stranger', such as the person who catches the same train every morning to whom we have never spoken.

4. Was the rude stranger just another member of the general public, or were they working in a job at the time?
5. Now, how about you, were you working in a job at the time?

These two questions were to eliminate problems associated with role performance. As with the familiar stranger, the person in a role is not really completely strange, new or ambiguous. We have clues as to who they are. People in some task-oriented role or uniform are less likely to generate fear in us, as are our clients. We have some expectations of worthy intentions and probable circumstances and can generate explanatory accounts for their actions. When the employee of the Department of Motor Vehicles starts abusing us, we can begin to imagine why this is. Perhaps there is a long queue and they are overworked? Perhaps we filled in the paperwork wrongly in our driving licence application? Further, sources of social support and legitimate authority are near at hand. We can appeal, for example, to the nearby supervisor if the rage of the DMV officer at our incompetence gets out of hand. With the true rude stranger we are in a situation of much stronger uncertainty, one where we must extricate ourselves from the encounter, or hope that a Good Samaritan comes to our rescue.

When it came to the content and format of the survey we faced a real challenge. We needed to be open to diverse respondent definitions and capture the full scope of human experiences. So the instrument had to be broad enough to accommodate a vast range of forms of incivility and the situational contexts within which these took place. Yet we also sought to capture the deep structure of the events, to probe their inner workings and narrative progress. In addition, we were looking to understand the social background of the respondent, their attitudes and the consequences arising from the victimization. The whole had to be intelligible to respondents on the end of a phone line, treat them with respect and hold their attention. The earlier phases of focus group research and some extensive piloting allowed us to develop and refine an instrument that came in three parts. The first section contained information on the most recent victimization. We looked at where the respondent was and what they were doing at the time of the event. Next, we collected information on the rude strangers and their actions. For example: What exactly did they do? What did they look like? Did they seem to act intentionally? By the end of this section we had information on the nature and context of the event itself. This brought us to the second part of the survey. Here we recovered information on the sequence step-by-step. We traced the emotional dynamics of the stranger/victim interaction at several points in time, looked at the unfolding of sanction and riposte and discovered how the interaction came to an end. In the final part of the survey we found out more about the demographics, social location and networks of respondents, investigated their attitudes towards crime and incivility and explored the ways that they coped with the event after it had concluded. This would allow us to discover if certain types of person were more likely to become victims, what the impacts of victimization might be and how experiences might be modified by wider cultural and social contexts. To sum up, the ELIAS Survey was designed to offer the first systematic glimpse into the world of everyday rudeness.

As we draw this chapter to a close, we note one special feature of our survey. The leading social theorist, Randall Collins (2000), has complained that most sociology – including most survey research – takes the individual as the unit of analysis. Really we should be looking at situations and interactions as the real atoms of social life. People do not live in isolation but in repeated instances of association. Ours is a study that conforms to this vision. It is an investigation of fleeting interactions, their meanings, drivers and consequences, made all the more unusual by virtue of the fact that it uses the survey research method rather than ethnographic observation. What we have is a sample of situations as reported by respondents from which empirical generalities can be extracted and with which contending explanations can be evaluated.

Outline of the book

This book consists of six data analysis chapters sandwiched between two more conceptual and reflexive contributions. There is also a brief summary given at the end. Generally speaking the data analysis increases in complexity as the book goes on. Where the logic of inquiry allows we have tried to keep our statistical techniques as simple as possible. We have also provided bullet-point summaries of the main points of each chapter. These offer core information for the statistics-fatigued or time-limited reader.

This chapter has set the scene and offered a rationale for the project. In the next chapter we begin our task of mapping and explaining everyday incivility. Chapter 2 looks at what people experienced as rude, identifies the social characteristics of rude strangers and their victims, finds out where this takes place and calculates some basic demographic risk factors. It maps out the banal world of what we call everyday incivility. In Chapter 3 we move on to explore the very ordinary qualities of this everyday incivility, showing how it is intimately connected to the time–space choreography of everyday life which distributes risks and allows strangers and victims to come together. Our finding is that most such events are akin to 'normal accidents'. They are inevitable and predictable – at least in aggregate. In Chapter 4 we move on to investigate the emotional and behavioural dynamics of incivil encounters. We evaluate the extent to which 'fear' and 'aversion' are common responses to rude strangers, and suggest that space needs to be opened up in research for a more diverse repertoire of interpretation and action. We also look at the drivers of 'self-help' solutions to rude strangers and see whether or not these lead to a repair of the social fabric. Finally, this chapter takes apart the unfolding sequences of action, emotion and interpretation that drive sustained exchanges between strangers and victims. Chapter 5 asks how gender, age and social class influence the distribution of incivil experiences and reactions to them. Specifically it highlights yet more the crucial role of routine activities and charts a demography of emotions. Chapter 6 continues this theme by looking at what happens after the event. Do people have to cope? Does the encounter with the rude stranger change them in any way? Our findings here suggest that the rude stranger encounter can indeed have lasting impacts for some individuals. In Chapter 7 we pull back the focus a little to explore general social attitudes towards strangers in our society. The emphasis here is on testing the widespread assumption that we live in a world without trust but with fear. The chapter further traces the social and experiential origins of such attitudes, including the role of the mass media. Informed by our findings Chapter 8 asks what can be done to reduce the levels of rudeness we encounter today. Looking to make our work policy relevant, the chapter reviews several candidate strategies and locates exemplars from around the world. We also briefly question the possibility and even desirability of eliminating rudeness. Chapter 9 is a quick and reader-friendly final summary. It offers a quick and accessible overview to the findings and arguments of this book. Directed towards the general reader who is short of time, this covers the main points in a question-and-answer format and directs readers to the chapters where they will find common queries answered in detail.

The main arguments of this chapter are:

• Existing research on incivility is too narrow in scope. It has a focus on poor urban areas, and is driven by a criminological and urban renewal agenda. We cannot generalize from this literature.

- There has been no real effort to explore systematically the distribution and dynamics of low-level interpersonal incivility as experienced across the social spectrum in everyday life.
- An incivility exists because of a human interpretation of an objective behaviour. It is culturally and personally relative and is situationally contingent. We need a method that can capture what ordinary people have experienced as incivil rather than imposing our own external definitions.
- Our Australian survey asked people about their recent encounters with rude strangers. It investigated the prevalence, contexts and nature of incivil encounters in a nationally representative sample.

2 | *The fundamentals of the incivil encounter*

Although this will be a simple and short chapter it will break new ground. Our aim is to answer some fundamental and often asked questions about public rudeness in a systematic way. How often do people encounter it? What is it? Where does it happen? Who does it? Is it deliberate or accidental? Who experiences victimization? Using some basic statistics we will be able to draw up a portrait of the kinds of events and people that are to be found in the world of everyday incivility. We can start with the most basic issue of all. What is logically needed for an incivil encounter with a rude stranger to take place in public? The answer is simple. There are three components: first, there must be an *action* interpreted as incivil that occurs in a public setting; second, this is committed by a *stranger*, either by accident or deliberately; third, it is experienced by a self-described *victim*. Here we look at each of these in turn. In effect, we will describe what happened and where, who did it and to whom.

The rude event

First, how prevalent are encounters with rude strangers? The ELIAS data show that about a third of respondents reported a rude event during the past month (508 of 1,621 respondents, or 31 per cent). As one might expect, the likelihood of encountering this type of incivility is substantially higher than more invasive interpersonal events such as crime victimizations. As a point of comparison, the 2004 International Crime Victimization Survey found that 17 per cent of Australians were crime victims during the past *year*, a figure far below the 31 per cent of our respondents reporting rude events in the past *month*. Many respondents further report that their latest incident was not exceptional. Of the 508 respondents reporting an event in the past month, approximately 42 per cent suggested that incivilities of this nature occur at least on a weekly basis. We do not probe more deeply into the incidence rate of incivility because of potential recall problems, but the data clearly suggest that rude stranger encounters are quite common.

As described in the previous chapter, we are more interested in the nature of the events and the characteristics of interactions than the raw prevalence or incidence of such conduct. To that end we begin with a fundamental question: what exactly was experienced as rude, inconsiderate or antisocial? Our survey generated an incredible range of events, one characterized by a long tail. This is reported in Table 2.1(a) below.

People who 'pushed in front of me' made up fully 25 per cent of all reported events, followed by 'rude bodily gestures' and 'swearing' at around 11 per cent each of the total. Notice that even a quick glance at the everyday incivilities listed here shows that they do not correspond in type or mood to those found in the criminological or urban policy literature. Although it is possible that some are perceived as signs of danger, this crop of antisocial behaviour does not on the face of it look too worrying. Respondents are not reporting 'being offered drugs' or 'having fireworks thrown at me', which are typical options in the British Crime Survey's effort to measure incivility (Home Office 2006). Most of what we have here look like ordinary low-key events of the kind that could take place anywhere. Because the level of detail in this table can be overwhelming it is useful to generate some aggregate categories. Looking down the list we notice a pattern to the kinds of things that are considered rude. Some are related to human movement, blocked human motion and the sharing of physical space and are of a strongly embodied kind (items 1, 4, 5, 7, 8, 9, 12, 13, 16). Others can be thought of as non-verbal actions that are culturally inappropriate, insulting and disgusting. We include here spitting, rude bodily gestures, throwing litter and behaving in poor taste (items 2, 14, 18, 19). A third group involves intrusive non-verbal sounds, such as cell phone ring tones, screeching children and background talk (items 6, 10, 15, 20). Finally, there is unwanted communicative or meaningful verbal activity like swearing, loud talking and sexual remarks (items 3, 11, 17, 21). If we sum the items in each group we find the distribution displayed in Table 2.1(b).

Later in this book we will also see the aggregated categories in Table 2.1(b) used in other analyses. Although many avenues for investigation are suggested at this early stage, movement would seem to

Table 2.1(a) *What the stranger did to the respondent to qualify as 'rude':*
rank order

Question: Now, what did the stranger do in the very
first instance that made you think of them as rude?

What exactly did they do?	%	N
1. Pushed in front of me	25.3	148
2. Bodily gesture	11.5	67
3. Swearing	11.3	66
4. Blocked my way	9.6	56
5. Bumped into me	9.4	55
6. Screaming, screeching or shouting	5.6	33
7. Invaded my personal space	5.1	30
8. Swerved in front of me	3.8	22
9. Tailed me	3.6	21
10. Motor vehicle noise	3.2	19
11. Prejudicial comments	2.2	13
12. Stopped abruptly in front of me	1.9	11
13. Took up too much personal space	1.4	8
14. Acting in poor taste	1.4	8
15. Loud talking	1.4	8
16. Sat or stood in front of me	1.2	7
17. Sexual remarks	0.9	5
18. Waste disposal	0.7	4
19. Spat	0.3	2
20. Mobile phone	0.2	1
21. Non-English language	0.2	1
Total	100	585

Note: The N exceeds 508 as respondents could report more than one type of
behaviour.

stand out as a dominant category worthy of study. We return to this
theme in the next chapter. For example, might there be something
distinctive about the impacts of rude events related to movement and
space management on victims' emotional reactions? Do men, with
their larger physique and a presumed sense of entitlement in public
space generate more movement-related incivilities than women (see
Gardner 1995)? How much does crowding matter?

Table 2.1(b) *What the stranger did to the respondent to qualify as 'rude':* aggregated categories

Question: Now, what did the stranger do in the very first instance that made you think of them as rude? What exactly did they do?	%	N
Movement and space management	61.2	358
Bad language	14.6	85
Bodily decorum	13.9	81
Intrusive sounds	10.4	61
Total	100	585

The setting

Now let's consider the public settings where these activities take place. Table 2.2(a) provides another rank ordering, this time of locations for the reported events. Note again the seemingly ordinary nature of the reported locations as well as their diversity.[1] Looking down the list a number of locations stand out as places where incivilities involving strangers are more likely to be found. The place most commonly mentioned by respondents was a roadway (30 per cent). Supermarkets and outdoor walkways (including bike paths) each contained 10 per cent of events. The remaining 50 per cent of events occurred across an amazingly wide array of publicly accessible settings.

Once again it is possible to establish a typology. First, there are the conduits, nodes and technologies that people use to get from A to B such as roads and footpaths (items 1, 3, 4, 5, 6, 14) and mass transportation (items 7, 11, 16, 20). Next, we have public places that we might think of as destinations. These are places where our respondents want or need to go and where they might also encounter a stranger, such as shops, banks, parks and bars (items 2, 8, 9, 10, 12, 13, 15, 17, 18, 19, 21, 22, 23, 24, 25, 26, 27). These are generally enclosed,

---

[1] Notice that some places are not present in this list. Parents waiting outside a school are unlikely to encounter the complete stranger who is central to our project. Places of work are excluded by the fact that one or the other of the parties is likely to be involved in a visible role and hence excluded from our sampling frame.

Table 2.2(a) *Locale where the encounter occurred: rank order*

Question: Where specifically were you?	%	N
1. On a residential street/main road	29.8	138
2. In a supermarket	10.4	48
3. On an outdoors walkway	10.2	47
4. On a freeway/highway	7.8	36
5. In a car park	6.7	31
6. On an indoors walkway	6.0	28
7. On a train	5.4	25
8. In a public bar	3.9	18
9. In a shop	3.0	14
10. In a department store	2.8	13
11. On a bus	1.9	9
12. In a cafe	1.5	7
13. In a takeaway food outlet	1.3	6
14. At a petrol station	1.3	6
15. At a branch of commercial service provider	1.1	5
16. On a tram	1.1	5
17. At a sports ground	1.1	5
18. In a restaurant	0.9	4
19. At a park	0.9	4
20. At an airline terminal	0.6	3
21. At an educational institution	0.4	2
22. In a food court	0.4	2
23. In a gaming room	0.4	2
24. At a gym	0.4	2
25. At an indoor leisure centre	0.2	1
26. In a cinema	0.2	1
27. At a branch of government service provider	0.2	1
Total	100	463

privately-owned public spaces. This understanding that rude events can occur either in a 'destination' or 'in the process of getting somewhere' is one that we will again look at in more detail in the next chapter. Meanwhile, we can observe in Table 2.2(b) that the process of moving through space in transit towards a destination ('getting somewhere') looks more risky for encountering the rude stranger than being at the destination. This is slightly counter-intuitive. We tend to think

Table 2.2(b) *Locale where the encounter occurred: aggregated categories*

Question: Where specifically were you?	%	N
In the process of getting somewhere – roads, footpaths, car parks, etc.	61.8	286
In the process of getting somewhere – mass transportation	9.0	42
Destinations	29.2	135
Total	100	463

of rude strangers as 'being somewhere', in part because the standard repertoire of images consists of people 'hanging out'. The alcoholic is to be found on the park bench, the gang of young men is at the night-club and so forth. Our finding about 'getting somewhere', however, is presaged in an item of pioneering research from the early-1950s. Looking at the experiences and emotions of 'negro' youth, Baker M. Hindman (1953) found that in a context of segregation public transport was a major locus of unpleasant social interactions, much of this involving verbal abuse.

When considered in combination with the finding from previous tables that problems related to bodily movement seemed to be a major experience of incivility (Tables 2.1(a) and (b); and 2.2(a) and (b)), the results on the places where such encounters occur allows for an interesting speculation. Are substantial proportions of encounters with rude strangers the outcome of problems of flow in the course of progressing from A to B? We investigate this hypothesis in detail in the next chapter. Meanwhile, we can offer the observation that destinations often have enforcers of norms of behaviour (bouncers, staff) and definitions of place as ludic or pleasurable, or formal and rule governed. These discourage the situational generation of incivil behaviour and/or adjust the interpretative matrix such that it is more flexible. The process of getting somewhere, however, involves a more anarchic environment, one without strong situational cues. 'Getting somewhere' might be characterized by competition, queuing and a sense of urgency. One might reflect, for instance, on an extreme example. Consider the difference between being in Disney World and driving down the freeway to get to Disney World.[2] Even if Disney World is crowded and the queues for the rides are long, we are likely to see norms of civility maintained.[3] The journey to get there, however, might be more anarchic.

Was there a connection between any of these three types of places (in the process of getting somewhere: by personal or mass transportation, or destinations) and the four kinds of everyday incivility? In other words, do we find particular forms of public rudeness to be associated with getting somewhere as against being somewhere? The findings in Table 2.3 show that the different places give rise to divergent forms of everyday incivility. Somewhat contrary to our expectations, movement and space management-related incidents are clearly associated with destinations rather than getting somewhere. By contrast events involving bad language, bodily decorum and intrusive sounds are especially prevalent in the process of getting somewhere, whether by personal or mass transportation. This is a puzzle that we return to in the next chapter.

The rude stranger

Enter the rude stranger, stage left. For the purposes of our research this rude stranger on our stage is the person the victim identified as the perpetrator of an event in the litany of incivil actions described at the start of this chapter (i.e., the person who 'pushed in front of me', 'gave me a dirty look', who 'swore' or 'screamed' and so forth). Criminological research has laid primary responsibility for commonplace incivility at the feet of young males, the group known to be responsible for a large proportion of crime and deviance more

---

[2] This was the central plot of the popular film *National Lampoon's Vacation*, which is about the trials and tribulations experienced by a regular American family in the course of driving the family station-wagon across the country to their holiday destination of choice, Wally World.

[3] The example of Disney World brings up another matter – the work of institutions to skilfully manage public behaviour in spaces for which they are responsible. Clifford Shearing and Phillip Stenning (1984) note that order is maintained through skilful and unobtrusive means by Disney employees and through careful modifications to architecture and design. Control is 'built in' to the setting. We return to consider this theme in Chapter 8.

Table 2.3 *Type of everyday incivility by locale where the encounter occurred*

Type of everyday incivility	Personal transportation		Mass transportation		Destinations	
	%	N	%	N	%	N
Movement and space management						
Yes	51.0	146	50.0	21	67.4	91
No	49.0	140	50.0	21	32.6	44
$\chi^2 = 10.6**$						
Bad language						
Yes	17.5	50	23.8	10	8.9	12
No	82.5	236	76.2	32	91.1	123
$\chi^2 = 7.6*$						
Bodily decorum						
Yes	21.3	61	19.0	8	6.7	9
No	78.7	225	81.0	34	93.3	126
$\chi^2 = 14.2**$						
Intrusive sounds						
Yes	14.0	40	19.0	8	6.7	9
No	86.0	246	81.0	34	93.3	126
$\chi^2 = 6.5*$						

* $p < .05$
** $p < .01$

generally.[4] How do our data align with this depiction? Our new information suggests a much more diverse profile for incivility than for criminality. Table 2.4 shows that although men were identified as behind the majority of events of commonplace incivility (69 per cent),

[4] Age and sex are arguably the two most stable and consistent correlates of criminal behaviour (see, e.g., Gottfredson and Hirschi 1990, ch. 6). Perhaps on account of this correlation, theory and research on incivility often points to the presence of teens, and implicitly young men, as an indicator of incivility and disorder. This was certainly the case in Wilson's and Kelling's (1982) classic statement on 'broken windows', where examples of incivility frequently

Table 2.4 *Visible social attributes assigned to the rude stranger*

Visible social attribute	%	N
Gender		
Male	68.8	340
Female	31.2	154
Age		
Elderly adult (80s or older)	0.4	2
Older adult (60s–70s)	8.7	42
Middle-aged adult (40s–50s)	40.3	195
Younger adult (20s–30s)	43.2	209
Teenager (13–19)	6.8	33
Child (12 or younger)	0.6	3
Visible minority (ethnic, racial, religious)		
Yes	16.1	77
No	83.9	402
Number of people in company of rude stranger		
They were alone	64.8	316
One	19.3	94
Two or more	16.0	78
Rough looking or respectable looking		
Very rough looking	4.4	21
Quite rough looking	17.1	81
Neither rough looking nor respectable looking	21.5	102
Quite respectable looking	47.6	226
Very respectable looking	9.5	45

we find an unexpectedly high proportion of incidents where women were seen as the instigators (31 per cent). With respect to age, young adults (twenties and thirties) were far from alone as the primary agents of everyday incivility (43 per cent). Middle-aged adults (forties

allude to rowdy teens, obstreperous teenagers and gangs of teens. In line with their vision of teens and incivility, empirical research in this vein consistently measures disorder and incivility with reference to 'teenagers hanging around on the streets' (e.g., Markovitz *et al.* 2001, p. 301; Skogan 1990), teenage loitering (Skogan and Hartnett 1997), 'peer groups with gang indicators' (Sampson and Raudenbush 1999, p. 618) and related measures.

and fifties) sat along side them as the age group most likely to have been identified in the study as rude strangers (40 per cent). Of interest, teenagers were largely absent from our sample of everyday incivil events, manifesting a presence as the rude stranger in only one in every fifteen cases (7 per cent). With respect to cultural status, in one in six events the rude stranger was deemed to be an ethnic, racial or religious minority group member (16 per cent). The rude stranger was generally alone, having the company of at least one other person in only one in three cases (35 per cent). Of particular interest, and contrary to all theoretical expectations, the rude stranger was overwhelmingly coded by our respondents as 'respectable-looking' (57 per cent). In only in one in five cases were they deemed to be 'rough-looking' (21 per cent). In sum, what our findings suggest is that it is too simplistic to say the rude stranger has a single identifiable profile. If the modal perpetrator is a white male, aged 20–50 and respectable looking, it is important to recognize that rude people can be found throughout the social spectrum.

We turn next to a further basic question about the rude stranger. Did the rude stranger deliberately intend to insult, disgust, frighten, disrespect or offend? Or were they merely selfish, self-absorbed or not mindful of the needs of others? Are certain kinds of person more likely to act in a deliberately rude way? Clearly we can have no definitive way of determining this without access to the minds of perpetrators, but in one sense this does not matter. There remains a qualitative difference between events that are interpreted as intended and those understood as being a product of thoughtlessness. Table 2.5 shows that victims felt the large majority of events were accidental in nature (78 per cent). Around one in five were viewed as having been deliberate (22 per cent). This finding is consistent with the speculation of the popular social commentator, Lynne Truss, that a 'my bubble, my rules' world has come into place. Here everybody feels entitled to do as they choose without regard to those around them. She suggests that 'we are all in our own virtual bubbles when we are out in public, whether we are texting, listening to iPods, reading ...' (2005, p. 28). Rudeness emerges from the self-absorbed and selfish attitude of the bubble dweller. So who is 'bubble rude' and who is rude in a more deliberately communicative and other-oriented way? Our findings suggest that teenagers, individuals-in-company and the rough looking were seen as more likely to have been deliberately rude. In some cases

Table 2.5 *Whether the event was accidental or deliberate by visible social attributes of the rude stranger*

Question: Now, what did the stranger do in the first instance that made you think of them as rude ... do you think their primary motivation was to do what personally suited them at the time, OR to deliberately go out of their way to offend or disadvantage you?

	Accident	Deliberate	%	N
All events[1]	77.7	22.3	100	494
Gender ($\chi^2 = 6.0*$)				
Female	84.6	15.4	100	149
Male	74.6	25.4	100	334
Age[2] ($\chi^2 = 6.2$)				
Older adult (60s–70s)	82.9	17.1	100	41
Middle-aged adult (40s–50s)	82.0	18.0	100	189
Younger adult (20s–30s)	74.5	25.5	100	204
Teenager (13–19)	66.7	33.3	100	33
Visible minority ($\chi^2 = 1.0$)				
Yes	82.7	17.3	100	75
No	77.6	22.4	100	393
Number of people in company of rude stranger ($\chi^2 = 4.1$)				
They were alone	79.8	20.2	100	307
One	75.6	24.4	100	90
Two or more	69.2	30.8	100	78
Rough looking or respectable looking ($\chi^2 = 11.8*$)				
Very rough looking	65.0	35.0	100	20
Quite rough looking	64.6	35.4	100	79
Neither rough looking nor respectable looking	80.3	19.7	100	102
Quite respectable looking	82.2	17.8	100	218
Very respectable looking	81.4	18.6	100	45

* $p < .05$
[1] In fourteen cases the respondent couldn't recall.
[2] Elderly adult and child were excluded as categories due to small Ns.

the differences are moderate to sizeable. For instance, nearly twice as many incidents involving teenagers as elderly adults were perceived as deliberate acts (33 per cent versus 17 per cent). Comparable differences are found for very respectful looking strangers (19 per cent) relative to very rough looking strangers (35 per cent). In this respect the profile of deliberately rude strangers comes closer to fitting the image of incivility proffered in much criminological literature. Yet this finding begets an additional question: do deliberate acts affect victims differently than accidental acts? Stated more generally, does it matter whether the stranger is merely self-absorbed and insensitive versus purposefully rude? Our goal for now is to simply establish the pattern, but we return to the above questions in Chapters 5 and 6 when we look at coping, behavioural changes, and the determinants of emotional reactions to the incivility.

Who is the victim?

The term 'victim' is a problematic one. It is possible that our respondents would not see themselves as 'victims'. In today's world this can be a somewhat degrading and pathetic label suggesting powerlessness (Walby and Myhill 2001). Such worries aside, the term victim is a convention in criminology, and it is one that captures well enough the contours of the events that were described to us in the focus group and survey research. People considered themselves to have been disadvantaged, insulted or annoyed by the actions of someone else. So let's move on from semantics to ask a question: who is at risk of being such a victim of a rude stranger? To investigate this question, we can simply compare respondents who reported an incivil encounter in the prior month (31 per cent) with those who did not (69 per cent). The results of a systematic comparison of these two groups on several dimensions are presented in Tables 2.6(a) and 2.6(b).

First, we can see from Table 2.6(a) that social class matters. Yet, rather than it being those at the lower end of the social order being most at risk as we might expect from the criminological literature with its focus on marginal neighbourhoods, we find it is those in the upper echelons of society who are more prone to experience problematic encounters. University-educated white collar workers on good incomes stood apart from poorly educated blue collar workers on basic incomes. They were *more* likely to experience everyday incivility. Yet, while these

Table 2.6(a) *Victims and non-victims of everyday incivility: a comparison of social attributes*

	Victims		Non-victims	
	%	N	%	N
All respondents	31.3	508	68.7	1,113
Education (χ^2 = 10.49**)				
Completed year 10 or less	26.0	105	74.0	299
Completed high school, trade certificate	30.6	189	69.4	428
Bachelor's degree or higher	35.6	209	64.4	378
Occupation (χ^2 = 17.43***)				
Skilled/semi-skilled/unskilled worker, farm	24.2	57	75.8	179
Clerical, sales	25.5	54	74.5	158
Professional, technical, high level administrator, service	36.7	234	63.3	403
Household income (χ^2 = 11.83**)				
Up to $25,999	26.3	71	73.7	199
$26,000 to $41,599	28.0	56	72.0	144
$41,600 to $77,999	37.6	156	62.4	259
$78,000 and above	33.9	132	66.1	257
Gender (χ^2 = 4.77*)				
Female	33.8	283	66.2	555
Male	28.7	225	71.3	558
Sexuality (χ^2 = 6.22*)				
Mainstream	31.0	486	69.0	1,082
Alternative	50.0	19	50.0	19
Age (χ^2 = 36.89***)				
18–25	40.8	78	59.2	113
26–35	38.4	117	61.6	188
36–55	31.7	214	68.3	461
56–65	23.8	61	76.2	195
Over 65	17.7	31	82.3	144

* $p < .05$
** $p < .01$
*** $p < .001$

Table 2.6(b) *Victims and non-victims of everyday incivility:*
a comparison of social attributes

	Victims		Non-victims	
	%	N	%	N
All respondents	31.3	508	68.7	1,113
Years in Australia (χ^2 = 8.51, ns)				
1–5	23.4	11	76.6	36
6–10	25.7	9	74.3	26
11–15	11.5	3	88.5	23
16–20	40.0	20	60.0	30
More than 20 years	31.8	465	68.2	998
Visible minority (χ^2 = 2.60, ns)				
Yes	22.4	15	77.6	52
No	31.7	493	68.3	1,061
Place of residence (χ^2 = 9.83**)				
Metropolis	33.6	328	66.4	647
Regional centre	32.4	80	67.6	167
Country town	25.1	100	74.9	299

* $p < .05$
** $p < .01$

differences are clearly present in the data, we would make the point
that the disparity between the more and less well off is not overly great.
Second, gender and sexuality have consequences. Women and people of
alternative sexuality are more prone to encounter rude strangers than
men and those with conventional sexuality. The difference is especially
pronounced in the case of sexuality, with one in two gays, lesbians and
trans-gendered persons in the study reporting having experienced everyday incivility within the last month. Third, age counts a lot. Younger
respondents were substantially more likely to have encountered everyday incivility than older respondents. In this case the result mirrors the
well-established finding in the criminological literature that the majority victims of interpersonal crime are young people.

Finally, what of the effects of race/ethnicity and place of residence?
To find out about this turn to Table 2.6(b).

Somewhat surprisingly, race/ethnicity was found to have negligible effects. We might well predict that the experience of everyday incivility will be heightened among subgroups who are less *au fait* with the lived conventions of everyday life in Australia (new arrivals) or who are more easily identified as members of a visible minority 'worthy' of targeting (probably Aboriginal and Torres Strait Islanders, and Asians, see Cowlishaw 1988). The culturally unfamiliar will be more prone to norm-reinforcing actions from the mainstream majority, while the visibly different will be more likely to face prejudice and discrimination from racists and nationalists. Yet our findings suggest there is little support for either of these propositions. By way of qualification, we note that the prospects for discovering statistically significant differences when comparing new arrivals and visible minorities with other subgroups in the study was diminished as a result of the smallish number of cases in these two subgroups. Yet the trends apparent in the available tabulated data are better than no information at all.[5] Finally, where you live counts for experiences of everyday incivility. Rude strangers are encountered with greater regularity by residents of the big city (34 per cent reported an encounter in the prior month) as against residents of the country town (25 per cent). This finding is broadly consistent with that from American data. According to the Public Agenda Survey (2002) from America there was a 17 per cent gap between urban and rural dwellers in responding that they 'practically never' encountered rude or disrespectful behaviour. However, the difference is nowhere near as big as we might have expected given the circulating stereotypes and myths – think, for example, on the film *Escape from New York* and then on *Anne of Green Gables*. Contra

---

[5] Studies of minority groups (whether defined by race, ethnicity, sexuality, religion) generally require over-sampling to compensate for higher refusal rates and a smaller relative population. They also need more sensitive data collection methods, such as ethnographic studies or survey administration by trained, culturally appropriate interviewers (see, for example, Gardner 1995). Our quest to derive a benchmark did not permit such detailed inquiry. We would like to think, however, that the experiences of minorities can be made more meaningful or poignant through a contrast with our benchmark data. For example, a finding on high levels of deliberate verbal and physical abuse (as detected in Hindman's (1953) study of African-American youth or Gardner's exploration of gendered cat calls and wolf whistles) could be set against our results that show the prevalence of unintended, embodied rude actions in the wider population.

Table 2.7 *Risk factors for experiencing*
everyday incivility: rank order

Social attributes	Epsilon[a]
Age	23.1
Occupation	12.5
Household income	11.3
Education	9.6
Place of residence	8.5
Gender	5.1

[a] Epsilon is the percentage difference between
the categories of the independent variable with
the most extreme values.

the imagery of unruly cities and Arcadian rural backwaters, people in
the country were not that far behind their metropolitan counterparts
with respect to the degree to which commonplace incivility is present
in their day-to-day lives.

From having looked at the different risk factors one at a time, we
now ask the question: how much importance do they have in a comparative sense? Which matters the most and which the least? To get
an indication of this, the results from the preceding two tables are
reconfigured and presented in Table 2.7.

Here we now find the array of different social attributes examined
as risk factors rank ordered by the strength of their association with
everyday incivility. (Results for sexuality, years in Australia and visible minority are excluded here due to a lack of robustness resulting
from small numbers in the categories of analytic interest.) The data
show that age clearly matters the most. Social class (whether measured as occupation, income or education) and urban/rural residence
come next, followed by gender. Another way of putting this is that
younger people are much more prone than older people to everyday
incivility. People at the upper end of the social echelon are somewhat
more likely than those in the lower social orders to encounter rude
strangers. Residents of the metropolis and women are marginally
more at risk than people who live in country towns and men.

These findings can be explained in a number of ways and it is worth
introducing these themes here in order to anchor later discussion.

First, certain groups might have divergent thresholds for labelling activities as incivil. Higher rates of reporting might reflect different settings of a 'rude behaviour detection' sensor. One might expect the affluent middle classes, for example, to be hypersensitive to the proprieties of public behaviour. They will tend to see rudeness where others might remain indifferent. Second, we have to think about the odds of encountering a rude stranger in a more statistical way. There might be something about the routines of certain social categories that puts them at risk. This is most obviously the case for young people, who are often out of the home in environments rich in alcohol where there is sexual and status competition. In a similar vein, it is possible that the findings of a positive rude stranger effect for the more affluent social categories reflects the fact that they are moving about the city more than others, perhaps on their way to work or to the leisure activities that are central to their consumption-driven, bourgeois lifestyles. Research in Australia, as elsewhere, indicates the centrality of this pattern in the middle classes (Mullins *et al.* 1999; Woodward 2003). One might profitably contrast these affluent members of the pavement café and chardonnay class with the equally stereotypical pensioner. Shuffling around in tartan slippers, they are trapped in their bungalow by lack of transportation and money, but ironically protected from the dangers of the rude stranger encounter by virtue of their social disadvantage. Third, certain groups might experience higher levels of victimization as they make attractive targets. Women might be presumed by both men and other women to be unlikely to rebuke the rude stranger. Those with alternative sexualities might present a symbolically pleasing temptation to bigots. Later in this book we attempt to disentangle the effects of each of these lifestyle and demographic variables as we unpack the experiences of diverse groups (Chapter 5).

We turn next, however, to investigate a theme suggested by Table 2.2(a). This indicated the very ordinary nature of the places where incivility was encountered. According to our respondents, this was taking place not in the ghetto but in the supermarket, car park and residential street. Could it be that incivility is structured into the familiar everyday life of everyday folk, that it is an ordinary and not an extraordinary event? The following chapter makes an investigation of this issue, before going on to look in more detail at the question of crowds and movements in public places.

The main findings of this chapter are:

- Incivilities are diverse and often trivial. At first glance they do not look criminal or dangerous.
- The majority of rude events involved issues of movement and space management.
- Events can be thought of as occurring in the course of getting somewhere and at destinations. They take place in diverse and ordinary places.
- Somewhat surprisingly destinations were associated with movement-based incivility.
- Rude strangers are surprisingly diverse in terms of social characteristics. They often look respectable. Men seem to be more rude than women.
- Most events were not perceived as intended or deliberately communicative, but were simply selfish or insensitive. However, teenagers, groups and rough-looking people were associated with deliberate incivilities.
- Risk factors for experiencing incivility were being younger (strong effect), being middle class (moderate effect), living in a city and being female (weak effect).

3 | Everyday incivility and the everyday round

Our major finding in our previous chapter was the very ordinary quality of incivility. It took place in everyday locations like the supermarket and car park. Rude people were generally not thugs, lurkers or even troublesome teens. They were as diverse in terms of age, gender and appearance as their victims. We also showed that rudeness could be found in a variety of low-level impolite acts. These were not threatening, malicious or crime-related deeds. Finally, a substantial proportion of events involved movement. Put together these clues suggest that rudeness should be studied as a commonplace rather than exceptional act. It is somehow structured into the opportunity spaces of daily life. It is a product of our mundane trajectories through public environments where there are strangers.

Routine activity and predictable incivility

One way to think about this finding is with routine activity theory (Cohen and Felson 1979). Developed in the field of criminology, this shifts our attention away from the study of deviants and offenders towards the analysis of situations and opportunities. The argument is that we can understand certain forms of crime without having to inquire into motivations, or without looking to faulty values and failed socialization for our explanatory context. Arguing that any given crime has to take place at a certain time and at a certain place, routine activity theory asks questions such as: when do victims and offenders come together? At what time of day are guardians away from attractive property? How do people keep safe? A typical and reliable finding is that many crimes like assault or the theft of mobile phones and iPods take place in 'hot spots', such as the bars and clubs where potential victims and possible offenders converge in space and time at an alcohol-rich environment. Similarly, people are known to break into houses when there is nobody around – the guardians are missing. So-called 'home invasions' are rare for this reason. Often they are mistakes – the criminal thought there was nobody in. Some findings in this literature defy folk wisdom. Contrary to expectations, such work has shown that old people are relatively safe from preda- tory crime. They stay at home more often than other people and so do not encounter would-be criminals. Moreover, their homes are safe from burglary as they have near-permanent guardians (the pensioners themselves) reading the paper, gardening, doing odd jobs and under- taking other kinds of pottering activity. Do such lessons about the time/space patterning of routine activity derived from the study of crime apply also to the distribution of public rudeness? Looking back to another era we find a hint that they do. An isolated, but prescient, study of 1950s African-American youth reported that 64 per cent of the negative inter-racial interactions they experienced took place in just three social locales: public transport; stores; and employment. Why? The answer, as Baker M. Hindman puts it, was that 'the points of contact between Negro youth and white persons are concentrated within a relatively small number of areas of civic and social life' (1953, p. 120). These three locations actually accounted for 60 per cent of all black youth contact with whites. For identical reasons related to rou- tine activity some 51 per cent of their pleasant social experiences with whites also took place on public transport, during employment or in stores. Where people come together seems to matter.

   To reiterate a point we made above in passing: what is particularly interesting about this routine activity perspective is that it does not see individual character as the primary explanatory factor. Common sense tells us that to explain rudeness we need to come up with an explanation for the existence of the 'rude people' who do 'rude' things. For example, that we can explain the distribution of racist incidents against those African-American southern youths in the 1950s by think- ing about the causes of racism among prejudiced rednecks. The routine activity perspective brackets out background issues of personality, cul- ture and dispositions and looks to the situation. What allows a rude encounter to take place has to be a coming together of an offender and a victim, perhaps on a bus ride. Turning to Figure 3.1 we see a major lesson from routine activity theory apparently confirmed. The distribution of events over the day and night is connected to the daily round. Although each individual experience of a rude stranger might be unpredictable to social science or appear to its victim to be simply

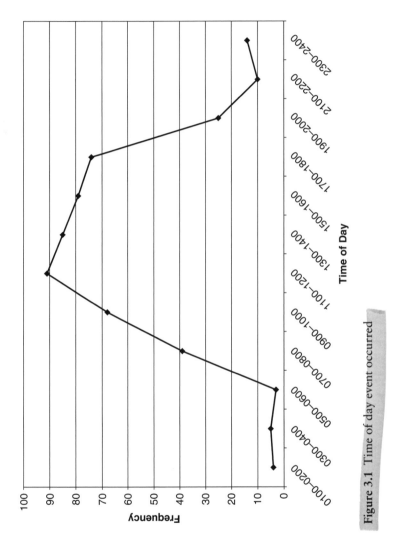

Figure 3.1 Time of day event occurred

the product of chance, in the aggregate we can identify a pattern. This is as robust as Emile Durkheim's (2006 [1897]) famous demonstration in the 1890s that suicide rates contained 'social facts': that Protestants were more suicide prone than Catholics and Jews, or that married people were protected relative to the never-married.

One might think that the sum total of rudeness increases after dark when alcohol-drinking troublemakers, antisocial night owls and assorted deviants stalk the streets. Our results show that the large majority of events occur during daylight hours. Some seven in eight events happen after 6 am and before 7 pm (88 per cent). There is a rapid rise in incivility in the morning and a rapid decrease in the late afternoon. Taken as a whole, events are fairly common between 9 am and 6 pm. The data further suggest the peak time for the occurrence of everyday incivility is between 11 am and 2 pm, or in more human terms 'around lunchtime'. We can explain this simply: rudeness happens where we find a greater density of human interaction.

So much for time. How are the events in the study distributed across different social spaces? In the previous chapter we showed that events could take place at a 'destination' or 'in the process of getting somewhere' (Table 2.2(b)). In overall terms, some seven in ten events occurred during the course of the victim going somewhere. This result is reiterated in Figure 3.2, which identifies five categories of social

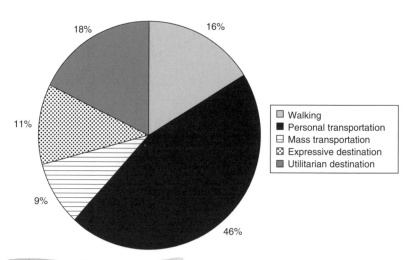

Figure 3.2 Setting of rude event

space in which an incivility might be encountered. The most common setting for experiencing incivility is in a personal vehicle going somewhere. A little over two in five events occurred under these conditions (46 per cent). Simply driving around in a car, then, is a significant risk factor for encountering rudeness. In around one in six incidents incivility was encountered in the process of walking somewhere (16 per cent), or while at a destination associated with utilitarian activities such as a bank or supermarket (18 per cent). The remaining events were spread across two settings: expressive destinations such as bars, clubs or parks (11 per cent) and while going somewhere on mass public transportation (9 per cent).

While our results suggest a general patterning of everyday incivility over both time and space, it is important to recognize that time *and* space might come together in particular ways. Table 3.1 shows the distribution of everyday incivility over different times of day for the five general types of social spaces we have just discussed. Using the time patterns for all events as a benchmark, we can see clearly how everyday incivility ebbs and flows in each type of social space over the course of the daily routine. The first finding we note is that the distribution of events at the most prevalent site of everyday incivility (personal transportation in the automobile) departs very little from the overall pattern of the bell curve. However, each of the other four social spaces of interest rises and falls in concert with the course of the daily round. We can easily chart these regularities with reference to a typical day.

Turning first to early morning, the results show mass transportation stands out as a pivotal site for everyday incivility. It generates some 19 per cent of its daily total of episodes around 7 am or 8 am in the morning (a vignette illustrating this is offered in Chapter 8). Also noteworthy at this time of day is the virtual absence of any events at some destinations. Potential victims and possible rude strangers have simply not yet arrived at these places making their space–time convergence impossible. By mid-morning (0900–1000), the situation on mass transport systems has calmed down, and we witness a fairly even distribution of events across different social spaces at this time. Yet destinations have now started to generate incivility as people arrive. Come the lunchtime period (1100–1400) there is a veritable explosion of everyday incivility on our public walkways. Around six in ten rude stranger encounters involving walking happen during this time. It is

Table 3.1 *Event setting by time of day*[a]

	Early morning (around 7–8 am)	Mid-morning (around 9–10 am)	Late morning/ early afternoon (around 11 am–2 pm)	Mid-afternoon (around 3–4 pm)	Late afternoon (around 5–6 pm)	Night time (around 7pm–6 am)	All events	N
All events	8.6	13.3	35.0	15.9	16.2	11.1	100	452
Public walkway	4.1	8.1	58.1	14.9	8.1	6.8	100	74
Personal transportation	13.3	14.3	29.1	16.7	17.2	9.4	100	203
Mass transportation	19.0	9.5	14.3	9.5	33.3	14.3	100	42
Expressive destination	1.9	13.5	23.1	17.3	17.3	26.9	100	52
Utilitarian destination	0.0	17.3	46.9	17.3	11.1	7.4	100	81

Note: N = 452; χ^2 = 77.3 ($p < .001$)

[a] Time of incident coded to the nearest hour.

an instructive speculation to imagine office workers pressing through crowded pavements as they try to run errands and find a bite to eat in a limited lunch break. As if to confirm this picture, utilitarian destinations come into the frame at this time of day as a key place for meeting the rude stranger (47 per cent of their daily total). By mid-afternoon, the scenario shifts again. We have a situation rather like that of mid-morning with incivility scattered over a range of sites. However, in the late afternoon the action shifts back to mass transportation which starts to generate significant quantities of incivility again (33 per cent of its daily total). Not only are more people travelling on public transport at this time of day – thus increasing the risk of an encounter – they are also crowded together and in a hurry. This is a recipe for rudeness. With the arrival of night-time, we see the expressive destinations finally begin to fire on all cylinders as pivotal zones for everyday incivility. They now generate 27 per cent of their daily total, while at the very same moment utilitarian places drop out of the picture. Banks and offices are closed, but bars, restaurants and cinemas are in full swing. Incivility, then, is intimately shaped by the time–space choreography of daily life. Movements through space, openings and closings, crowds and urgency all play a part in structuring the social distribution of encounters with the rude stranger. To find incivility we need only ask: where is everybody right now?

Routine versus non-routine activities

The findings just presented offer strong evidence for our claim that the daily round drives the risks and distributions of incivility. Rude stranger encounters should be thought of as the normal and predictable output of our normal and predictable lives, the socially choreographed flow of bodies through time and space. There is a crucial test we can perform here to lock in this finding. An alternative hypothesis is that incivility arises on those rare occasions when ordinary people break with the ontological security of their routine and enter new social spaces. Perhaps our survey has recorded unusual events, and we have simply assumed commonplace activity in assembling our story. In such situations people might be unfamiliar with prevailing norms or be more likely to encounter those dubious characters lacking in good manners. It is easy to imagine the scenarios: taking a wrong turn at the lights; making the annual trip to the refuse tip with junk from the attic; visiting our alcoholic cousin who lives on the wrong side of the tracks; going to a distant city on a business trip – these infrequent breaks with respectable and socially familiar settings might be a recipe for trouble. Further, they would not be distinguished by a survey item asking just about time of day or mode of transportation.

Fortunately, we are able to refute this contending interpretation. Figure 3.3 shows the large majority of events happened at a place the respondent goes to at least once a week (70 per cent). Only a small proportion of all events occur in strange locations, those never visited or only once a year. True enough, in relative terms such places are more risky. Places visited only once per year provide more than the 1/364th of all incivility that we might expect, all things being equal. Given an hour in such a location the odds of encountering a rude stranger are disproportionate. Yet in absolute terms people are tending to encounter rude strangers where they go most frequently.

Yet another way to see whether routine activity is the driver of rude encounters is to look at the qualities of the place where they occur. It is reasonable to assume that most upstanding people will want to avoid unpleasant locations and seek to spend more time in those where they might feel safe and which are aesthetically pleasing.

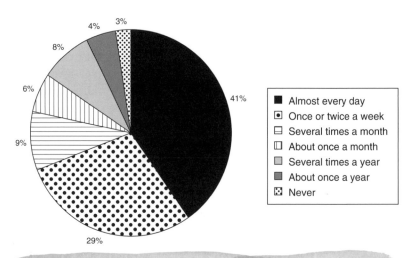

Figure 3.3 Regularity with which the respondent goes to the place where the event happened

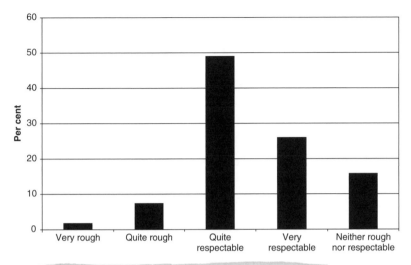

Figure 3.4 Perception of the place where the event happened

Figure 3.4 indicates that some three in four places where the event happened were seen as respectable (75 per cent). Less than one in ten places were perceived to be rough (9 per cent). In short, most events take place on the 'right side of the tracks'.

This finding is consistent with our discovery in the previous chapter that the rude stranger was generally speaking a respectable-looking person. Table 2.4 showed that around three out of every five of the rude strangers were seen as respectable looking (57 per cent), while only one in five were read by their victims as rough looking (21 per cent). We also showed in the previous chapter (Table 2.5) that most events were seen as accidental or as the result of 'bubble' or selfish behaviour (78 per cent) rather than as deliberate efforts to be rude (22 per cent). Also consistent with this picture of ordinary people and ordinary places, we note that respondents were by and large surprised by the action of the rude stranger. Figure 3.5 shows that in the large majority of cases, the respondent was at least quite surprised by what happened (70 per cent). However, in a solid minority of cases, we can see the respondent was not that surprised at all by having experienced the event (30 per cent). In general, though, the behaviour was seen as unexpected and as out of kilter with the ordinary, respectable setting. Rude behaviour in a rough setting, by contrast, would not be surprising.

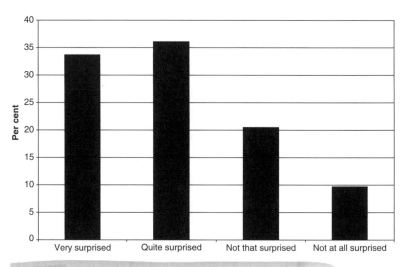

Figure 3.5 Level of surprise at the rude stranger's behaviour

We need next to consider an interesting issue. Is there anything different about those rude events in places visited rarely when contrasted with those visited often? As stated a few paragraphs ago, it seems reasonable to common sense to suppose that occasional visits are made to areas on the wrong side of the tracks. These would place our respectable informants in contact with rough people in problematic areas. Here they might become magnets for deliberate harassment by the antisocial elements so often researched in criminology and in government surveys on popular experiences of antisocial behaviour. Table 3.2 strongly contradicts this hypothesis. For the most part it is important to observe here the *lack* of statistically significant correlations. Respondents were no more prone to see the place as rough if they visited it almost every day, or as respectable if they visited it infrequently (Table 3.2(i)). Consistent with this hypothesis, respondents were no more prone to be surprised by events that occurred at places they visited infrequently, nor less surprised by events that happened at places they attended regularly (Table 3.2(iv)). Whether the person was seen as rough or respectable, or as motivated by bad intentions, seems to be unrelated to the regularity with which the place where the event occurred was visited. What does all this mean? The finding suggests that by and large the usual rules apply. Rude encounters in places visited rarely are not of a special type. They do not involve good people

Table 3.2 *Regularity of presence at place of event by event characteristics*

	Almost every day	Once or twice a week to several times a month	About once a month at most
(i) Rough or respectable place ($\chi^2 = 6.8$, ns; N = 500)			
Rough	10.4	9.1	3.9
Neither	15.9	20.8	10.5
Respectable	73.8	70.1	85.5
Total	100	100	100
(ii) Rough or respectable person ($\chi^2 = 1.1$, ns; N = 475)			
Rough	20.8	24.6	21.5
Neither	22.6	18.8	19.0
Respectable	56.6	56.5	59.5
Total	100	100	100
(iii) Perceived motivation of rude stranger ($\chi^2 = 2.0$, ns; N = 494)			
Simply acting in own self-interest	78.3	81.1	72.0
Deliberately trying to offend or disadvantage	21.7	18.9	28.0
Total	100	100	100
(iv) Level of surprise at the rude stranger's behaviour ($\chi^2 = 7.8$, ns; N = 507)			
Very surprised	31.5	32.9	44.3
Quite surprised	35.2	42.1	34.2
Not surprised	33.2	25.0	21.5
Total	100	100	100

who find themselves in bad places where they get their annual quota of rude stranger activity.

The social similarity of victims and offenders

Another means of assessing the importance of routine activities is to compare the demographic characteristics of offenders and victims.

With respect to criminal offending, the prevailing public discourse views offenders and victims as categorically distinct, with morally corrupt criminals preying on innocent victims (Singer 1981, p. 779). Criminals and victims are narrated within a melodramatic frame, one in which they have few social or moral commonalities (Sacco and Kennedy 2002, p. 71). The image that comes to mind is of unruly teens victimizing an elderly person, or intoxicated men harassing upstanding women. This mixing of offenders and victims is seemingly at odds with the routine activities perspective. The latter proffers that social life and daily routines entail a fair degree of segregation. Women are likely to spend more time in supermarkets, while men spend more time at sporting events. Younger people spend more time using public transportation and visiting night clubs, while the elderly are more apt to stay at home and potter.[1] From this perspective, the demographic pattern of routine activities and leisure preferences suggests that victims of crime will typically resemble the demographic profile of their offenders. People are likely to congregate in places with others who share similar backgrounds and lifestyles, which increase the odds of victimization by someone of the same age, gender or social class. We might expect a similar association for rude encounters. The young would presumably direct rude behaviour at other youths, men would victimize other men and so on, simply because people more frequently find themselves in the presence of socially similar strangers.

The ELIAS data allow us to compare two demographic characteristics of rude strangers and their victims – gender and age. If we are correct in our speculation about rude behaviour and routine activities, we should find more evidence of *intra*-group than *inter*-group victimization. There is indeed some evidence of this. Let's first consider gender, which is presented in the first part of Table 3.3. Sixty-nine per cent of incidents involving female rude strangers also involved female

[1] We do not simply rely on stereotypes and conjecture when making these claims or generating heuristic images. The ELIAS Survey included questions about time spent in various types of public places, and indeed there are correlations between gender and time in supermarkets as well as age and use of public transportation. We draw more heavily on these indicators of time spent in public in Chapters 5 and 7.

Table 3.3 *Victim and rude stranger similarities: age and gender*

	Rude stranger's gender		
Victim's gender	Female (%)	Male (%)	
Female	68.8	49.4	
Male	31.2	50.6	
	100 (N = 154)	100 (N = 340)	

	Rude stranger's age		
Victim's age	Child or teenager (%)	20s–30s (%)	40s or older (%)
18–25	19.4	21.0	10.6
Older than 25	80.6	79.0	89.4
	100 (N = 36)	100 (N = 205)	100 (N = 236)

Note: χ^2/degrees of freedom ratio for the gender comparison is 16.2/1 ($p < .001$). The χ^2/degrees of freedom ratio for the age comparison is 9.3/2 ($p < .01$).

victims, whereas females were victims in only half of the incidents perpetrated by males. Males were on the receiving end of 51 per cent of rude acts committed by other males compared with 31 per cent of rude acts perpetrated by females. The victim–offender association for age is comparable, although not quite as strong. Here we split our respondents into two groups to enable a comparison of teens and young adults (18–25 years old) relative to adults and the elderly. The bottom portion of Table 3.3 suggests that about 20 per cent of rude events involving a child or teenage stranger are directed at respondents between 18 and 25 years old. Practically the same percentage is found for rude acts committed by rude strangers in their twenties or thirties (21 per cent). By comparison, fewer than 11 per cent of rude acts committed by strangers in their forties or older are directed at young respondents. We also see that adult respondents are more likely to endure rude behaviour from strangers in their forties or older (89 per cent) than from strangers in their twenties or thirties (79 per cent) or teenagers (81 per cent). As with gender, we thus see some congruence between the ages of rude strangers and their victims. We find less evidence of men preying on women or the young singling out older respondents.

Table 3.4 *Victim's gender by offender's gender and type of setting*

Victim's gender	Transportation settings Rude stranger's gender		Destination settings Rude stranger's gender	
	Female (%)	Male (%)	Female (%)	Male (%)
Female	60.3	52.5	78.6	42.2
Male	39.7	47.5	21.4	57.8
	100 (N = 73)	100 (N = 244)	100 (N = 70)	100 (N = 64)

Note: χ^2/degrees of freedom ratio for transportation settings is 1.4/1 (ns). The χ^2/degrees of freedom ratio for destination settings is 18.6/1 ($p < .001$).

Before moving on we refer to one additional analysis germane to routine activities and victim–offender dyads. If we are right in our speculation about routine activities and rude encounters then we should expect intra-category incidents to be especially common in destination settings, but less common where there is more social mixing, such as transportation settings. We suspect the former is where people are most likely to come into contact with their own, while the latter tends to be more heterogeneous. The comparisons for gender reported in Table 3.4 align with this expectation.[2] The correlation between victim's gender and offender's gender is fairly weak and not statistically significant when looking at events that occurred while in transit. In contrast, the correlation is quite strong when looking at destinations. In the latter type of setting over 78 per cent of rude acts committed by females involved a female victim, while only 42 per cent of acts committed by men were directed at female victims. Male victims were also much more likely to describe a male rude stranger (58 per cent) than a female (21 per cent). This finding is consistent with our argument that rude encounters and the characteristics of rude strangers are fundamentally related to routine activities that enable strangers to converge in time and space.

---

[2] We did not present the results for age by destination because some of the cell frequencies were quite small. For instance, only four incidents involved children or teenage rude strangers in destination settings.

Dromology

In the past few pages we have seen routine activity theory providing a fruitful lead for our inquiry. We have seen that most incivility takes place where people go regularly, and its nature is patterned by the time–space choreography of daily life. The performance of tasks and movement around the city allocate risks of encounters. This vision of human circulation through the dimensions of time and space is one that offers a vivid alternative to the conventional approach to incivility which allocates the problem to neighbourhoods and their populations (see Phillips and Smith 2006a). Most research designs envisage the city and the suburb in static terms and take citizens as defined by their residential communities. In such an account incivilities occur in zones (such as blocks or census tracts) and at no particular time of day, not along the vectors and nodes through which subjects move and accomplish their daily routines. An alternative account of the city that we find appealing has been advanced by the French urban theorist, Paul Virilio. According to Virilio (1986), modernity is fundamentally characterized by speed. Lives are lived in a continual blur of motion. A fundamental problem for social and cultural systems is the regulation of speed and the coordination of multiple velocities. He calls the study of speed in social life 'dromology', and insists that we live in a dromological condition. As one commentator puts it, for Virilio 'the relentless logic of speed plays a crucial part ... in the organization of territory and the transformation of social, cultural and political life' (Armitage 1999, p. 6). Virilio is sometimes called a 'hyper-modern' theorist, yet this is a vision that finds its way back to the writings of nineteenth-century crowd theorists and onwards to the futurists of the early twentieth century, thence to critical writers of the 1930s like Walter Benjamin (1983). This latter figure highlighted the presence of the strolling flâneur in the emergent consumption spaces of urban capitalism and recognized the possibility for both voluntary and involuntary *derivée* or 'drift'. This is the process in which the citizen is carried along with the flow of human movement down sidewalks and through the spaces of the city like a leaf in a stream.

Such a vision of perpetual movement finds a recent ally in the work of the social theorist, John Urry, who has pointed to the need for a sociology of what he calls 'flows'. He contrasts this to the more methodologically convenient approach that assumes stasis. According to

Urry, the social sciences have been traditionally concerned with the analysis of spatial regions, operating, for example, through the mapping and analysis of national societies. We need, however, to also study the 'flows of people' within and between spatial zones and the ways that such flows might relate to 'desires for work, housing, leisure, religion, family relationships' and so forth. Urry's primary concern is with the long-distance transnational flows that have accompanied the globalization of social life, but he recognizes that this paradigm shift is one that can and should accommodate movements within 'the geographical intersections of region, city and place' (Urry 2000, p. 186). Indeed, his own slightly later explorations of 'automobility' conform to this pattern. Here Urry analyses the ways in which the car has had a profound impact upon our daily lives. It has both made possible and compelled new and freer time–space routines, and has reshaped the city: 'automobility divides workplaces from homes, producing lengthy commutes into and across the city'. Further he notes that 'people inhabit congestion, jams, temporal uncertainties and health-threatening city environments, as a consequence of being encapsulated in a domestic, cocooned, moving capsule' (2004, p. 28). Movement, then, is part of our lives. We do not simply move from A to B, but rather spend a large proportion of our time in motion or, more broadly, in the process of moving.

Our findings to date have indicated that a focus on flows through space might be a fruitful line of attack for the investigation of incivility. Transportation, walking, transit nodes and vectors all looked strongly predictive of the rude encounter. Just how far can we push this understanding? If there is a shortfall to routine activity theory it is that it adumbrates 'routine' without looking at 'activity' in more micro-detail. It is the study of what people do in general rather than just how they do it. Or, put another way, there is no study of embodied and vehicular *movement*. In the previous chapter we determined that collisions and bumps, blocked motion and invasions of personal space were common forms of incivility. These suggest the need for a study of the micro-contexts of movement. We were also puzzled by the fact that movement-based incivilities seemed to take place at 'destinations'. Perhaps we might understand incivility as generated by both the macro-level context of the daily round, which distributes risks, and by proximate and local environments that are the efficient cause of many specific incidents involving bodies themselves.

Table 3.5 *Crowding and mass movement*

	%
(i) Level of crowding in the social setting (N = 503)	
Very crowded	15.7
Quite crowded	28.8
Not that crowded	33.0
Not at all crowded	22.5
Total	100
(ii) Status of crowd (N = 506)	
Crowd in motion	69.2
Crowd stationary	30.8
Total	100
(iii) Status of victim/status of crowd (N = 506)	
Victim moving/crowd moving	50.2
Victim moving/crowd stationary	5.7
Victim stationary/crowd moving	19.0
Victim stationary/crowd stationary	25.1
Total	100

Are rude events, for example, the result of individuals disrupting the flow of movement within shared public space? Or are they simply the product of the density of bodies in a space? How strongly do crowds and flows predict incivil encounters? We turn next to this issue of the dromology of settings.

The social environment of crowds and mass movement

One of the characters famously remarks in Jean-Paul Sartre's (1987 [1944]) play, *Huis Clos*: 'Hell is other people.' Our results confirm Sartre's plea for the widely misunderstood remark to be taken as an existential literary gesture rather than as a claim to positive knowledge. A high density of 'other people' does not look to be a strong predictor of a rude encounter (or 'hell'). We are being a little playful here, but still, as Table 3.5 shows, the majority of events took place in locations that were not particularly crowded (56 per cent). Nevertheless, the theme of dromology, or movement in space as a

pivotal aspect of social life, stands up quite well. Looking down
the table we see that in seven out of the ten cases, incivil encounters
occurred under wider conditions of mass movement (69 per cent) and
in half of all cases both the victim and the wider crowd were moving
(50 per cent). Only a quarter of events took place in contexts where
both the individual and the wider crowd were stationary, a situation
we might find at the cinema, for example.

So, it is *moving* victims and crowds that are particularly risky.
This finding is augmented by the first result in Table 3.6. This shows
that fully three in four rude strangers were moving at the time of
the encounter (76 per cent), as well as just over half of victims (56
per cent). Now to three specificities of this domain: relative speed;
mental states; and agility. We know from driving down a smooth
flowing highway that the social organization of speed is possible. As
long as all drivers are moving at more or less the same velocity and in
the same direction there are few problems. It is when we encounter a
slow moving truck, a *peleton* of cycling enthusiasts, a horse and cart,
or on the other hand are subjected to tailgating that trouble starts.
This problem of regulating mobilities is one that is recognized in
diverse social settings. Some highways in Europe stipulate *minimum*
speeds. Norms regulate whether to walk on the left or the right of
the sidewalk. Failure to observe the norm can cause problems. In
Manhattan, for example, British tourists are a nuisance as they follow their habit passing to the left in places like Fifth Avenue. In the
world of ballroom dancing, the dancers always circulate counter-
clockwise in what is known as the 'line of dance'. The faster dancers
are expected to stay on the outside, the less nimble shuffle around
the centre. Accidents happen when ignorant novices or arrogant and
overconfident experts ignore protocol. Perhaps the most graphic illus-
tration of society's ability to regulate speed and direction is the cult
film *Koyaanisqatsi* (Reggio 1982). Set to an hypnotic Philip Glass
soundtrack of repetitive arpeggios, this dialogue-free documentary
features time-lapse photography of cars streaming down freeways,
planes lining up to take off, crowds surging onto and off escalators
and so forth. The movie is generally interpreted as an indictment of
modernity, technology and alienation, these being reflected in the
regimented flows of mass mobility. Reading against the grain, however, we could also see this film as an acknowledgement or even celebration of our remarkable capacity to move large numbers of people

Table 3.6 *Movement-related qualities of victims and rude strangers*

	%
(i) Status of participants (N = 506)	
Victim	
Moving	55.9
Stationary	44.1
	100
Rude stranger (N = 506)	
Moving	75.5
Stationary	24.5
	100
(ii) Desired velocity (N = 254)	
Victim	
Faster than everyone else	10.3
Around the same speed	73.6
Slower than everyone else	16.1
	100
Rude stranger (N = 298)	
Faster than everyone else	58.4
Around the same speed	30.2
Slower than everyone else	11.4
	100
(iii) Company (N = 508)	
Victim	
Alone	54.7
One other	27.2
Two others	7.1
Three others	4.7
Four or more others	6.3
	100
Rude stranger (N = 488)	
Alone	64.8
One other	19.3
Two others	6.8
Three others	4.7
Four or more others	4.4
	100

Table 3.6 (*cont.*)

	%
(iv) Victim felt rushed (N = 506)	
Felt very rushed	4.3
Felt quite rushed	7.5
Felt a little rushed	10.7
Did not feel rushed	77.5
	100

rapidly through space in a synchronized and collision-free manner. Certainly, our data suggest that this is a non-trivial dimension of everyday social life whose presence should not be carelessly wished away: unpleasant and unwanted consequences follow when flow becomes problematic.

As Table 3.6 shows, in less than one of four cases did victims report that they had been trying to travel either faster (10 per cent) or slower (16 per cent) than everyone else. For the most part they were simply going with the flow. Nearly six in ten of our rude strangers, however, were thought to be trying to go faster than everyone else. While we need to be a little cautious about this result, due to variation in actor subjectivities in the interpretation of speed – what they perceive in others and themselves (Dant 2004) – the pattern in the data is strong. An image is suggested. Rude strangers are trying to move fast through crowds or through traffic, perhaps initiating unwanted interactions by barging and pushing. Victims are blockages to flow. The strangers are the active party, the comparatively passive victim the recipient of this action. We find this possibility illustrated quasi-experimentally in a report by *Guardian* fashion correspondent, Jess Cartner-Morley (2009, p. 4). An habitual multi-tasking, frantic Londoner she was instructed by her editor to 'write a piece about the Go Slow movement' and to 'stop rushing about'. Now standing still on the escalator for the first time she found herself on the receiving end of mixed-velocity incivility. There were 'passengers racing down the stairs on either side', and 'barely concealed huffs as they were forced to deviate centimetres from the fastest route from A to B'. By going with the flow rather than being the faster moving 'active' agent as usual, she had become a victim rather than a perpetrator.

What about psychological states? Today our lives are often full, yet the supply of time is limited. Perhaps a feeling of urgency might also contribute to curt social relationships and brusque movements. Certainly, this is a common speculation (Public Agenda 2002; Truss 2005). We are not able to report on the thinking of the rude stranger, but whether they were in motion or stationary, a surprisingly small minority of our victims reported feeling very or quite rushed at the time the incivil event took place (12 per cent). Finally, we come to the question of agility. Whether in motion or stationary, encumbrance – the quality of being physically large, loaded up or possibly overloaded – can have the effect of interrupting the steady flow of human traffic. Slow speed, large dimensions and unpredictable movements are all connected with encumbrance. Movement in a group can also be disruptive to the flow of bodies. The group can become a blockage or clot to the general motion, or if faster than the crowd (unusual) it can become a bulldozer pushing a way through. Lovers will find that sometimes just holding hands is difficult on a busy sidewalk. Although our data showed that most victims and strangers were on their own, a significant minority were with one or more others. In nearly half of all cases victims were travelling in company (45 per cent). While in the majority of these cases there was only the one other person alongside the victim (27 per cent), it is noteworthy that in a little over one in ten incidents there were at least three others with them (11 per cent). Intuitively this seems a rather large number. As we reported before in Table 2.4 and repeat in Table 3.6, rude strangers were usually on their own. Only a third of them were with one or more other people. In general, then, victims were slightly more likely to be in a group than rude strangers. It is important not to speculate too wildly from this finding, but we are able to dispute the 'broken windows' common sense that gangs of rude strangers embolden themselves in packs and, armed with squeegees or waving their beer bottles, predate on hapless individuals. If we have a rival image it is that victim groups get in the way of fast moving, rude individuals.

In Table 3.7 we unpack group transit in more detail and with a particular focus on non-autonomous burdens, or, put another way, those people and objects that require supervision. We can see that the victim was in charge of at least one child in one in seven events (15 per cent), and responsible for conveying someone else (for example,

Table 3.7 *Payload-related qualities: victim and rude stranger*

	%
Overseeing children	
Victim	
Yes	15.0
No	85.0
	100
Rude stranger	
Yes	5.7
No	94.3
	100
Victim was conveying others (carrying, pushing, pulling, leading)	
Yes	10.0
No	90.0
	100
Transporting payload	
Victim	
Yes	18.1
No	81.9
	100
Rude stranger (N = 489)	
Yes	11.9
No	88.1
	100
Total payload index	
Victim	
One load	12.2
Two loads	6.5
Three loads	2.4
Cumulative %	21.1
Rude stranger	
One load	12.6
Two loads	2.2
Cumulative %	14.8

Note: N = 508 unless otherwise noted. No data were available on 'conveying others' for the rude stranger.

a frail elder) in one in ten incidents (10 per cent). Furthermore, in nearly one in every five incidents the victim was involved in transporting some kind of 'payload' at the time (i.e., groceries, stroller, trolley, trailer – 18 per cent). On average, around one in five victims was burdened with some kind of encumbrance (21 per cent), as against about one in seven strangers (15 per cent). Put together with our results on speed, it seems once again as if there is a slim tendency for victims to get in the way and rude strangers to be making haste.

To get one last and more general oversight of how individual trajectories through space matter for everyday incivility, it is interesting to bring all the incidents together, and to look at how they are distributed with respect to the mobility status of both the victim and the rude stranger at the time (moving or stationary). A first interesting point to note about Figure 3.6 is that only a small proportion of

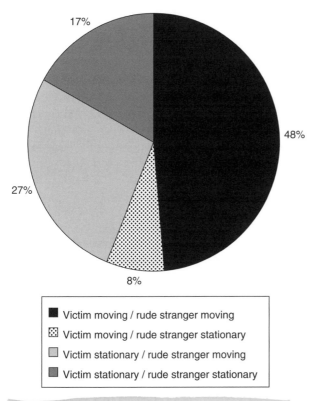

Figure 3.6 Mobility status of victim and rude stranger

incidents did not involve either a victim or rude stranger in motion (17 per cent), a finding consistent with the fact that only 31 per cent of events involved stationary crowd situations (reported earlier in Table 3.5). Indeed, the most common configuration of mobility statuses under which everyday incivility occurs is when both the victim and rude stranger are in motion – these amounted to around half of all cases (48 per cent). For incidents where there was only one party in motion, this was far more likely to be the rude stranger than the victim, with a ratio of around 3.5 to 1 (27 per cent as against 8 per cent). Again this finding is consistent with our image of passive victims getting in the way of active strangers. In sum, not only do the data show being in motion matters pivotally for the occurrence of everyday incivility, but that discordant mobility statuses contribute to a significant proportion of incidents – around one in three. In other words, the meeting of a moving vehicle and a stationary vehicle; a moving pedestrian and the person at the bus stop; the window shopping *flâneur* and the person rushing for a train – these all provide potentials for commonplace rude events.

Perhaps we have overloaded the reader with information in these last few paragraphs. The summary story is quite simple. Our data suggest that movement, especially when difficult, disjunctive and out of step with the general flow can play a role in a substantial proportion of incivil events. The failed coordination of mobilities does not account for all situations, but it does seem to cover a large number of contingencies. Here, then, we have a finding that dromology matters.

The major findings of this chapter are:

- Incivility is patterned by the daily choreography of collective human movements. Most takes place during daytime. Particular social locations become hot spots when people converge there to perform daily tasks.
- Incivility arises from routine. Most takes place in locations where people go frequently, not from occasional visits to bad locations.
- True enough, some rude strangers are found in locations where people go infrequently. These places are generally seen as 'respectable' rather than as 'rough'. The incivil encounter is not expected.

- People are often victimized by social similars, especially in destinations.
- Situations of mass movement are a common attribute of the settings where incivility takes place. Rude strangers are often seeking to move at a higher velocity than the rest of the crowd. Victims are not infrequently slower and encumbered by other people or by baggage.

Week #4
Readings
(end)

4 | *Emotions and sequences*

So far we have mapped out some basic issues. We know about the identities of perpetrators and victims. We also know what the commonplace forms of incivility look like. We have found out where and when and even why many encounters with rude strangers take place. In this chapter things become a little more complex. As we explained at the outset, this book is a study of encounters between two people. Here we look at how these meetings unfold over time. We focus on two important questions: just how do people *feel* when they encounter the rude stranger? What, if anything, do they *do* to remedy the situation?

Emotions and incivility

The existing literature suggests that we already know the answer to both these questions. Writing back in the early 1970s the famous symbolic interactionist Erving Goffman (1971) established the template with his work *Relations in Public*. Here the life of city dwellers is described as one revolving around suspicion and mistrust. As they navigate urban spaces they scan for dangers, constantly on guard and feeling unease. The emotions of fear and anxiety are barely suppressed and the encounter with the incivil other is traumatizing. Individuals develop action strategies of retreat and avoidance. This vision has been amplified more recently in the critical sociology of Zygmunt Bauman (2003), who identifies 'mixophobic' sentiments in the metropolis and suggests that social life is organized such that individuals avoid encounters with difference and risk as they move between secure bubbles dotted around the city: the home in a gated community, the mall, the country club, the office. For Bauman such lifestyle routines have become a strategy to reduce pervasive fear and anxiety, but at the cost of increasing homogeneity and inequality.

Although these respected authors write from the camp of interpretative social theory, there is surprising congruity with the spirit
of policy relevant criminological research of a more positivistic bent.
As we pointed out in an earlier chapter, the 'broken windows' tradition of research suggests that minor incivility might lead to major
crime and urban decay. The emotion of fear plays a key role in this
dynamic. Rude strangers are perceived as threatening signs in the
landscape. They generate worries about crime and good citizens take
flight. Although many aspects of this approach are highly contested
(Harcourt 2001) – such as the causal link of disorder to actual crime –
the fact that incivility can result in fear has indeed been demonstrated
to some extent (Borooah and Carcach 1997; Warr 1994).

This might all seem perfectly reasonable were it not for the fact that
such research and interpretative speculation is predicated upon the
investigation or imaginative reconstruction of 'worst case scenarios'
for incivility. These are episodes in which respectable citizens find
themselves in encounters with dubious individuals in rough locations.
Fear might well make sense if an apparently alcoholic or mentally-ill
homeless person approaches us with a squeegee at an on-ramp stoplight
as we return from the opera late at night. Our research, however, has
uncovered a very ordinary quality to incivility. If the occurrence has a
routine quality, perhaps the emotional register will be different. Our
confidence in the existing fear–avoidance paradigm should be further
reduced due to the nature of conventional research protocols. Having
decided that 'fear' is the dominant response, or the only response
of policy relevance, researchers ask only about this. Respondents are
often primed to respond 'I would fear, I would avoid' by the wider
context within which specific questions on incivility are asked. For
example, they might have been told by the interviewer at the outset
that they are participating in a 'crime victimization survey'.

What might be the alternative ways that people deal with incivility?
Somewhat surprisingly, turning to the resources of classical social theory can help us be more imaginative. Writing around the turn of the
nineteenth century the German theorist Georg Simmel (1997) noted
that urban life in modernity had a divergent affective tone from that
which had gone before. Unlike the village and the market town it was
full of incessant stimuli that threaten to overwhelm the senses. City
dwellers had, therefore, developed a blasé attitude, responding with
an affect-neutral orientation towards an ongoing cascade of events

and even ignoring much of what was going on around them. A few decades later the aesthete Walter Benjamin (1983) modified this perspective by suggesting that city life had generated forms of *flâneurie*. Citizens had now become wandering spectators observing the life of the city with amusement and interest, but not participating in it in any way requiring deep personal commitment.

This narrative of a loss of affect need not be our only option. The work of Norbert Elias (1978 [1939]) on the 'civilizing process' traced the shift in manners and emotions over the centuries in Western Europe. He noted the role of the emotion of 'disgust' in the long-term process through which bodies and behaviours became ever more tightly regulated. As norms shifted, activities which had once passed without notice (defecating in the street, public sex, spitting) started to be viewed as repulsive, first by the upper strata of society but subsequently by the lower classes to whom novel behaviour rules slowly trickled down. Strategies of avoidance and aversion were generated by the desire to avoid this internal emotional response. How many readers of this book have visited – or would like to visit – an abattoir? Pieter Spierenburg's (1984) discussion of the history of the public execution nicely demonstrates this thesis. Displays of public torture and the gibbet, once seen as a form of amusing entertainment, were later abandoned by the middle classes as revolting spectacles. Respectable people simply did not show up. Soon the working classes followed.

The founding father of sociology, Emile Durkheim (1980 [1893]), offers yet another possibility. Way back in the 1890s he asserted that normative breaches were rarely trivial. Deep down they were violations of the collective conscience and of a sacred moral bond that held society together. The result had to be anger. Coming with this was a desire for punitive vengeance. By exacting sanctions against the offender society could repair the damage to its cultural codes, reaffirm its moral boundaries and express its disapproval in a therapeutic way. Durkheim's speculation has received diverse empirical support, one of the more interesting examples of which is a result from Baker M. Hindman's (1953) survey of African-American youth in the early 1950s – an intriguing early study which we have already mentioned on two occasions. He noted that being called 'nigger' by whites tended to generate aggressive feelings. With other, more subtle forms of rudeness and discrimination this was not so much the case. Hindman comments, 'the youth feel a considerable amount of

Table 4.1 *Emotions at three time-points*

Emotion	At the time of the event, in the first instance (%)	Immediately after the rude stranger had gone (%)	Looking back on the event today (%)
Level of surprise			
Very surprised	33.7	22.0	n.a
Quite surprised	36.1	32.5	
Not that surprised	20.5	28.9	
Not at all surprised	9.7	16.5	
Type of emotion			
Anger	59.6	40.7	15.2
Fear	11.2	6.3	2.8
Disgust	26.8	21.9	9.4
Shame	3.5	2.8	1.6
Didn't really care	6.1	17.1	51.2
Other emotion	16.5	24.8	22.0
Can't recall	0.6	0.4	0.2
Satisfied	n.a.	2.0	2.8
Emotional intensity			
Very strong	27.3	20.6	6.0

Note: Types of emotions were not mutually exclusive categories and thus the column percentages do not sum to 100.

resentment over the use of the term. It may represent a frustration of their basic need for recognition and self-respect' (1953, p. 127). This line of reasoning points, perhaps, to a flaw in Durkheim's collectivistic reasoning about norm violation. Perhaps anger arises not from a sense of attack on general shared values, but rather from insults to the dignity of the self.

How do these varying perspectives fare? Table 4.1 offers a concise overview. We note first the prevalence of surprise, an emotion we reviewed in another context in the previous chapter. Moving down the table, the left-hand column allows us to adjudicate on the clash of theoretical Titans that we have set up in recent paragraphs. Durkheim comes out of the fray looking good. Around six in every ten events resulted in anger. Elias also makes a respectable showing. Disgust features in around a quarter of all encounters. Fear and Simmel's indifference did not fare so well, being found in 11 per cent and 6 per cent of events, respectively. As we move from left to right through the table we note that the emotions had a short half-life. Respondents were significantly less likely to feel any emotion once the stranger had gone. In the case of anger, for example, only around one in seven respondents reported still having this emotion at the time of interview. An aggregate measure of all 'very strong' emotions reported at the bottom of the table confirms this picture. Although more than a quarter of all events generated a 'very strong' emotional reaction at the time of the first rude action, when looking back only 6 per cent of respondents still reported having strong feelings. We finally note that the blasé attitude ('didn't/don't really care') grows in significance over time. In other words, the modal path is from strong feelings of anger and disgust towards weak emotions or indifference. This suggests that Simmel is both right and wrong. At the time of the encounter individuals are rarely able to call upon a blasé buffer as he would predict, but as time goes by they are generally able to neutralize the strong affect engendered by the initially shocking event. We return to this theme in Chapter 6, where we explore the coping behaviours through which actors come to deal with their encounters.

Action in the face of incivility

If the dominant Goffmanian and criminological approaches to thinking about incivility fare poorly when it comes to predicting emotions, they do somewhat better when it comes to behavioural responses. Figure 4.1 shows that only around a third of events resulted in a direct response to the rude stranger. This would be in the form of a sanction or a communication that the stranger had done something wrong. However, in two-thirds of cases the victim did not respond directly to the stranger. Put another way, they were avoiding confrontation. We find this pattern reflected in another and more serious aspect of social life: interpersonal violence. As Randall Collins (2008) discovered in a far-reaching investigation, most individuals will avoid fights if given the chance.

Turning to Table 4.2 we can see what happens in the smaller section of the pie shown in Figure 4.1. What of the range and distribution

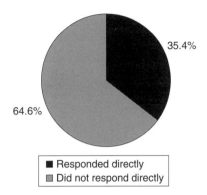

35.4%

64.6%

■ Responded directly
▨ Did not respond directly

Figure 4.1 Type of response to rude stranger's conduct

of direct responses used by victims? We reported in Chapter 2 that many rude encounters involved bodily movement, bodily collisions and competition for space (see Tables 2.1(a) and 2.1(b)). It is surprising to see that responses to rudeness rarely took this form. Only 4 per cent of incidents saw our victims blocking, bumping, tailing and so forth in response to the initial rude action by the stranger. Language violations such as swearing made up only a small proportion of the initial rude events. We find, however, that verbal responses are very common, being found in around three in every five events where there is a direct engagement with the rude stranger. Finally, we see that paralinguistic gestures, looks and sounds are not uncommon, and take place in around one event in every four. So efforts to communicate rather than compete seem to be central. When people have been victims of rudeness and they respond, it seems that their priority is generally to make the offender know that they have done something wrong. There is something of an inversion here. If rudeness is often accidental, physical and not intended to send a message (see Table 2.5), direct responses to the rude stranger are intentional and communicative.

What exactly might be the purpose of this communication? We believe that the integrity of the self is central. If Erving Goffman was a little wrong when writing of the prevalence of fear as a response to incivil society, he was correct in pointing to the fact that everyday life is organized around incessant rituals of deference and demeanour (see Collins 2004; Goffman 1967). Drawing upon Durkheim's

Table 4.2 *Types of direct responses to rude stranger and reported motivation*

(i) Types of direct responses	%
Movement	
(a) Bumped into them	1.1
(b) Blocked their way	1.1
(c) Tailed them	0.5
(d) Invaded their personal space	0.5
(e) Made an exaggerated show of making way for them	1.1
	4.3%
Language	
(f) Made short statement: self-directed	11.0
(g) Made short statement: other-directed	46.1
(h) Verbally abused them	5.8
	62.9%
Sounds	
(i) Sighed or muttered loudly	1.1
(j) Increased own noise level	6.8
	7.9%
Gestures	
(k) Remonstrative facial gesture	8.9
(l) Remonstrative hand gesture	3.1
(m) Other remonstrative gesture	1.1
(n) Impassive facial gesture	2.1
(o) Impassive hand gesture	2.1
(p) Other impassive gesture	1.6
	18.9%
Criminal offence	
(q) Assaulted or attacked them	0.5%
(r) Other	11.0%
Total	100%

(ii) Reported motivation	
To disadvantage them	5.6
To advantage yourself	6.7
To offend them	6.7
To get them to give you some respect	72.6
Total	100%

Note: N = 179 respondents and 191 reported responses (respondents could report more than one response).

idea that modernity had a 'cult of the individual', Goffman elaborated a theory of everyday life in which various interactional micro-rituals continually testified to the integrity and worth of interacting subjects. Simply by saying 'please' or 'thank you', or by respecting other people's personal space we signify that we perceive others as valid equals. Further, belief in the need to defend the sacred self is deeply internalized. Because feelings of humiliation, shame and anger can result if a stigmatized status is imposed through interaction, individuals will take steps to protect and defend their dignity (see also Hindman 1953).

Consistent with this theory, when we presented respondents with a range of different possible intentions behind their direct response to the rude stranger, the most commonly selected motivating factor was to 'get them to give you some respect' (see bottom of Table 4.2). Nearly three in four respondents selected this option (73 per cent). In comparison, neither of the three alternative reasons presented to respondents – 'disadvantage them', 'advantage yourself' and 'offend them' – were nominated in more than one in fourteen cases (7 per cent). In short, responding to the rude stranger is mostly about meaning and identity, not competition for scarce resources (e.g., space), or self-interest conceived in more competitive or Darwinian terms. It is interesting to reflect that this finding is consistent with a wider body of research. The ethnographer Elijah Anderson's (1999) investigations of the 'code of the street' in poor African-American ghettos indicates that the search for respect and the need to defend status are central characteristics of urban minority cultures and can lie behind deadly vendettas in a context of gang culture. In his study of 'righteous slaughter' the sociologist Jack Katz (1988) comes to a similar conclusion. He shows that many people are killed in puzzlingly trivial incidents. Perhaps a driveway is blocked or some food is splashed by the eventual victim, with this precipitating their murder. Katz explains an emotion–interaction dynamic in which the humiliation of the victim turns into a kind of rage in which they stand up for themselves and what they believe in, perhaps property or dignity. What unites these two studies with ours is the finding that sanctions are a way for individuals to affirm their own worth.

This desire to communicate extends through to situations where there was no direct remonstration or sanction against the offender. Consider the first six response categories in Table 4.3, which looks at

Table 4.3 *Types of indirect responses to rude stranger*

	%
(a) Told someone I was with about it	5.7
(b) Told another member of the general public about it	3.5
(c) Told an employee working in their job about it	1.4
(d) Let someone I was with know what I felt about it by a gesture	2.2
(e) Let another member of the general public know what I felt about it by a gesture	2.4
(f) Let an employee working in their job know what I felt about it by a gesture	1.9
(g) Simply left the situation	21.2
(h) Turned away/looked away	8.7
(i) Carried on as if nothing had happened	43.8
(j) Other	9.2
Total	100%

Note: N = 329 respondents and 369 reported indirect responses.

types of *indirect* responses to the incivility. When summed these show that about 17 per cent of the time victims let onlookers know that a breach had taken place (rows (a)–(f)). Perhaps they were looking for affirmations of solidarity in the face of the antisocial or were dealing with personal embarrassment. That said, simple avoidance was the dominant response. In nearly 75 per cent of those cases without any rejoinder the victim simply moved on, turned away or left the situation (rows (g), (h), and (i)).

This might seem to indicate a retreat of the social. Close inspection shows a more differentiated picture. In his noted work on difficult, conflictual and unstable situations, Albert O. Hirschman (1970) noted that strategies of exit (getting out of the system) and voice (trying to change things) were logical possibilities in political life. Perhaps something similar is going on here. Sometimes people try to deal with the problem of incivility by 'doing something' in the setting, but at others they just move on. When we reconsider the sum total of 560 responses summarized across Tables 4.2 and 4.3 in this light, a notable pattern emerges. We find responses are fairly evenly divided along an exit and voice distinction. Categories (g), (h) and (i) in Table 4.3

all suggest a victim strategy of exit (48 per cent of all responses). The array of direct responses depicted in Table 4.2 and categories (a)–(f) in Table 4.3 are unified by suggesting some form of voice (45 per cent of all responses). There was a literal or figurative speaking up that was directed either at the rude stranger or towards someone else present at the scene of the incivility with the intent of repairing or affirming a normative order.

How emotions and actions combine

Having looked at emotions and behaviours in isolation we can now see if they are systematically connected. The theoretical traditions we have used to shape our investigations in this chapter predict not only emotions, but also behavioural responses consequent upon these. The dominant paradigm links fear with avoidance. Durkheim suggests that anger leads to expressive sanctioning. For Elias the emotion of disgust will result in avoidance. Finally, Simmel predicts emotional and behavioural indifference. How do these predicted ties stand up? In the middle part of Table 4.4 we are looking for differences between the behavioural responses of those who nominated a given emotion to the survey interviewer and those who did not. Here the theories of Durkheim and Simmel came in as statistically significant. Respondents who said they 'didn't care' can be thought to exhibit Simmel's blasé attitude. Consistent with the theory, this subgroup was distinguished by a propensity to exhibit indirect voice or exit as behavioural responses to the rude stranger. Those who reported feeling anger were significantly more likely than those not mentioning anger to engage in what we term a 'direct voice' intervention against the rude stranger (such as a gesture, look or verbal remonstration). This association between anger and remonstration is also consistent with more contemporary work on emotions. In his description of people who get 'pissed off' at the conduct of other drivers on the streets and highways of Los Angeles, Katz (1999, e.g., pp. 60–1) finds that irritated drivers are seemingly unable to keep their anger boxed in or simply ponder what just transpired. 'Sitting on it' may indeed generate more frustration than resolve. Rather, angry drivers need to respond, for instance by flipping the finger, in order to dramatically express their emotions and thereby 'create a sensuality through which they can overcome their anger' (p. 61). Not unlike Durkheim's

Table 4.4 *Initial behavioural response by three types of initial emotional reactions*

| | Behavioural response | | | | |
	Direct voice (N = 179)	Indirect voice (N = 53)	Exit (N = 244)	Total	χ^2
All respondents	37.6	11.1	51.3		
Level of surprise					12.1*
Very surprised	46.0	8.1	46.0	100	
Quite surprised	38.5	11.5	50.0	100	
Not surprised	27.1	14.3	58.6	100	
Type of emotion					12.7**
Anger					
Mention	44.0	11.0	45.0	100	
No mention	28.4	11.3	60.3	100	
Fear					n.s.
Mention	35.3	5.9	58.8	100	
No mention	37.9	11.8	50.4	100	
Disgust					n.s.
Mention	38.2	10.7	51.1	100	
No mention	37.4	11.3	51.3	100	
Shame					n.s.
Mention	35.3	5.9	58.8	100	
No mention	37.7	11.3	51.0	100	
Didn't care					7.1*
Mention	19.4	22.6	58.1	100	
No mention	38.9	10.3	50.8	100	
Intensity					10.1*
Very strong	44.6	9.9	45.5	100	
Quite strong	40.7	12.4	46.9	100	
Not strong	29.7	7.2	63.1	100	

Note: Behavioural response in 32 cases was not ascertained.

   * $p < .05$
  ** $p < .01$
n.s. = not significant.

thoughts on sanctioning and consistent with the above findings, Katz sees remonstration as in some sense a cathartic release of the anger through communicative activity.

Two other findings are worth reporting from Table 4.4. Looking to the top of the table we see that those experiencing high levels of surprise at what happened were more likely to engage in direct voice and less likely to exit than those who were not surprised. We speculate that this reflects the quality of rude strangers and locales. Surprise at an incivility is more likely where the perpetrator and setting are perceived as respectable. The data indeed lend some support for this premise. As shown in Table 4.5, 37 per cent of respondents who identified the rude stranger as 'respectable looking' were very surprised by the incident and another 39 per cent were quite surprised, while 33 per cent of respondents identifying 'rough looking' strangers were very surprised and only 28 per cent were quite surprised. The percentages are similar when comparing respectable versus rough places, although the latter association is not statistically significant. People thus seem more likely to be caught off guard when experiencing incivilities perpetrated by respectable-looking strangers and to a lesser extent respectable locations, and this emotional charge sometimes manifests in direct remonstration with the stranger. Finally, the bottom of Table 4.4 shows that the strength of an emotion matters. As predicted by basic social psychology, when people feel strongly about something – for example, as suggested by Table 4.2 that they have been disrespected – they are more likely to do something to rectify the situation. Direct voice ties to strong emotions, and exit to weak ones. Given the general tendency to avoid confrontation we noted in Figure 4.1, it would seem that emotions override the powerful inhibitors in the self that turn us away from potential conflict.

One final note about the correlations in Table 4.4 is in order. It appears that emotional intensity, type of emotion (e.g., anger), and level of surprise at the incivility have independent effects on behavioural responses. Although we do not show this series of partial tables and multinomial logistic regression models here, we examined whether the associations between the respective measures of emotions and behavioural responses remained consistent when controlling for the other indicators. The results for anger were quite clear. The emotion of anger increases the probability of responding in the direct voice even when controlling for the level of surprise and the intensity

Table 4.5 *Perception of rude stranger and place of incident by level of surprise*

	Level of surprise				
	Very surprised	Quite surprised	Not surprised	Total	χ^2
Perception of rude					10.0*
** stranger**					
Rough	33.3	27.5	39.2	100	
Neither	29.4	39.2	31.4	100	
Respectable	36.5	39.1	24.4	100	
Perception of place					5.7
Rough	32.6	26.1	41.3	100	
Neither	26.9	39.7	33.3	100	
Respectable	35.2	36.8	28.0	100	

* $p < .05$
Note: N = 475 for perception of rude stranger and N = 499 for perception of place where incident occurred.

of the emotion. Indeed, the magnitude of the 'anger effect' hardly changed. Supplementary analyses further indicate that some of the effect of emotional intensity is attributable to the level of surprise at the incident, but not enough to say that emotional intensity matters because of the level of surprise. In short, the respective associations between emotions and reactions shown in Table 4.4 are largely independent of one another.

Duration of incidents

We have established that strategies of initial exit are frequent. In fact, very few encounters with the rude stranger endure. As Table 4.6 shows, at each possible interaction stage far more situations are terminated than continued. Interactions with rude strangers are overwhelmingly brief, with neither the victims nor the offenders looking especially keen to keep them going. They do not conform to the vendetta and honour archetype so often found in drama – for example, Shakespeare's *Romeo and Juliet*, or a John Wayne Wild West bar

Table 4.6 *Frequency of sustained encounters*

Stage	Percentage of all encounters	Number of responses
(1) Stranger does initial rude act	100	508
(2) Victim does something back to them (direct voice)	35.3	179
(3) Rude stranger responds	15.2	77
(4) Victim responds again	3.9	18

scene – where an insult leads to a protracted and wordy interchange, this to be followed by fighting. Nor do they match the pattern found in subcultures of violence, where individuals are quick to flare up to defend their status. Our individuals seem keen to move on. We can only speculate, but it is possible that conditions of anonymity and mobility make exit an attractive option. This is not the case in places like the prison, where leaving the environment is impossible and a failure to respond would simply lead to future interactional degradation and predation (Sykes 1958). Further, in a culture of modernity where there is presumed equality there is no deep public need to defend honour, only a private one. By contrast, the historical evidence suggests that hierarchical cultures had to develop elaborate institutions for formal and visible status repair, such as duelling.[1] In the contemporary urban and suburban landscape the cost of terminating the interaction might be simply a small amount of fleeting humiliation in the eyes of onlookers who are strangers. To continue to interact brings the risk of negative emotions, the attention of others and sustained and unrewarding interaction with a person who has already been coded as 'rude'. Why not simply move on? Life is short.

This rapid rate of attrition created unexpected problems for our data analysis. In designing the survey we had expected to trace the life history of our interactions. We had hoped, for example, to identify the specific emotions, behaviours and situational factors most associated

[1] Randall Collins, personal e-mail communication to authors concerning findings of Chapter 4, May 2009.

with conciliatory and conflictual endings. In the analysis reported so far in this chapter we have made use of data pertaining to stage (2) identified in Table 4.6. For stages (3) and (4) we have less statistical power, but the data still allow us to make a few summary statements about the characteristics of events in relation to their duration. By scanning Table 4.7 from left to right we can identify patterns in which the percentage of cases in a given category changes from one stage to the next. Mindful of the relatively small number of cases at the latter two stages, a few trends stand out as intriguing. First, emotions generated at the time of the event appear to drive sustained encounters. This is particularly the case for anger and fear. Anger was initially present in around 60 per cent of events that started up. Yet some 72 per cent of those that reached stage 4 had this as their initial victim emotion. We also see a higher proportion of fearful respondents at the latter two stages (20 per cent and 28 per cent) than the earlier stages (11 per cent and 10 per cent).[2] Likewise, strong emotional intensity and level of surprise appear to drive sustained encounters. A strong initial emotion and a high level of surprise are more likely found to be at the start of enduring confrontations. In contrast, the nature of the initial incivility does not seem to make a difference. Here we see the proportions reported in the table are very stable across the four stages. Whether the stranger or the place was perceived as rough or respectable is rather inconsequential for incident duration. Nor does it seem to matter whether or not the initial incivility was perceived as deliberate.

What are we to make of this? In his theory of interaction ritual the sociologist Randall Collins (2004) points out that social interaction thrives upon what he calls 'emotional energy'. For the most part his work discusses the emotional rewards and drivers of solidaristic

---

[2] The organization of Table 4.7 is descriptive and intuitive but does not permit a direct assessment of statistical significance. However, in a separate set of analyses not shown here we created a single variable indicating the stage at which the encounter was terminated (ranging from 1 to 4) and correlated this variable with the event characteristics presented in the left column of Table 4.7. In the latter analyses the following predictor variables were statistically significant ($p < .05$): level of surprise, anger, fear and very strong emotional intensity. We do not show the latter analyses in a table because it was quite cluttered and, frankly, a bit cumbersome. Table 4.7 provides a cleaner presentation of the data and drives home the same point.

Table 4.7 *Drivers of incident duration*

	Behavioural response			
	Stage (1) Stranger does initial rude act (N = 508)	Stage (2) Victim does something back to them (direct voice) (N = 179)	Stage (3) Further relations (N = 77)	Stage (4) Final act (N = 18)
Nature of initial incivility				
Movement	54.3	54.2	54.5	61.1
Body	15.6	15.1	18.2	11.1
Sounds	11.5	11.2	15.6	—
Language	15.7	15.6	19.5	11.1
Victim initial emotion				
Very surprised	33.7	41.3	46.8	38.9
Anger (mentioned)	59.6	69.3	67.5	72.2
Fear (mentioned)	11.2	10.1	19.5	27.8
Disgust (mentioned)	26.8	27.9	27.3	22.2
Shame (mentioned)	3.5	3.4	3.9	0.0
Didn't care (mentioned)	6.1	3.4	1.3	11.1
Emotional intensity				
Very strong	27.3	31.4	42.1	43.8
Perceived motivation of rude stranger				
Accidental	77.7	75.3	73.7	77.8
Deliberate	22.3	24.7	26.3	22.2
Perception of rude stranger				
Rough	21.5	18.9	24.3	22.2
Respectable	57.1	59.8	59.5	61.1
Perception of place				
Rough	9.2	10.1	13.0	11.1
Respectable	75.0	76.4	74.0	77.8
Regularity of visitation				
Once a week or more	68.9	66.0	55.9	50.0
Less than once a week	30.8	34.0	44.1	50.0

interaction rituals, such as everyday conversation, smoking and sexual intercourse. Essentially, people are emotion junkies, engaging in extended mutually satisfying and reciprocal exchanges in order to boost their feelings of subjective wellbeing and collective belonging. Here we see hints of a different and somewhat darker universe, one in which social relations persist in a potentially conflictual setting thanks to the strong emotional currents at play. We might understand these as internalized psychic forces which steer the victim away from the low risk, low cost exit strategy that is almost ever present in the world of strangers.

The main findings of this chapter are:

- Surprise and anger are the two most frequent emotional responses to commonplace incivility. Emotions usually diminish quite rapidly in intensity. This does not support the image of people expecting incivility and living in fear that characterizes the majority of the literature and policy debate.
- Direct responses to the rude stranger were found in around 30 per cent of cases. These tended to be communicative rather than instrumental. They were efforts to assert 'voice' and were generally motivated by the desire for respect. In around 17 per cent of cases victims communicated to those around them that a breach had taken place.
- Strategies of initial exit were to be found in nearly half of all incidents. People often just walked away or continued with what they were doing. Exit continued to be a popular option at later stages of encounters.
- Anger, surprise and strong emotions all predicted a direct response to the rude stranger. Weak emotions and indifference predicted a quick exit from the encounter.
- Interaction sequences are overwhelmingly brief. Those that persisted were more likely to be characterized by strong emotions and anger.

5 | *Gender, age and class: divergent experiences?*

Our analyses so far in this book have concerned 'people in general'. We have focused for the most part on outlining the features of events and their aftermath as they impact upon the woman or man in the street. Once or twice we have noted that victims with certain social or demographic characteristics have divergent experiences from the average, but we have not given sustained attention to the ways that categorical identities might shape the distribution and interpretation of victimizations. In this chapter we move the analytic spotlight onto three sociodemographic background variables: gender; age; and class.

In the backlash against universalism, a major theme in postmodern and poststructural social theory has been the claim that the experience of life is radically shaped through identity. The argument goes that when thinkers talk about generic human experience they are usually talking about or projecting the worldview of the affluent white male. General statements cloaked particular experiences. Goffman himself became prey to such critique, the case being made that he drew large conclusions from his own impressions of walking down the street. His observations about the subtleties of eye contact, the averted gaze and interpersonal space in public reflected *his* reality. For Goffman these behaviours were all about tact and mutual respect. The case was made that for women such body management in public might be about avoiding sexual harassment; for persons of colour the issue might be to dodge racism or to appear non-threatening. We do not wish to intervene in such debates here, but we do see them as sensitizing this project to a particular set of issues. This 'tuning in' to difference finds validation from what the poststructuralists might well consider an unlikely source – mainstream quantitative work in criminology. Criminologists have repeatedly found substantial variation structured by race, age, class and gender as these relate to issues such as fear of crime, attitudes towards the police and the experience of victimization.

Incivility: the rude stranger in everyday life

Explaining demographic variation in victimization

Let's focus for a while on the last of these. One of the most useful resources we have in criminology is the crime victimization survey. Our survey replicates the logic of these by asking people directly
about their experiences in a defined prior time period. Victimization
surveys are particularly useful in mapping crime because they bypass
the filtering that takes place before crimes are brought to the attention
of the police. Most crimes are not reported because they are trivial,
there is nothing the police can do, the victim is ashamed, they have
something to hide, or there is fear of reprisal, among other reasons.
Hence, official statistics often tell us more about the process of reporting and recording of crime than they do about the actual crime rate
(see Black 1970; Kitsuse and Cicourel 1963 for classic discussions).
For this reason criminologists often make use of victimization surveys
to gauge the extent of the crime problem. In crime victim surveys
randomly chosen respondents are typically asked if they have been
subject to assault or if their property has been damaged or stolen in
the prior year. One of the major and most consistent findings from
these in recent years has been that crime victimization is unevenly distributed over the general population. To speak of a 'national average'
is not very helpful given that risks are strongly skewed by social location and demographics. In America the National Crime Victimization
Survey has consistently found that people who are younger, poorer,
male and unmarried are at a higher risk of crime victimization than
those who are older, more wealthy, female and married. It is interesting to note that this first group also provides a disproportionate number of offenders. The image that comes to mind is of young males in
public engaging in risky activities in problematic social spaces (and
victimizing each other), older married people sitting at home and
watching television. Accurate or not, such a stereotyped picture can
help us get a fix on just how demographic and social characteristics
might play out in the distribution of crime victim vulnerability. The
life cycle combines with routine activity to shape opportunity structures for would-be offenders.

In looking for a point of comparison with our Australian survey
data of 2005 we are drawn to the findings of the 2004 International
Crime Victimization Survey. This had a substantial Australian component, with over 7,000 interviews recorded (Johnson 2005). The

survey found that 17 per cent of respondents had been victimized in 2003. Those most at risk of 'personal crime' victimization (assault, theft directly from the person) were the unmarried, the unemployed, the more wealthy (perhaps because they have more things worth stealing), those who had lived at their postcode less than one year (i.e., the transient or newcomer, probably renting) and those with an active lifestyle outside the home. We see this category of 'personal crime' as in some ways similar to that of rude stranger victimization given that it more or less requires the physical movement of a body into a public space. Surprisingly, there was no substantial gender difference in victimization rates. Let's put some numbers on these generalities. According to research from the Australian Institute of Criminology, some 14 per cent of those aged 16–24 experienced personal crime victimization in 2003, in contrast to just 4 per cent of those aged 60 and over. About 14 per cent of singles had been a victim, compared to 6 per cent of those married. Those who went out almost every evening were victimized at 18 per cent, while of those who went out once a month just 8 per cent had been a victim. Those looking for work came in at 17 per cent, students at 13 per cent and pensioners at 4 per cent. A logistic regression analysis confirmed the potency of each of these variables (Johnson 2005, tables 3 and 6). The exact numbers don't matter much for our purposes. What is important is to notice that risks vary substantially, and that household structure, age and routine activity would seem to play a role as predicted.

It is interesting to ask whether and how such factors protecting some people from crime victimization and putting others at risk play out in the case of rude stranger encounters. Is the underlying dynamic essentially the same, or is it very different? Looking back to the earlier chapters we drew a picture of commonplace encounters with ordinary people taking place during daytime in ordinary or 'respectable' places. This contrasts somewhat with the criminological literature's finding that night-time activity, single young people and perhaps alcohol are a perfect storm for thefts from handbags and pockets, brawling and predatory assault. So our hypothesis for this chapter is that we will find few significant effects for the major socio-demographic variables: rude strangers are widely distributed in the social landscape, but crime victimization is clustered. However, we share the prediction that time outside the home is important. Rude strangers cannot be found in our living rooms. Yet we qualify this by suggesting that this time need not be concentrated in the evenings.

Before moving further in the analysis we should recap what we already know and discuss some measurement and reliability issues with the ELIAS data. In Chapter 2 we looked at some of the risk factors for being a victim of incivil behaviour (Table 2.7). These results are largely recapped in Table 5.1, but in this table the far right column also shows the associations between the background variables and experience with crime victimization.[1] We discuss the similarities and differences between incivility and crime victimization in a moment, but we first need to demonstrate that the crime victimization measures we put into the ELIAS Survey are reliable. That is, do the patterns of victimization in our data resemble those from other victimization surveys? We examine this by comparing the predictors of crime victimization in the ELIAS data with those found in a sample of Australians in the International Crime Victimization Survey (ICVS) discussed above (Johnson 2005). As one might expect, the specific percentages differ between the two surveys because each employs distinctive measures of victimization. Also, and unlike the ICVS, we asked about victimizations *in public places* instead of victimizations anywhere. Mindful of these measurement differences, it is evident that the ELIAS Survey results are largely consistent with the ICVS and crime victimization surveys from other countries (e.g., the National Crime Victimization Survey in the United States). For instance, both the ELIAS data and the ICVS show that the risk of victimization declines with age. Each survey also indicates that males are more likely than females to experience crime victimization, although the latter correlation is stronger in our survey.[2] In addition, the ICVS shows that people who spend more time out of the house are at higher risk of victimization, while we find that respondents spending more time in public places are at higher risk of victimization (not shown in Table 5.1). Moreover, both the ELIAS

---

[1] Respondents were coded as 'victims' if they mentioned any of the following five types of victimization *in a public place* within the past year: someone (1) stole something from you; (2) attacked or assaulted you; (3) deliberately damaged your property; (4) threatened to attack you; or (5) subjected you to personal vilification.

[2] In this respect our survey is more consistent with extant literature on crime victimization and the results from the U.S. National Crime Victimization Survey.

Table 5.1 *Rude stranger encounters and criminal victimization by respondent background characteristics*

	Rude event (%)	Crime victim (%)
Gender		
Male	28.7*	30.1*
Female	33.8	24.8
Age		
18–25	40.8***	44.0***
26–35	38.4	31.4
36–55	31.7	28.4
56–65	23.8	16.1
Over 65	17.7	15.0
Education		
Less than 10 years	26.0**	22.3***
High school, trade or Certificate	30.6	32.7
Bachelor's degree	35.6	25.3
Occupation		
Professional, technical, high-level administrative, service	36.7***	29.0
Clerical, sales	25.5	25.5
Skilled/semi-skilled/unskilled worker, farm	24.2	31.1
Income		
Up to $25,999	26.3**	29.7
$26,000–$41,599	28.0	28.5
$41,600–$77,999	37.6	28.8
$78,000 and above	33.9	26.7
Place		
Country town	25.1**	22.2*
Regional centre	32.4	28.7
Metropolis	33.6	29.1

* $p < .05$
** $p < .01$
*** $p < .001$

Note: Comparisons are based on the full sample of 1,621 respondents. The occupation and income variables included a larger number of missing cases than other variables. The valid N for the occupation variable was 1,085 and the valid N for income was 1,274. Percentages represent the proportion of respondents within the category of the variable in the left-hand column that experienced the event. For example, 28.7% of males reported a rude event, compared with 33.8% of females.

Survey and the ICVS show that students and the unemployed are at higher risk of victimization, while retirees are at reduced risk (results not shown). Perhaps the only notable difference concerns income. We find no association between crime victimization and income in the ELIAS data, while the ICVS indicates a positive association. This difference between the surveys is likely to be attributable to our focus on crime in public places, which precludes the reporting of victimizations in the home. This is an important distinction, because those with higher incomes are likely to have more goods worth stealing in their homes, and thus they are at an elevated risk for some types of victimization. Mindful of this difference, we generally find a high degree of congruence between the respective data sources.

Having demonstrated this general consistency between the ELIAS Survey and the ICVS, we now highlight ways in which the sociological distribution of incivility differs from more conventional measures of crime victimization. As suggested in Chapter 2, there are some similarities. For instance, younger respondents are more likely to report encounters with rude strangers and also more likely to report a criminal victimization in a public place. We also see comparable results for place of residence. Residing in the country rather than the city reduces the risk of incivility and crime victimization alike.

These similarities with respect to age and place are balanced by notable differences for gender and several measures of social class. Males are significantly more likely to report a criminal victimization, while a higher percentage of females described a run-in with a rude stranger. We also see differences for education. The likelihood of reporting incivility is about 10 per cent higher for those with at least a bachelor's degree compared with those with less than ten years of schooling. Crime victimization, however, showed a different pattern in which those who had completed high school or trade school (or equivalent) were most likely to be victimized in public places. In addition, crime victimization did not significantly vary across occupational categories, yet professionals and those working in technical fields were much more likely to report rude events than respondents in other occupations. The latter results are comparable to the results for income, which shows no association with criminal victimization in public places, but is positively correlated with incivility.

We can thus make two summary statements based on Table 5.1. First, with the exception of age and place of residence, risk factors for rude events differ in meaningful ways from the predictors of crime victimization. Second, it appears that rude encounters are more likely for the young, for women and for members of the upper-middle class. But why? In Chapter 2 we hinted at several relevant factors. For instance, we suggested that some demographic groups might have higher thresholds for proper and civil conduct. To the extent that incivility is in the eye of the beholder, members of the upper class and women may be more sensitive to uncouth mannerisms or foul language, and to that end more apt to categorize behaviour as rude in comparison with lower-class respondents and men. This interpretative explanation aligns with work on other behaviours that require a fair degree of subjective interpretation, such as sexual harassment. Uggen and Blackstone (2004), for instance, find that women are more likely than men to label offensive conduct in the workplace as sexual harassment. Unfortunately, the ELIAS data do not permit us to probe more deeply into this explanation. We suppose that such an empirical assessment would entail a carefully controlled experiment in which the same person behaves in the same manner in the presence of dozens of subjects, each of whom would subsequently complete a questionnaire about rude behaviour that day. This would certainly be clever, but to our knowledge such an experiment has yet to be undertaken.

We also proposed a second explanation for variations in rude stranger victimization rates in Chapter 2. This was more structural in nature and drew attention to movements through time and space. We then elaborated on this theme in Chapter 3, for instance, by pointing to the role of movements outside the home. Rude stranger encounters followed a bell curve, peaking between 10 am and 2 pm. They also took place in familiar environments, such as mass transit, shopping malls and city sidewalks (Table 3.1). However, we have not yet explored how our socio-demographic variables map onto those daily routines, although this is clearly an urgent task. As we suggested earlier in this chapter, the literature on crime victimization suggests that the demographic characteristics of individuals are converted into victimization rates through the mediating influence of routine or regular activity (Hindelang, Gottfredson and Garofalo 1978; Messner and Tardiff 1985; Miethe, Stafford and Long 1987). That is, some demographic groups are at higher risk of victimization because their lifestyles lead them to places where predatory or opportunistic offenders are more abundant. Others stay at home. Relative to incivility, from this perspective we might expect the young, the educated and members of the upper and middle classes with surplus income to spend more time in public places where the likelihood of encountering a rude stranger increases. In this case the ELIAS Survey allows us to probe more deeply. Specifically, towards the end of the survey all respondents were asked to report the amount of time they typically spent in what we label 'landscapes of mass culture'. This variable is an index based on the frequency with which respondents typically visit fourteen types of public places, for example, shopping malls, casinos, public transport and sports facilities. For each location respondents reported the amount of time according to a seven-point ordinal scale ranging from 'never' to 'almost every day', and our index represents the sum of these indicators.[3] As illustrated in Figure 5.1, there is substantial variation in the amount of time people spend in these locations. The variance closely resembles what statisticians refer to as a normal distribution in which a small proportion of respondents rarely set foot in these domains, while an equally small proportion move through them almost incessantly. The vast majority, however, enter and exit landscapes of mass culture on an occasional to regular basis.

Looking into this issue in detail, Table 5.2 further indicates that time spent in places that are populated with strangers varies along several dimensions. For convenience of presentation we split the continuous variable measuring time in landscapes of mass culture at the median value, thereby creating two groups indicating 'high' and 'low' exposure. With the exception of gender, we find rather strong and predictable associations with each of the variables included in Table 5.1 above. Exposure to strangers as indicated by time spent

---

[3] Survey respondents were asked about how often they engaged in the following: (a) shop in an enclosed shopping mall; (b) shop in an open-air shopping mall; (c) eat in a food court; (d) shop in a supermarket; (e) shop in a department store (or superstore); (f) go to the movies at a large cinema complex; (g) go to a large casino; (h) eat at a large takeaway food chain (McDonalds); (i) go to a large video/DVD rental store (Blockbuster); (j) go to a large sports ground to watch a major sporting event; (k) travel in a motor vehicle on a main road/freeway/highway; (l) use a mass parking lot; (m) ride on public transport; and (n) catch a plane.

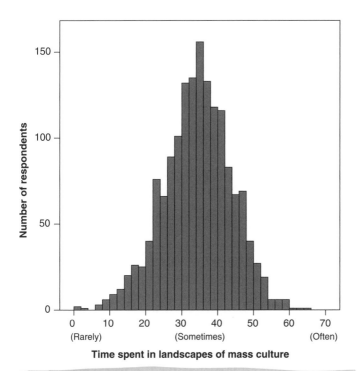

Figure 5.1 Histogram of time spent in landscapes of mass culture

in landscapes of mass culture is substantially higher for the young, the more educated and those working in professional and clerical occupational sectors. Exposure to strangers is also higher among wealthier respondents and those residing in regional centres and metro areas, rather than in rural locations. Another way to think about this is that the potential for exposure to rude strangers has a social gradient that maps onto our earlier findings concerning the likelihood of experiencing incivility. On this note, and as we might expect, exposure is also strongly correlated with the probability of encountering a rude stranger. Using the same high–low dichotomy as employed in Table 5.2, Figure 5.2 shows that 24 per cent of respondents who spend less time in such populated domains reported a run-in with a rude stranger. This proportion is substantially smaller than the 39 per cent of those spending more time in public places who reported a rude event.

Table 5.2 *Time spent in landscapes of mass culture by respondent background characteristics*

	Time in landscapes of mass culture (% within each group above the median)
Gender	
Male	48.7
Female	50.1
Age	
18–25	83.1***
26–35	57.8
36–55	49.8
56–65	29.8
Over 65	22.6
Education	
Less than 10 years	36.6***
High school, trade, or certificate	52.6
Bachelor's degree	55.1
Occupation	
Professional, technical, high level administrative, service	57.7**
Clerical, sales	54.3
Skilled/semi-skilled/unskilled worker, farm	43.6
Income	
Up to $25,999	38.2***
$26,000–$41,599	45.5
$41,600–$77,999	53.1
$78,000 and above	57.1
Place	
Country town	29.7***
Regional centre	48.4
Metropolis	57.6

* $p < .05$
** $p < .01$
*** $p < .001$

Note: Comparisons are based on the full sample of 1,621 respondents. The occupation and income variables included a larger number of missing cases than other variables. The valid N for the occupation variable was 1,085 and the valid N for income was 1,274.

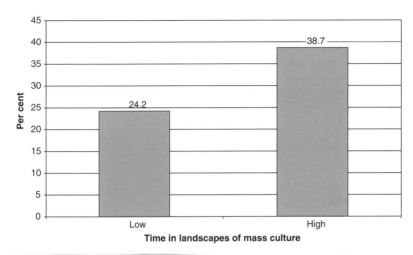

Figure 5.2 Probability of encountering a rude stranger by time spent in landscapes of mass culture

The above findings lead to an additional question: to what extent does spending time in landscapes of mass culture explain the above-mentioned associations between rude encounters and other background variables? To answer this question we present pairs of logistic regression coefficients in Table 5.3. For each variable discussed above, we first report the bivariate regression coefficient indicating the log odds of encountering a rude stranger. A second model then estimates the effect when controlling for the continuous measure of time spent in landscapes of mass culture. We can then compare the coefficients to assess approximately how much of the association between the demographic indicator and rude events is explained by exposure to places where strangers are abundant. For instance, consider the association between age and encounters with rude strangers (model 1). The age coefficient in the bivariate model is $-.29$ ($p < .001$), which indicates that the odds of reporting a rude event decrease by about 25 per cent for each unit increase in age, which is measured in five categories ($1 - e^{-.29} = .25$). When we control for time spent in public places the partial correlation between age and experiencing a rude event drops to $-.16$ ($p < .01$), which implies a 15 per cent decrease in the odds of a rude encounter for each unit increase in age ($1 - e^{-.16} = .15$). Stated differently, the magnitude of the age coefficient decreases by

Table 5.3 *Logistic regression coefficients: rude stranger encounter on background variables with and without controlling for time spent in landscapes of mass culture*

	Model 1	Model 2	Model 3	Model 4	Model 5	Model 6
Age						
Bivariate	− .29***					
Control for exposure	− .16**					
Male						
Bivariate		− .23*				
Control for exposure		− .28*				
Bachelor's degree[a]						
Bivariate			.31**			
Control for exposure			.21			
Professional[b]						
Bivariate				.57***		
Control for exposure				.49**		
Income						
Bivariate					.14**	
Control for exposure					.07	
Regional centre[c]						
Bivariate						.36*
Control for exposure						.18
Metro area[c]						
Bivariate						.42**
Control for exposure						.10
% change	− 45%	+ 22%	− 32%	− 14%	− 50%	− 50%
						− 76%

   * $p < .05$
  ** $p < .01$
 *** $p < .001$

Note: Analyses are based on the full sample of 1,621 respondents. The occupation and income variables included a larger number of missing cases than other variables. The valid N for the occupation variable was 1,085 and the valid N for income was 1,274.
[a] Reference category is respondents with less than a bachelor's degree.
[b] Reference category is respondents working in sales, clerical work, skilled/semi-skilled/ unskilled work or farming.
[c] Reference category is residence in a country area.

45 per cent when we account for time spent in landscapes of mass culture ([– .29 – – .16]/ – .29 = .45). Age thus retains a significant and negative effect on experiencing a rude event, although a sizeable proportion of the association is attributable to exposure to landscapes of mass culture. Gender is unique in that the coefficient is slightly stronger when controlling for exposure, which is not entirely surprising given the low correlation between gender and time spent in public places (see Table 5.2). Yet for all other variables we find that a healthy proportion of the association with rude events is explained by exposure to landscapes of mass culture. In some cases the slope coefficient is reduced by a small but non-trivial amount. For instance, the effect of occupation decreases by about 14 per cent. But in other cases the change is quite substantial. The income coefficient, for example, is 50 per cent smaller and no longer statistically significant once we control for exposure. The percentage change is even more drastic for residence in a metro area, where the slope coefficient declines from .42 in the bivariate model to .10 when the control variable for exposure is added to the model (a 76 per cent change). For the latter variables we might say that time spent in places with numerous strangers is the linchpin that connects the demographic profile with the likelihood of a rude event.

Before moving to the next section we briefly recap our results and discuss them in the context of a broader literature on victimization and movement through time and space. As discussed in Chapter 3, an influential line of criminological theory suggests that people differ in their routine activities – their daily patterns of movement that dictate how much time is spent in the home, at work, on route to locations and in other (e.g., leisure) activities – and this pattern of movement puts some people at greater risk of criminal victimization than others. In a classic statement on this perspective, Lawrence Cohen and Marcus Felson (1979) argued that routine activities that lead people away from their homes will increase the probability of offenders and victims converging in space and time, and thus people spending more time away from their homes are increasingly at risk of predatory victimization. Put simply, some kinds of people are out and about more than others, and in doing so they put themselves at higher risk. We have demonstrated how this ecological approach to crime victimization is also applicable to the study of incivility. A key finding from our analysis is that people who spend more time in public settings are at higher risk of encountering a rude stranger. Moreover, we showed that exposure to places with crowds and strangers fits a demographic profile. We can thus make a few summary points with respect to the three demographic indicators that are central to this chapter: age; gender; and class:

- Age and class: we measured class with reference to the occupation, education and income of respondents. Regardless of the measure, higher status people experienced more rudeness, yet this is largely because they spend more time in public places and are thus more frequently exposed to strangers. The same can be said for younger respondents. The young are, in part, more likely to report a rude event because they spend more time in the public sphere.
- Gender: in contrast to crime victimization, women were *more* likely to report a rude encounter than men. Unlike age and class, however, we cannot say that exposure via routine activities in public places accounts for this gender gap. This suggests that thresholds and interpretations, or the interpersonal behaviours themselves (Gardner 1995), might have a strong gender dynamic independent of time outside the home.

We make two additional points about time, space and interpersonal contact before moving on. First, we demonstrated that the amount of time spent in public increases the risk of undesirable events such as contacts with rude strangers. Still, we should keep in mind that time in public might also increase the risk of prosocial interactions. From an ecological perspective, the same people who experience incivility are also apt to report exceptional instances of civility, such as strangers offering to open doors, giving up a seat on the subway, or covering the fare on a shared cab ride. We were able to investigate only one consequence of exposure, but we are mindful that it likely cuts both ways, good and bad.[4] Second, focusing on the occurrence of a rude

[4] This argument would be consistent with demographic research on cordial and conflictual types of intergroup relations. For instance, areas with higher rates of inter-racial marriage also have higher rates of inter-racial crime (South and Messner 1986). An intriguing question extending from our findings is whether persons reporting incivility are equally likely to report acts of civility. The research of Baker M. Hindman (1953) suggests this is a strong possibility. As we reported earlier, his study of African-American youth in the 1950s found pleasant and unpleasant encounters with whites taking place in the same locations and with similar frequency.

event tells only part of the story. Perhaps a more consequential set of questions revolves around the interpretation of the event. Are rude acts seen as benign episodes or do they pack an emotional punch? Moreover, *who* is most likely to experience emotional shocks in the wake of a rude encounter? We now turn to these questions.

The interpretation of experience

So far in this chapter we have explored the distribution of encounters as these map onto activities and demographics. Next, we need to consider the question of the interpretation of experiences. Are there also significant patterns here that are structured by age, class and gender? Extant theory gives us some guidance on what to expect. Recall that in Chapter 4 we discussed the types of emotional reactions people might have to rude behaviour and incivility. We noted that Norbert Elias emphasized the emotion of disgust, Emile Durkheim pointed to indignation and anger, the 'broken windows' advocates and related lines of criminological scholarship predicted fear, and theorists such as Georg Simmel suggested that city dwellers developed a sense of indifference, a sort of blasé attitude, towards everyday incivility. But are these reactions equally likely among professionals and labourers? The poorly and highly educated? Men and women? The young and the elderly? The above lines of scholarship offer less precise predictions with respect to the 'demography of emotions', but they at least hint at some expected correlations.

Consider the work of Elias and the emotion of disgust. Elias envisioned the development of etiquette as a top-down process. Manners and standards of decency were typically determined by the elite, where proper displays of etiquette and the occasional show of sophistication became indicators of class distinction. Over time the expectations of courtly society diffused outward, or perhaps downward, so that refinement was an expected facet of social interaction across society. Elias thus envisioned refinement as intimately associated with class and saw disgust as the reaction of interest to poor displays of self-control. A logical extension of Elias' work is that the well educated, professionals and members of the upper and middle classes are more apt to express disgust in response to incivility. This reaction is in contrast to the more 'medieval' emotion of anger, which is presumably the province of the lower classes.

Simmel offers some additional insight with respect to indifference. His work revolved around the orientation of urbanites who routinely contend with the crowds, noise and strangers that pervade modern city life. For Simmel, nonchalance is a defensive posture for city dwellers – a way of dealing with the daily grind in the modern metropolis – and thus we can expect residents of metropolitan areas and those who spend more time in places populated with strangers to remain blasé in the wake of a rude encounter.

Modern criminology is perhaps more specific in its predictions concerning fear. This line of work repeatedly shows that women, the elderly and the poor are more fearful of crime. Women and the elderly tend to be more fearful because they perceive themselves as *physically* vulnerable to violence (Skogan and Maxfield 1981), while the poor see themselves as *socially* vulnerable to victimization. In other words, the former two groups fear injury, while the latter worry about the likelihood of victimization. Following this line of thinking we would expect women and older respondents to express fear when encountering a rude stranger. Theory suggests they would worry about an escalation of the encounter and, accordingly, fear that it could intensify to a more serious type of victimization.

We are mindful that the fear of crime literature is related only indirectly to incivility. After all, we are looking at rude encounters, not criminal events. Still, the criminological literature makes two points that bear on the present set of analyses. First, fear of crime is often correlated with non-criminal experiences. Incivility, in particular, has been the subject of much criminological scholarship on fear of crime (Garofalo and Laub 1978; Markowitz *et al.* 2001; Skogan and Maxfield 1981; Taylor and Hale 1986). Second, even if the distribution of rude encounters differs from crime victimization (see above), the processing of emotions may be consistent. Just as women fear crime because of a perceived sense of vulnerability, they may react to a lewd look, an uninvited grope, or road rage in much the same way. The same might be said for the elderly.

We test these theoretical assumptions by correlating the emotions of interest – indifference, disgust, anger and fear – with several characteristics of respondents and the nature of the rude encounter (Table 5.4). Specifically, respondents were asked to recall their emotional reaction at the time of the event, which we then break down by our predictor variables.[5] Looking first at indifference and testing the ideas of Georg Simmel, the results show no significant differences across our indicators of gender, age, class, place or time spent in public places.[6] The blasé attitude, it seems, is pretty random in terms of its demography and other predictors. Simmel may be correct that some respondents remain nonchalant when encountering rude behaviour, but we find no support for the notion that residents of the metropolis or those spending significant time in public places are more desensitized to rude behaviour than those residing in the country or respondents spending less time in the presence of strangers. The same might be said for disgust, which is not significantly correlated with characteristics of respondents. In fact, the pattern of emotions depicted in Table 5.4 seems to run in the opposite direction to that predicted by Elias. Less educated respondents in our sample were slightly more likely to mention disgust than well educated respondents, and those working in the professional or technical sectors were the least likely to express disgust, although these correlations are not statistically significant.

Unlike indifference and disgust, the emotions of anger and fear show clear patterns. For instance, and consistent with the criminological literature, women are more than twice as likely to express fear as men (15 per cent versus 7 per cent). Age is also significant. Older respondents – namely those in their mid-fifties or older – are much less likely to express anger and more likely to express fear. Again, the latter finding is likely to be attributable to perceptions of physical vulnerability among the elderly. In addition, anger is correlated with education and type of occupation. Here we see an intriguing pattern. Respondents with more education and those working in the professional, clerical and sales sectors are more likely to express anger than the less educated and skilled or unskilled labourers. In some

---

[5] We also ran a series of correlations that incorporated the intensity of the emotional reaction. In this case respondents were coded '1' if they reported strong or very strong emotions (e.g., strong disgust, strong anger, strong fear) at the time of the event. There was no substantive difference in the correlations when using this measure, and thus we do not show the table here.

[6] Our indicator of time in public places, which at times we also refer to as time in landscapes of mass culture, might be rather crude in that we split this continuous variable at the median. We note that the correlations are also non-significant when we regress the outcome variables on the continuous measure.

Table 5.4 *Emotional reactions to incivility by demographic and incident characteristics*

	Indifference (%)	Disgust (%)	Anger (%)	Fear (%)
Expressing emotion	6.1	26.8	59.7	11.2
Gender				
Male	8.0	24.9	60.0	6.7**
Female	4.6	28.3	59.4	14.8
Age				
18–25	10.3	18.0	64.1**	6.4*
26–35	6.0	29.1	63.3	11.1
36–55	4.2	29.9	63.1	9.8
56–65	6.6	24.6	47.5	13.1
Over 65	9.7	25.1	32.3	29.0
Education				
Less than 10 years	9.5	32.4	46.7**	9.5
High school, trade or certificate	5.8	22.8	65.1	11.6
Bachelor's degree	4.8	27.8	60.8	12.0
Occupation				
Professional, technical, high level administrative, service	5.6	26.1	63.3*	9.0
Clerical, sales	3.7	29.6	75.9	11.1
Skilled/ semi-skilled/ unskilled, worker, farm	10.5	33.3	50.9	1.8
Income				
Up to $25,999	9.9	22.5	57.8	9.9
$26,000–$41,599	8.9	30.4	51.8	14.3
$41,600–$77,999	5.1	24.4	66.7	10.3
$78,000 and above	5.3	31.1	60.6	12.1
Place				
Country town	4.0	31.0	55.0	13.0
Regional centre	7.5	20.0	61.3	12.5
Metropolis	6.4	27.1	60.7	10.4

Table 5.4 (*cont.*)

	Indifference (%)	Disgust (%)	Anger (%)	Fear (%)
Time in pubic places				
Low	5.6	30.3	56.4	11.3
High	6.3	24.7	62.5	11.5
Rude stranger acted deliberately				
No	5.7	24.2	63.8**	8.3***
Yes	6.4	32.7	49.1	22.7
Language				
No	7.0*	23.6***	62.4**	10.1
Yes	1.3	43.8	45.0	17.5
Movement				
No	5.2	31.9*	48.7***	11.6
Yes	6.9	22.5	68.8	10.9
Sounds				
No	6.9*	26.5	60.1	10.0*
Yes	0.0	28.8	55.9	20.3
Body				
No	6.3	25.4	61.8*	11.4
Yes	5.1	34.2	48.1	10.1

* $p < .05$
** $p < .01$
*** $p < .001$

Notes: Comparisons are for the 508 respondents who reported a rude event. The occupation (N = 345) and income (N = 415) variables had more missing cases than other variables. Percentages indicate the percent within the category that expressed the emotion. For example, 6.7% of males expressed fear while 93.3% of males did not, and 14.8% of female respondents expressed fear while 85.2% of females did not. Emotions refer to those felt at the time of the event.

respects this turns Elias on his head. Where he predicted disgust, we find expressions of anger.

We next turn to the bottom portion of Table 5.4 and assess whether the nature of the rude event is associated with emotional reactions.

We first home in on whether the rude stranger's conduct was perceived as deliberate or accidental. The last two columns in Table 5.4 suggest that deliberate acts of rudeness are correlated with anger and fear, although the effects run in opposite directions. Anger is actually more likely when the conduct was perceived as accidental, while fear is much more likely for intentional (23 per cent) than unintentional rudeness (8 per cent). This pattern is somewhat intuitive. We might picture a man working his way through a busy sidewalk or navigating a crowded transportation hub who is accidentally bumped in the shoulder by a discourteous stranger. This event is unlikely to conjure up a fearful reaction, but it likely leaves the guy on the receiving end a bit perturbed, even downright furious. Alternatively, we can picture a woman making her way through traffic at rush hour who accidentally cuts off another car. The other driver lays on the horn and flips a finger – an obvious deliberate and pointed act. The latter is likely to instil a momentary sense of fear of what the stranger might do next. These images of rude behaviour and the subsequent emotional processing are consistent with other findings in Table 5.4. For instance, the emotion of anger is much more likely when the rude event entails movement, such as bumping, blocking an entrance or taking up too much space. This correlation is quite sizeable, as anger is reported by nearly 69 per cent of respondents reporting rude events involving movement, compared with 49 per cent of those not entailing movement. In addition, fear is twice as likely in the context of rude events involving sounds. When we look more closely at the specific context, the association between sounds and fear is almost entirely attributable to actions involving motor vehicles, such as beeping horns or revving engines (not shown in Table 5.4).[7] Finally, we note that reactions of disgust are also related to the nature of the incivility. Approximately 44 per cent of respondents who mentioned a rude event involving language (e.g., swearing, sexual or prejudicial comments) felt disgusted. This percentage is notably higher than the 24 per cent of respondents who experienced other types of rude events.

We close this chapter with a few summary points and additional methodological notes about reactions to incivility. First, we presented

[7] Fear was reported by 26% of respondents who mentioned a rude event entailing sounds from motor vehicles, compared with less than 11% for those reporting other types of incivility.

the bivariate associations as opposed to partial correlations in a set of logistic regression models because some of our variables of interest – namely, income and type of occupation – had a sizeable number of missing cases (e.g., valid N for occupation is 345 in Table 5.4). However, we note that the pattern of associations discussed above remained significant in logistic regression models that controlled for all variables from Table 5.4 with the exception of occupation (which was omitted; analyses not shown). Second, we see that reactions to rudeness are patterned according to the nature of the act. Events entailing movement beget anger; language often evokes disgust; and sounds are more likely to yield fear, particularly when in the context of road rage. On that note, one reason why anger is such a prevalent emotion is that the most common type of incivility reported by our respondents involved movement. Third, the pattern of reactions to rude behaviour parallels what we see in the criminological literature on fear of crime. Women and the elderly are not only more likely to possess a heightened general sense of fear about crime victimization, but in the context of even mild, non-criminal victimizations they are also more apt to be fearful at the time of the event. Fourth, in Chapter 4 we noted that emotional reactions dissipate rather quickly, and to that end the correlates of emotions also attenuate over time. Emotions are anything but sticky, and even demographic subgroups with penchants for fear or anger drift towards indifference as time passes. In the next chapter we further explore the relationship of time and emotions, only we look further down the track. Specifically, we explore the process in which individuals come to cope with the emotional residue of their encounter. We also examine whether longer-term attitudes and behaviours subsequent to a rude stranger event might also change.

The main findings of this chapter are:

- With the exceptions of age and place of residence, the risk factors associated with rude encounters differ from those associated with crime victimization. This is particularly evident for gender and social class.
- A significant predictor of rude events is the amount of time spent in public places. Time in public settings also explains much of the association between rude events and demographic characteristics of respondents, with the exception of gender.

- Women and the elderly are more likely to express fear when encountering a rude stranger. Anger is more likely among the young, those in clerical and professional/technical occupations and those with more education. Indifference and disgust are not correlated with respondent demographics.
- The nature of incivility is correlated with emotional reactions. Events involving language more often lead to disgust; movement-related incidents more often lead to anger; deliberate acts and road rage incidents more frequently produce fear.

Week #5
Readings
(end)

6 | *After the event: coping, avoiding and changing*

When unexpected or bad things happen to people they try to make sense of them or to cope in various other ways with the shock of what has happened. This is particularly the case with traumatic events. Further, unusual, dangerous or serious episodes can change our mental outlook and behaviours. In this chapter we explore the implications of rude stranger encounters. We start with coping.

Coping and ontological security

Much of what we know about coping is informed by the literatures in social-psychology and criminology and concerns how people cope, and hopefully recover, from very serious events: rape; incest; predatory violent crime; domestic violence; bereavement; life threatening injury. We do not wish to claim that an encounter with a rude stranger is in the same domain as such tragic misfortunes. Most obviously intense physical or psychological harms are missing. Still, the case could be made that the encounter with the rude stranger requires some adjustments. Further, it is important that as outside observers we do not prejudge. What might seem trivial from our Olympian perspective could be deeply meaningful as a personal experience.

The argument that the rude stranger encounter well might require some coping is suggested circumstantially by findings from earlier in this book. We reported in Chapters 3, 4 and 5 that in a large number of cases people were surprised by what had happened to them. Further, many times our victims had strong initial emotional reactions, including anger, disgust and fear. Although others of our respondents appear to have been able to remain blasé, for a significant minority it might be reasonable to describe the event as one that violated, if only briefly, some of their taken for granted assumptions about everyday life.

Just how and why does this violation matter? Sociologists, such as Anthony Giddens (1984), have written on the centrality of 'onto-logical security' to the way that we live. This is the sense we have that things are normal, the world is predictable, that our bodies are safe and that we are surrounded by reasonably civil, likeminded people. This feeling of ontological security allows us to get on with daily activity and to trust others. In part it means we do not have to relent-lessly scan the street for dangers and that we can do whatever we are doing somewhat efficiently as a result – perhaps to walk to the Post Office with a valuable gift rather than calling for an armed security escort. But it also means a little more than this. Metaphorically one might say it implies that there is some ground beneath our feet as we make that walk. According to the extensive literature on coping in social psychology, traumatic events damage this ontological secur-ity, this ability to believe in a business as usual world (Updegraff, Silver and Holman 2008). Shocks and emotional upheavals, even if short in duration, can challenge our assumptions about our envir-onment, about other people and about ourselves. They might sug-gest that the world is malicious and capricious; that it is chaotic and random, or else deterministic and so equally outside of our control. Coping, the psychologists say, is about rebuilding buffering beliefs that things are 'normal' or allowing us to find an answer to the 'why me?' questions.

It is difficult to convey in writing in a book like this the centrality of ontological security for the self and as a lubricant for social process. An extreme case is helpful. Drawing on the work of the psychologist Bruno Bettelheim, Giddens (1984) notes the traumatic experience of life in a concentration camp marks perhaps the powerful form that the removal of ontological security can take. Bettelheim (1960), a Nazi death camp survivor, had observed first-hand how persistent danger, the new awareness that some people could be radically evil, arbitrary decision making on who should live or die, random violence, lack of privacy and the impossibility to plan ahead due to wild swings in pol-icy, led to the erosion of personality, the emergence of fatalism and a dimming of the human spirit. People would stumble and shuffle around like the living-dead. Real death would come quickly to those who could not retain some core of self or self-control.

We would like to stress here that the rapid and near complete loss of autonomy and belief came about not just due to concerns about physical safety, but from also immersion in a more general environment that was anything other than orderly, stable and predictable. As Primo Levi (1996) recorded when writing of his own Holocaust experiences, life and death could hinge upon the chance allocation of a pair of wooden clogs on arrival at Auschwitz that were a good fit. A bad fit would mean foot sores; these would become infected. The prisoner would then be unable to walk. Unable to walk, they were unable to work. Being unable to work, they would be 'useless'. Selection for death in the gas chamber would follow. Yet there was no way to control the contingency of having a good pair of clogs. Further, even to predict on arrival that having a good pair of clogs would save your life would be impossible. Those able to adapt psychologically to this sort of perverse, unknowable environment where small things could have colossal implications had some chance of surviving.[1]

Everyday incivility is in absolutely no way equivalent to the evils of the Holocaust. Yet the commonplace has lessons of its own to teach on the centrality of ontological security to self-confidence, self-belief and social intercourse. This possibility was illustrated in the famous 'breaching experiments' of the ethnomethodologist Harold Garfinkel (1967) in the 1960s. He had his students act in ways that simply did not make sense to those around them. For example, some would relentlessly ask questions or behave in ways that looked irrational. Others acted like lodgers in the family home. In a game of chess one might make illegal moves or simply take pieces off the board for no obvious reason. Garfinkel discovered that strong anger towards the norm-breaker often resulted. This arose not from fear, nor even from the act itself, but rather from the implication of what had happened. A

---

[1] It is interesting to note that those equipped with a strong ideology, for example, a belief in communism, seemed to have been better able to cope. The doctrine gave them a way to make sense of what was going on. Having been long suspicious of the Nazi Party, for example, they half-expected imprisonment and atrocities. Put another way, their worldview was confirmed. Famously, Jehovah's Witnesses had a low suicide rate in the camps and they converted many other inmates. Their faith offered a way to interpret the event (it was material evidence of the Devil's evil and of his existence) and a meaningful cosmological role (to witness this evil and to struggle against Satan). Those who suffered the more comprehensive psychological collapse seem to have been unsuspecting members of the Jewish middle class who had thought of themselves as harmless law abiding citizens, not as potential targets. In a curious and oblique way this perhaps fits with our finding that 'surprise' predicts the need for coping.

tacit understanding about the mutual intelligibility of action had been broken, a veil of trust torn. The experiments suggested we depend in a deep way on knowing – or better said, on believing we know – how the social world works and trusting that others will cooperate with us on this task. Shared trust, belief, faith – these are building blocks for social life (Wright 2005). Without such complicities everything will crumble.

Understanding this, Anthony Giddens helpfully notes that that ontological security depends on 'predictable routines' (1984, p. 50). Building on Goffman he adds that 'tact ... seems to be the main mechanism that sustains trust or ontological security' (1984, p. 75). So small-scale, repeated rituals of politeness are pivotal to keeping everyone on an even keel. Rude behaviour might be understood as worrying because it signals the fragility of such a negotiated social order. As the popular commentator Lynne Truss (2005, p. 54) puts it, when someone fails to thank you for holding a door open, a complex chain of reasoning can sometimes follow: 'Instead of feeling safe, you feel frightened. You succumb to accelerated moral reasoning. This person has no consideration for others, therefore no imagination, therefore is a sociopath representative of a world packed with sociopaths.' The situation is somewhat analogous to what happens when a previously smooth flight is interrupted by a nasty little air pocket. Suddenly we realize that we are in a tin tube 6-miles high moving at 500 miles per hour. Social life is kept airborne by mutual respect and a mutual faith, the incivil moments are bumps that remind us how things can easily go wrong. Coping is the repair activity – perhaps analogous to an intensified focus on that in-flight movie, or another free alcoholic drink – that allows a feeling of normality to be restored and worries to recede to the back of the mind.

Such a capacity for rude encounters to shake to the core the premise of ontological security is nicely captured by Madeleine Bunting (2008b) writing in *The Guardian*. Here she comments on the online responses that were posted on her newspaper's website in response to her own narrative of incivility (we return to this in Chapter 8):

As I trawled through the anecdotes of people's transport horrors, what became very clear is just how important these experiences are in shaping our understanding of the world and our place in it. These seemingly trivial incidents really get to us; we think about them and remember them for a long time. What disturbs us is not just the nasty people we might encounter, but how we react, as one person pointed out in an email; he described how in an encounter with an aggressive motorist, he was as much shaken by his own anger as that of the motorist. These bits in between work and home, these places where we bump up against people we might have absolutely nothing in common with and have totally different life experiences from, are the one place where we are most aware of our shared humanity – all we might have in common is the fact that we are human beings.

A journalist rather than a psychologist, Bunting understands the challenge of rudeness to prior and deeply ingrained world- and self-views. Coping is about rebuilding damage to these. All this said, we arrive at some interesting questions to explore in the first part of this chapter: (1) how widespread is coping activity?; (2) what are the more common forms it takes?; (3) what kind of person is more likely to engage in this?; and (4) how might event characteristics drive coping?

The first question we might ask is: did people do anything to cope? The answer is provided in Figure 6.1.[2] As can be seen, only a very few respondents engaged in no coping activities at all. Most victims of the rude stranger reported between one and four coping behaviours. So people seemed to use multiple strategies. There is also a 'long tail' of individuals reporting five or more techniques. The picture provided here is somewhat interesting. People were sufficiently impacted by their rude stranger experiences not only to remember them and to report them to our survey team, but also to do things in an effort to deal with the experience.

What exactly were the kinds of things that people did to cope? Table 6.1 shows the frequency of various kinds of commonly reported coping activity. Our respondents were able to nominate more than one category. Looking at the items we can see that most coping involved respondents trying to 'move on' mentally. Other coping strategies that one might predict would be common were in fact not common at all. Less than 1 per cent of responses involved hitting something or yelling out, only 2 per cent entailed thinking of ways to get revenge, and only 9 per cent were about engaging in a mental fantasy leading to what we might think of as *esprit de l'escalier*. This is an attractive

---

[2] See Table 6.1 for types of coping behaviours.

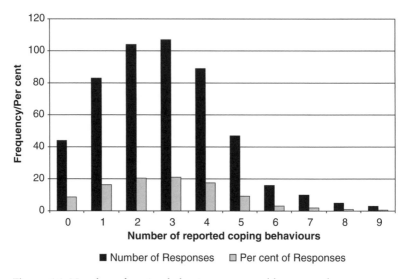

Figure 6.1 Number of coping behaviours reported by respondents

French term for when you think of something cutting, witty or appro-priate, a bon mot or gesture that a Molière or an Oscar Wilde might have produced – but only as you are leaving the building. In sum, only a small minority of people remained tied to the event in a confronta-tional way, coping by keeping hostility or competition active in their psyche. What we might think of as active or behavioural efforts at distraction were equally infrequent. Watching television was a strat-egy 3 per cent of the time, getting some exercise also constituted 3 per cent of responses and using drugs or alcohol to relax was surpris-ingly uncommon at just .6 per cent of all responses. Some 11 per cent entailed 'trying to forget what was happening by doing something else'. The most popular responses involved mental work organized around a kind of 'letting go' or 'coming to terms', something that we also find, for example, in the literature on bereavement. Hence, we find 28 per cent of responses involved 'trying to accept what hap-pened' and 17 per cent were about 'waiting for their feelings to pass'. Although mental work is involved here it is not strongly cognitive in orientation. Rather, these respondents sought a kind of inner peace or an emotional de-escalation of the event in their consciousness. The aim was to let time do its work. By contrast only 7 per cent of responses

Table 6.1 *Coping behaviours*

Coping behaviour	%	N
Tried to accept what happened	27.8	399
Talked to someone about how I felt about what happened	17.8	255
Waited for my feelings about what happened to pass	17.4	250
Tried to forget what happened by doing or thinking about something else	11.4	163
Fantasized about what I should have said or done to the rude stranger	8.6	124
Tried to think about what happened in a different way	7.0	101
Went out to get some exercise to make me feel better about what happened	2.7	39
Watched television	2.7	39
Thought about how to get revenge on the other person	2.0	29
Prayed to God for help	1.3	19
Yelled or hit something to let out my pent-up feelings about what happened	.7	10
Had a drink or took a pill	.6	8
Total	100%	1,436

N = 508 respondents reporting 1,436 coping behaviours.

involved 'trying to think about the issue in a different way', which suggests a more active and creative effort at reframing the experience. Talking to others, especially friends and family, is an important way of dealing with our problems. It is often how we deal with health issues, for example, as we seek advice or meaning-making words from others. Rude stranger encounters are also good conversation pieces, one would think. Somewhat surprisingly, only one respondent in six reported talking about the event as a form of coping.

So, most people did engage in coping. This was largely, but not exclusively, oriented around a kind of letting go. Our victims might be thought of as engaging in a series of low-key efforts to get back to normal. Now we are in a position to move on to a couple of more complex issues. Is there anything about the victim, the rude stranger or the event that generates the amount and nature of coping activity?

Predicting coping

To answer this question we employ a series of regression models. Model 1 in Table 6.2, for instance, reports the coefficients for the number of coping activities regressed on respondent demographic variables. This model indicates that men report fewer coping activities than women, but aside from this gender difference the victims' demographic characteristics are poor predictors of coping activity. Model 2 adds several variables to capture offender and incident characteristics, and here the results yield some interesting findings about the aftermath of incivility. For one, neither the demographics of the rude stranger, the type of setting where the offence unfolded, nor the type of incivility displayed by the offender have any discernable consequences for coping. Respondents cope to a similar extent regardless of whether the offender was rough looking or respectable, male or female, making obscene gestures or invading personal space.[3] In some respects these findings are counter-intuitive. Classic statements on 'broken windows' point to the pernicious impact of unruly youth and the obstreperous looking (Wilson and Kelling 1982), yet we find no evidence that acts by the young or rough looking are more likely to result in coping. Perhaps this is because they do not really challenge our commonsense world – in a way we expect these people to behave in a particular way. Still, coping is not completely divorced from characteristics of the encounter. As depicted in model 2, respondents appear to be most affected when they are caught off guard and when they attribute motivation to the offence. That is, victims engaged in significantly more coping activity when they were surprised by the rude stranger's conduct and when the stranger appeared to act deliberately. Earlier we found that surprise is a more common emotion in encounters with 'respectable'-looking perpetrators (see discussion of Table 4.5), and here we see that the shock of the event requires some coping. Taken together, it seems as if the occasional bump on the subway can be easily shrugged off.

---

[3] We also found no significant association between the race of the rude stranger and coping. We omitted the race variable from the analyses shown in Table 6.2 because it included 29 missing cases and added nothing to the model.

Table 6.2 *OLS regression coefficients: coping on predictor variables*

Variables	Model 1	Model 2	Model 3
Respondent characteristics			
Male	− .457**	− .406*	− .258
	(.163)	(.171)	(.168)
Age	− .010	.025	− .007
	(.077)	(.080)	(.077)
Education	− .050	− .055	− .090
	(.110)	(.111)	(.108)
Native Australian	− .030	.078	.053
	(.203)	(.208)	(.201)
Lives in inner-metro area	− .061	− .113	− .132
	(.179)	(.180)	(.174)
Rude stranger characteristics			
Male		− .007	− .116
		(.192)	(.187)
Approximate age		− .085	−.085
		(.114)	(.110)
Rough looking[a]		.199	.247
		(.228)	(.224)
Neither rough nor respectable looking[a]		− .001	.031
		(.217)	(.209)
Incident characteristics			
Very surprised by rude stranger[b]		.856***	.589**
		(.214)	(.219)
Quite surprised by rude stranger[b]		.402*	.336
		(.204)	(.199)
Rude stranger acted deliberately		.592**	.450*
		(.216)	(.211)
Duration of encounter		− .020	− .111
		(.098)	(.096)
Place was rough looking[c]		− .335	− .420
		(.297)	(.288)
Place was neither rough nor respectable looking[c]		− .116	− .082
		(.231)	(.224)
Respondent on foot[d]		.052	.155
		(.188)	(.184)
Respondent on public transportation[d]		.628	.772*
		(.360)	(.350)

Table 6.2 (*cont.*)

Variables	Model 1	Model 2	Model 3
Nature of the incivility			
Movement		– .004	– .112
		(.193)	(.189)
Body		.247	.317
		(.243)	(.235)
Sounds		.031	– .073
		(.269)	(.247)
Language		.049	.074
		(.255)	(.247)
Emotions			
Anger			.148***
			(.031)
Fear			.196***
			(.051)
Disgust			.040
			(.037)
Constant	3.222***	2.627***	2.406***
	(.404)	(.587)	(.572)
Valid N	496	485	485
R^2	.017	.100	.167

   * $p < .05$
  ** $p < .01$
 *** $p < .001$

Notes: Standard errors are in parentheses. Dummy variables indicating missing cases for gender of the rude stranger and whether the stranger was rough looking were included in the analysis to reduce the number of missing cases. These coefficients are not shown in the table. The substantive results are consistent when omitting these cases from the analysis.
[a] 'Respectable looking' is the reference category.
[b] 'Not that surprised' or 'Not at all surprised' is the reference category.
[c] 'Place was respectable looking' is reference category.
[d] 'Respondent in vehicle' is reference category.

Yet, a well-dressed person intentionally blocking one's way leaves a bad aftertaste that requires some mental readjustment or other coping activity. Deliberate acts and surprise at the conduct are most likely to damage ontological security.

Model 3 in the table adds some perspective as to why gender, level of surprise at the incident and attribution of motive require more coping. This model includes a block of variables measuring the respondents' emotional reactions. As discussed in previous chapters, respondents were asked about their emotions *at the time of* the event and also *immediately after* the incivility transpired. More specifically, victims reported the type of emotion (fear, anger, disgust, something else) and its intensity (e.g., very strongly, not strongly at all). For each time point – during and immediately after the event – we created a variable ranging from 0 to 4 indicating the strength of the emotion. Values of '0' indicate the complete absence of the emotion, '1' implies that the emotion was present but not felt strongly at all, and a maximum value of '4' implies that the emotion was felt very strongly. We then summed the variables (during + immediately after) to create an emotional reaction index that ranges from 0 to 8. It is evident from the coefficients in the final model of Table 6.2 that the emotional reaction during and immediately after the incident, particularly feelings of fear and anger, drives the need to cope. Put another way, the interpretation of the event is crucial. If victims were able to remain nonchalant and aloof following an encounter with a rude stranger, then they engaged in little coping. Yet respondents with such a casual demeanour are clearly in the minority (about 6 per cent of respondents during the episode and 17 per cent immediately after; see Table 4.1). Rather, the vast majority of incivilities results in a strong emotional response; for instance, nearly two-thirds of ELIAS respondents reported strong feelings of anger, fear or disgust at the time of the initial incivility, and over 40 per cent expressed these sentiments immediately after. We also note that the emotions variables help to explain the victim and incident effects noted above. Comparing model 3 with the model 2, we see that the gender coefficient is reduced by over 35 per cent, the motivation effect (i.e., the stranger acted deliberately) is nearly 25 per cent smaller when the emotions variables are considered and the level of surprise coefficient is more than 30 per cent smaller.

The nature of coping

The coefficients in Table 6.2 speak to the amount of coping, but not to the nature of it. As shown in Table 6.1 above, victims express a range of coping mechanisms. Some do the mental work necessary to find acceptance or come to terms with the event. A few resort to relaxing intoxication or seriously ponder revenge. But to what extent are the types of coping associated with characteristics of the persons involved and the nature of the event?

We are particularly interested in the 'high harm' victims who evidence more than passive coping after the incident; i.e., those who went beyond merely trying to accept what happened. Specifically, we look at the determinants of three types of coping: (1) active mental work, such as trying to reframe the event in one's mind; (2) actual behavioural coping of any kind, be it constructive (e.g., exercising) or potentially injurious conduct (e.g., popping pills); and (3) a measure of coping that signifies a higher level of distress for the victim, such as using intoxicants, praying for help, and hitting and yelling.[4] The results from a series of logistic regression models (not reported here) closely resemble the OLS models shown in Table 6.2. Only a few incident and victim characteristics are significant, yet these largely wash out when accounting for the emotions felt by victims during or immediately after the incident. Strong feelings of anger and fear, in particular, are significantly associated with the type of coping. We demonstrate the magnitude of these emotions by graphing the predicted probabilities of experiencing each type of coping in Figure 6.2. When we hold all other variables from the logistic regression models constant at their mean values, we find that the likelihood of coping via the three means described above increases dramatically if the respondent reported a strong sense of fear or anger. For instance, the model estimates that about one in five victims of incivility that

---

[4] Specifically, active mental work refers to affirmative responses to the following: 'Tried to think about what happened in a different way', 'Fantasized about what I should have said or done', 'Prayed to God for help', or 'Thought about how to get revenge on the other person'. Behavioural coping is coded '1' if respondents reported any of the following: 'Had a drink or took a pill', 'Talked to someone about how I felt about what happened', 'Went out to get some exercise to make me feel better about what happened', or 'Yelled or hit something to let out my pent-up feelings about what happened'. Finally, the measure of coping that signifies a higher level of distress for the victim was based on affirmative responses to the more detrimental aspects of the previous two variables, including the following: 'Had a drink or took a pill', 'Fantasized about what I should have said or done', 'Prayed to God for help', 'Yelled or hit something to let out my pent-up feelings about what happened' or 'Thought about how to get revenge on the other person'.

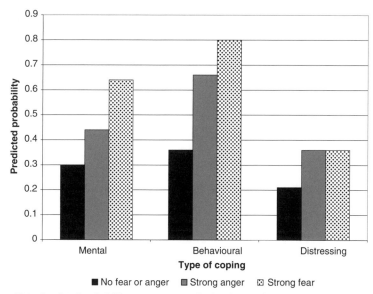

Figure 6.2 Effects of emotions on types of coping

Note: Predicted probabilities were generated using the 'clarify' procedure in Stata (King, Tomz, and Wittenberg 2000). Estimates are based on separate logistic regression models for each of the three outcome variables described in footnote 4. Each model controls for all factors included in the full OLS model shown in model 3 of Table 6.2. Control variables were held at their mean values to generate predicted probabilities. 'Strong' emotions are indicated by a value of six on the eight point scale for the emotions variables. The value for the fear indicator was fixed at zero when generating predicted probabilities for anger, and anger was held at zero when generating estimates for fear.

reported no sense of fear or anger would engage in a type of coping that might be considered distressing or potentially injurious (e.g., hit something, pray, yell). Yet for those reporting strong feelings of anger or fear the expected probability exceeds 35 per cent. The differences are equally as stark for the other types of coping.

New attitudes and behaviours in public

Aside from coping, there are many other possible responses to the incivil encounter that we must consider. Coping is something often done at home. But when they are back out in public people might think or behave differently as well. In the criminological literature the theme of 'constrained behaviour' has been well established in the context of the study of the impacts of victimhood. The idea here is that victims of crime change what they do. They might stay inside more, avoid certain parts of the town or change their routines so as not to encounter problem individuals (Garofalo 1979; Markowitz *et al.* 2001; Skogan and Maxfield 1981). Essentially, the freedom of movement of the victim is eroded due to caution or lack of confidence. Further, the argument is made that there are negative consequences for the wider community. Constrained behaviour is important because it contributes to 'broken windows' effects. If 'good people' stay off the street, then these are further colonized by bad elements. A vicious circle is then initiated as the probability of negative social encounters for everyone else increases as each good citizen retreats from public space. Table 6.3 looks at such constrained behaviour, but within a wider context of diverse attitudes and actions.

A clear pattern emerges. The most common response is that being a victim of the rude stranger makes many people more sensitive to the prevalence of such people. The experience in a sense amplifies perception in this particular direction. One way to think about this is in terms of 'scanning', something that Erving Goffman (1971) suggests we do as we walk down the street or move through other public places. According to Goffman, we are perpetually on the lookout for possible trouble, trying to spot problem individuals, such as the pickpocket, the mentally ill, the homeless or the alcoholic. Something analogous is going on here, only with our respondents the perceptual antenna is tuned into signs of rudeness. The most common set of behavioural responses were about becoming more tolerant, civil and polite. This awareness of the need for civility was more commonly invoked than the response categories in the survey that spoke of the self becoming hardened, as remonstrative or shut off. Being a victim, then, opens people up to the need for civility more often than it makes them confrontational and cold. Aversive behaviour was quite rare. Two other response categories were extremely rarely invoked. Only seven people in the entire survey said that they had become ruder themselves. The same number said they had gone back to the scene of the incivil encounter looking for the rude stranger. We can think of this as something of a vigilante scenario, a scaled-down version of that in the *Deathwish* movie (Winner 1974), where the character played by Charles Bronson stalks the streets seeking revenge after his wife is murdered by a gang of low life criminals.

Table 6.3 *Changes in emotions and behaviours since the event*[a]

	%	N (of responses)
(a) Becoming more aware of rude strangers	28.0	221
(b) Becoming more tolerant and understanding of other people in general	20.3	160
(c) Becoming a more polite person	15.9	126
(d) Remonstrating with rude strangers I come into contact with	12.7	100
(e) Becoming more hardened to other people in general	6.2	49
(f) Becoming more shut off from other people in general	5.1	40
(g) Avoiding busy public places in general	3.7	29
(h) Avoiding places like the one where 'the event' occurred	3.4	27
(i) Avoiding the place where 'the event' occurred	3.0	24
(j) Becoming a ruder person	.9	7
(k) Going back to the place where 'the event' occurred looking for the rude stranger	.9	7
Total	100%	790

N = 474 respondents reporting 790 emotions and behaviours.

[a] The survey question reads as follows: 'Okay, now during the time you have spent in public places since the event, have you found yourself doing any of the following things?'

The findings of Table 6.3 are reconfigured and simplified in Figure 6.3, which shows the percentage of responses falling into each generic category.[5] The most common response is increased sensitivity or awareness of rude strangers (category (a) from Table 6.3); then

[5] For Figure 6.3 we first grouped the categories and then ran a multiple response frequency. Hence, the percentages in Figure 6.3 do not represent the simple summation of categories in Table 6.3.

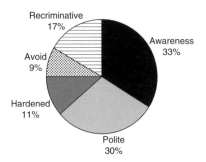

Figure 6.3 Behavioural and emotional changes following rude stranger encounter

trying to be more civil ((b) and (c) in Table 6.3). Around one in three responses were of the latter type. By contrast, a third of responses involved becoming hardened ((e) and (f)) or recriminative ((d), (j) and (k)). Only one in ten responses conformed to the avoidance pattern ((g), (h) and (i)). In general, then, the experience of incivility does not seem to easily or automatically generate incivility. Or, at least at first glance, this is the story of our pie chart. If we further pool our responses we might observe that being antisocial, withdrawing and avoiding add up to 37 per cent. This is slightly more than the 30 per cent who had found themselves trying to be more polite in public. Here we have a classic case of how to cut up the pie.

However we read them, these are interesting findings given the large quantity of work documenting the 'brutalising' effects of exposure to violence and that civic engagement is reduced when rude behaviour is witnessed. Some of this has been in the experimental tradition of social psychology. Diana Mutz and Byron Reeves (2004), for example, exposed experimental subjects to videotaped political debates conducted by actors. In one rendition the actors were civil, making the appropriate signs of listening with respect. In the other, they traded insults, rude facial expressions and gestures. The intellectual arguments were the same in each case. The experiment showed that trust in government was eroded by the rude version of the debate, yet enhanced by the civil interchange. Mutz and Reeves come to the conclusion that witnessing rudeness leads to disengagement and cynicism. Another study by Christine Porath and Amir Erez (2009) involved the experimental subjects witnessing incivility not on tape, but in real time between real people. Essentially, their experimental subjects were told to turn up for a test on personality and task performance. They sat doing anagrams and other activities. A confederate of the experimenter arrived late in the test room and was given a harsh dressing down in front of the experimental subjects – 'you are irresponsible, you will never hold down a job' etc. Porath and Erez found that those who witnessed the incivil encounter were less likely to engage in a subsequent citizenship behaviour (staying behind voluntarily to do some extra tests) and more likely to engage in 'dysfunctional ideation' (coming up with violent or hostile uses for a brick in a standard test of creative thinking) than the control group. So the picture from social psychology indicates that there is an erosion of the social goodwill that comes from experiencing even indirect rudeness. In the case of real world incivility our data suggest a mixed picture, one that perhaps mirrors the complexity of real social settings rather than experimental environments. Various strategies and resolutions seem to be available and used in everyday life.

But who, exactly, becomes disengaged or otherwise alters their behaviour following the event? Are there characteristics of the encounter that make some victims more eager to remonstrate with rude strangers in the future? In Chapter 4 we showed that initial reactions to rude behaviour significantly influence the likelihood that the victim would directly remonstrate with the stranger (see Table 4.4). Some emotions, such as anger, even prolonged the duration of the exchange (Table 4.7). But do the respondents' attitudes about others and behaviours in public settings meaningfully change in the days or weeks after the encounter in question?

To shed light on these questions we again employ a set of regression models, this time to assess the determinants of three measures of behavioural change. First, we test facets of the fear–avoidance paradigm professed by 'broken windows' advocates by assessing whether characteristics of the victims, offenders or event result in avoidance of public places following the incident. The latter variable is coded '1' if the victim responded affirmatively to any of the avoidance questions from Table 6.3 (otherwise coded '0'). Second, we decipher whether some victims become increasingly hardened and shut off from people in general following the incivility. Finally, a non-trivial proportion of ELIAS respondents reported that they remonstrated with rude strangers since their recent bout with incivility (see the fourth category in Table 6.3). What is not clear, however, is whether incident characteristics affect whether victims will remonstrate with other rude strangers.

The logistic regression coefficients are reported in Table 6.4. The coefficients differ with respect to strength and magnitude for each outcome variable, although three general patterns seem apparent. First, and akin to the coping analyses discussed above, demographic characteristics of the victim and offender have only marginal effects on behavioural changes. Whether respondents are old or young, urban or rural, native Australian or immigrant, has no bearing on behavioural or attitudinal alterations following the incivility. In addition, respondents react no differently if the rude stranger appeared old or young, rough looking or respectable, or appeared to act deliberately or unintentionally. The one exception with respect to victim and offender demographics is gender. For instance, the coefficients in model 1 show that female victims become more avoidant than male victims. The same is true for those encountering a male rude stranger. These findings on the gendered nature of incivility (see Gardner 1995) and its aftermath map fairly cleanly onto the fear of crime literature, which consistently shows that women often feel physically vulnerable (Box, Hale and Andrews 1988; Katz, Webb and Armstrong 2003) and view strangers as more threatening (Cobbina, Miller and Brunson 2008). On account of these concerns women employ a range of precautionary strategies that often revolve around avoidance and retreat from public spaces (Day 2000). The criminological literature, as we discussed in Chapter 1, has long been focused on measurable incivilities that often border on criminal (visible prostitution, graffiti, syringes on the ground). Our findings suggest that seemingly trivial acts of rudeness – acts that rarely make their way into fear of crime surveys and coder clipboards – are also consequential for women. In addition, few victimization surveys consider other reactions beyond avoidance, such as the proclivity to intervene when confronting rude behaviour in public. Looking at model 3, we see nearly the inverse of model 1. On average, men report a higher proclivity to remonstrate with rude strangers after the incident, while respondents encountering a male rude stranger are less apt to remonstrate after the event. Taken together, we might conclude that female victims are more likely to avoid potentially troublesome areas, while males are more likely to intervene.

Table 6.4 *Logistic regression coefficients: behavioural changes on predictor variables*

Variables	Model 1 Avoidance	Model 2 Hardened	Model 3 Remonstrate
Respondent characteristics			
Male	−.825*	.016	.598*
	(.358)	(.300)	(.267)
Age	.102	−.276	−.046
	(.158)	(.149)	(.121)
Education	−.034	−.024	−.549***
	(.211)	(.198)	(.173)
Native Australian	.156	−.160	.173
	(.417)	(.357)	(.332)
Lives in inner-metro area	.019	.244	.409
	(.347)	(.303)	(.270)
Rude stranger characteristics			
Male	.860*	.071	−.904**
	(.401)	(.349)	(.295)
Approximate age	−.082	−.244	−.062
	(.214)	(.198)	(.177)
Rough looking [a]	−.427	.414	.312
	(.458)	(.388)	(.365)
Neither rough nor respectable looking [a]	−.248	−.363	.097
	(.440)	(.395)	(.331)
Incident characteristics			
Very surprised by rude stranger[b]	−.303	−.227	.093
	(.443)	(.392)	(.352)
Quite surprised by rude stranger [b]	−.252	−.106	.199
	(.419)	(.369)	(.320)
Rude stranger acted deliberately	.732	.614	−.388
	(.379)	(.355)	(.343)
Duration of encounter	−.057	−.009	.348*
	(.190)	(.163)	(.143)
Place was rough looking[c]	.825	−.182	.012
	(.492)	(.498)	(.454)
Place was neither rough nor respectable looking[c]	.206	.025	.224
	(.443)	(.395)	(.343)
Respondent on foot[d]	.838*	.413	.386
	(.679)	(.332)	(.300)

Table 6.4 (*cont.*)

Variables	Model 1 Avoidance	Model 2 Hardened	Model 3 Remonstrate
Respondent on public transportation [d]	.837 (.679)	.529 (.597)	.336 (.536)
Nature of the incivility			
Movement	− .001 (.383)	.255 (.345)	.049 (.293)
Body	− .359 (.450)	.855* (.397)	.973** (.338)
Sounds	− .109 (.526)	− .303 (.490)	.233 (.389)
Language	− .171 (.451)	.088 (.420)	.417 (.382)
Emotions			
Anger	.049 (.060)	.272*** (.057)	.103* (.049)
Fear	.162* (.080)	.106 (.085)	− .001 (.087)
Disgust	.112 (.066)	.049 (.063)	.025 (.057)
Constant	− 3.506** (1.174)	− 2.006* (1.017)	− 1.086 (.882)
Valid N	458	457	458

* $p < .05$
** $p < .01$
*** $p < .001$

Note: Standard errors are in parentheses. Questions about behavioural changes were only asked of 474 respondents who reported that they have been back in public since the event in question (34 had not been). Dummy variables indicating missing cases for gender of the rude stranger and whether the stranger was rough-looking were included in the analysis to reduce the number of missing cases. These coefficients are not shown in the table. The substantive results are consistent when omitting these cases from the analysis.

[a] 'Respectable looking' is the reference category.
[b] 'Not that surprised' or 'Not at all surprised' is the reference category.
[c] 'Place was respectable looking' is reference category.
[d] 'Respondent in vehicle' is reference category.

Conversely, encounters with male offenders seem to propel avoidance and repel remonstration.

A second notable finding in Table 6.4 concerns the nature of the stranger's conduct. Offences involving bodies and bodily management (spitting, dirty looks, reading porn) appear particularly irksome, even to the point of altering the victim's subsequent behaviour. According to the results in model 2 of Table 6.4, experiencing this type of incivility increased the probability that victims would feel more shut off and hardened towards others. In addition, witnesses to bodily mismanagement were also more likely to remonstrate with rude strangers after the incident (model 3). In contrast, other types of incivility were not significantly associated with any behavioural changes. Victims seem willing to endure mild physical altercations (getting cut-off, pushed, tailed) and tolerate foul language or loud noises without altering their behaviour after the rude stranger encounter. This set of findings chimes with classic scholarship on the rise of etiquette in modern societies. As discussed in an earlier chapter, Norbert Elias (1978 [1939]) proposed that the absence of self-restraint with respect to bodily control violates a fundamental dimension of good manners that is pivotal for modern society. It appears that ringing cell phones, beeping horns and dropping the f-bomb may be irritating, but not to the point where witnesses to such conduct become themselves hardened or remonstrative. Bodily etiquette, it would seem, is a different animal.

Finally, emotional reactions are again salient.[6] For example, the extent to which victims were fearful during and immediately after the incident is associated with subsequent avoidance of select public places. It is worth emphasizing that the event and perpetrator characteristics did not fare well in the statistical analysis of avoidance. Yet emotions, in this case fear, seem to have more predictive power. How are we to explain this? Put into commonsense language, events do not carry their own emotional freight. There is a moment of contingency between the event, its interpretation and its translation into an emotional landscape. When this act of translation generates a strong emotional pattern, *then* we see impacts on coping, attitudes and behaviour.

---

[6] We use the same measures of emotional reactions that were used in the analysis of coping (see above).

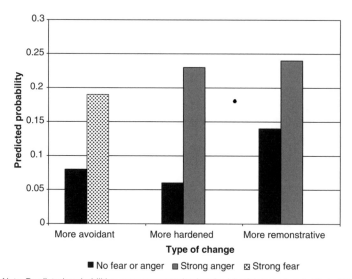

Note: Predicted probabilities were generated using the 'clarify' procedure in Stata (King, Tomz, and Wittenberg 2000). Estimates are based on separate logistic regression models for each of the three outcome variables described in the text. Each model controls for all variables included in Table 6.4. Control variables were held at their mean values to generate predicted probabilities. 'Strong' emotions are indicated by a value of six on the eight point scale for the emotions variables. The value for the fear indicator was held at zero when generating predicted probabilities for anger, and anger was held at zero when generating estimates for fear.

Figure 6.4 Effects of emotions on behavioural and attitudinal changes

Given their relative importance, let's talk a little more about emotions. The magnitude of the 'fear factor' discussed above is noteworthy. As illustrated in Figure 6.4, the predicted probability of avoiding certain types of public places after the most recent encounter with a rude stranger is more than twice as high if the victim expressed a strong sense of fear as compared with not feeling afraid at all. This finding aligns with multiple theoretical perspectives on incivility discussed – and generally critiqued – earlier in the book. Goffman, for instance, argued that residents of modern cities view rude strangers as potentially threatening and, accordingly, city dwellers tend to retreat from persons and places seen as unruly. From a very different perspective, 'broken windows' advocates and routine activities theorists posit that encounters with disorderly and disreputable people instil a sense of fear, which subsequently constrains social interaction in public settings and even leads some victims to withdraw from certain public areas altogether. This fear–avoidance paradigm clearly finds some support in model 1 of Table 6.4 and the corresponding figure (Figure 6.4). Yet we have repeatedly argued that 'broken windows' theory and the related literature on fear of crime remain myopic with respect to emotional reactions to victimization. That is, the emotion of interest is almost exclusively fear. We have already demonstrated that victims report a wider range of emotions and that fear is far less common than anger or disgust (see Table 4.1). In addition, we reported in Chapter 4 that victims were more likely to respond directly to rude strangers when respondents were surprised, felt intense emotions or felt angry about the stranger's behaviour. The latter two emotions also led to more back-and-forth between the actors in question (see Tables 4.4 and 4.7). However, it still remains unclear whether such emotions exhibit any demonstrable effect on the attitudes and behaviours of victims after the initial event transpires.

The coefficients in models 2 and 3 of Table 6.4 speak to this issue and suggest that feelings of anger have enduring consequences. Stronger feelings of anger at the time of the incident leave victims more indurated, at least in the short term (see model 2). In addition, model 3 shows that a stronger sense of anger yields a higher likelihood of remonstrating when other rude strangers cross the respondent's path. Emile Durkheim might have anticipated the latter finding. In contrast to the fear–avoidance paradigm, Durkheim (1980 [1893]) argued that deviant conduct left onlookers feeling indignant, and this indignation translated into some degree of sanctioning. Our results indicate that victims are indeed more likely to intervene and sanction *other* rude strangers in the days or weeks after the event. As shown in Figure 6.4, the magnitude of this effect is sizeable.

We close with a few observations about the findings in relation to extant scholarship on incivility. Unarguably the dominant school of thought on incivility and its consequences over the past two decades has been the 'broken windows' model. This paradigm emphasizes the purportedly inextricable linkages between incivility, fear, the withdrawal of 'good citizens' from dilapidated public spaces and ultimately serious crime. To wit, fear and avoidance are paramount concepts. Our analysis of a unique survey that taps into a range of incivilities, most of which have remained beyond the purview of 'broken windows' research, lends some support to the fear–avoidance paradigm. Yet, we caution that although fear is associated with constrained behaviour, it is an emotion expressed by a very small proportion of respondents and one that decays rather quickly over time (see Table 4.1 in Chapter 4). It is also intriguing that some of the most common reactions to incivility were self-reported *increases* in politeness, tolerance and remonstration. We are by no means discounting the negative repercussions that rude and unruly behaviour can have. Our agenda, after all, is not to advance some Pollyannaish vision of incivility as a social good. Still, we suggest here as we did in previous chapters that prior scholarship has far too rarely considered these possible reactions to incivility, and future work in this vein should broaden its conceptual arsenal and look beyond the old standbys of fear and avoidance. Akin to Durkheim's (1980 [1893]) observation that crime serves a positive function in society by bringing people together in a collective show of disdain for the violation, our investigation into rudeness similarly suggests that the occasional discourtesy might serve as a reminder about our own tolerance and politeness. In some cases it might even reignite our willingness to intervene or perhaps sanction the next rude stranger.

The main findings of this chapter are:

- Most victims of the rude stranger engage in one or more coping activities.
- These coping strategies are generally low key and involve somewhat passive mental work.
- Behavioural and attitudinal responses to the encounter are common, including very frequently increased awareness of rude strangers, the resolution to be more polite and also the evolution of hardened attitudes. The 'broken windows' paradigm does not capture this diversity.
- Women engage in more coping behaviours than men. They are also more likely to engage in avoidance.
- Strong emotional responses to events are a predictor of coping behaviour and other behavioural or attitudinal changes. Event qualities predict less than the implication or interpretation of the event into an emotional landscape.
- Remonstration with the rude stranger is associated with bodily display incivility and the emotion of anger.
- Fear and avoidance do go together, but this is a relatively uncommon response.

Week #5 Readings (3) (start)

7 | General attitudes towards the stranger: exploring fear and trust

In traditional societies most people lived in bands or in villages, their geographic horizons usually defined by how far one could walk in a day. Such familiar environments were largely without strangers. Passing migrants, gypsies, tinkers, charlatans and traders were noteworthy interruptions in biographies filled with known others, mostly family and neighbours. Even in courtly society unknown outsiders were something of a novelty. One thinks of the stir caused by the arrival of a company of travelling players in Shakespeare's *Hamlet*. By contrast, much of lived experience in modern societies takes place in the close physical presence of strangers. Urbanization and the evolution of affordable technologies for daily travel have led to the increased social densities and circulations that see strangers thrown against each other. Of course, at home and at work the stranger is relatively absent. Yet out in public the situation is very different.

Remarkably little objective information is known about our social connectedness with, beliefs about, or quality of interactions among those anonymous people with whom we must share public space. Still, respondents to surveys seem to be confident in claiming that things have gone to the dogs and are getting worse. The Public Agenda (2002) survey of 2001 found 79 per cent of American respondents saying that 'lack of respect and courtesy is a serious problem for our society', and 73 per cent believing that there was more respect around in the past. These impressions are generally supported rather than critiqued in the academic literature. This scholarship suggests, on the back of a certain quantity of evidence (but also a good deal of theory-inflected speculation) that this connectedness to the unknown or general other is very tenuous. The academic and philosophical majority opinion seems to be that trust, concern and interest in the stranger are declining precipitously.

Writing back in the 1960s the German philosopher Jürgen Habermas (1984, 1989) famously painted a picture of the eighteenth century as

129

a time when strangers could meet and have careful debate on crucial social issues. In coffee houses they would assemble to discuss in a rational, civil and informed manner the topics of the day. According to Habermas the idyll of high-trust, intimate and communicative public settings has been replaced by a dystopia of commodified media power, efforts at opinion manipulation and advertising culture. This image of falling sociability has been elaborated in more empirical detail by the cultural historian Richard Sennett (1992). Looking to accounts from prior centuries he notes that there was once a celebration of what he calls 'public man'. People would talk to strangers, literally wear their political colours on their sleeves and seek out the company of unknown others. Starting in the nineteenth century, he sees this orientation being replaced by increasing introspection, concerns for privacy and a retreat into the domestic sphere. Life starts to be lived for the self rather than for the other, and moreover in a non-communicative way. The popular author Lynne Truss (2005) takes the case even further, arguing that an epidemic of rudeness has emerged in recent years in response to such a shift. She suggests that the Goffmanian analysis of tact with its core concepts like 'deference' and 'respect' is perhaps no longer analytically relevant to explaining public life. Rather, we need new ways to understand the self-centred, self-absorbed and volatile personalities to be found in public places. Much the same point is made by Stephen L. Carter (1998), who in his book on incivility paints a picture of a self-indulgent and spoilt society where people are unwilling to invoke moral standards, to listen or to be held accountable for their actions.

A strong, if somewhat circumstantial, evidentiary basis for such claims of decline and fall can be seen in studies of social capital, such as those of the influential political scientist Robert Putnam (2000). These suggest that social networks and civic engagement can play a crucial role in augmenting the quality of life. Yet they conclude with sadness that generalized trust and goodwill between strangers is diminishing. For example, the case is made that there is not just an unwillingness to talk about issues as Habermas noted, but even that people will not acknowledge co-presence. Putnam shows that membership of clubs and sports leagues is declining, and that today nobody is much interested in community picnics. Television in particular has been accorded an important role in this process. It shifts the location of leisure from the park and plaza to the home, and its images foster a view of the world as threatening (Putnam 1995). In such a context the living room becomes a sanctuary. Criminological research has painted a broadly similar picture, sketching out a scenario in which fear of crime is bringing about a withdrawal from public life among strangers in urban settings (Gendleman 2006; Miethe 1995). Likewise, writing from the perspective of critical humanism, Zygmunt Bauman (2000) sees a somewhat irrational fear of strangers as endemic in the postmodern condition. This has directed middle-class lives into fragmented private domains and sealed safety bubbles, such as the gated community and guarded shopping malls.

The vision of retreat and distrust is endorsed in the media studies field too. Certainly, the case can be made that circulating images or representations of strangers have become increasingly negative over recent years. Recently, sociological research has taken a special interest in analysing the ways in which different social types are presented in mass media discourse: the terrorist, the criminal, the asylum seeker, the serial killer (Anleu, Martin and Zadoroznyi 2004). What these icons share in common is their distillation of the stranger into an emblem of uncertainty and danger, rather than romance and opportunity. Media studies scholars suggest that public life is increasingly represented as a 'mean and dangerous world' (Gerbner *et al.* 1980), while the people who inhabit it are ever more depicted as 'risky strangers' – as potential aggressors or stalkers. Towards such people our default position should always be 'stranger danger' – a term originally used to instruct children that has now been generalized as a prudent social attitude (Furedi 1998). In terms of connectedness to wider social conditions, the emergence of this hardening and accelerating representation has occurred alongside an increasingly nostalgic orientation towards the past. According to the leading historian Eric Hobsbawm (1991) a 'Golden Age' lasting from 1945 to the early 1970s was associated with growing prosperity and a sense of stability and community. This has given way to the 'Crisis Decades'. Lasting from the early 1970s to the present, these are viewed as an era of polarization, moral decline and economic instability. Here in the Crisis Decades we are said to feel uneasy. One result of this general unease has been audience resonance for a plethora of 'reality TV' shows. Some, such as Big Brother or Survivor, deliberately throw strangers together in uncomfortable or downright confrontational situations and wait for conflict to erupt. It is no accident that in Australia one of the most highly rating programmes over the last couple of years is all about the analysis of potentially threatening strangers. It follows immigration officers as they try to figure out whether newly arriving individuals to the country can be trusted (Dale 2006). So the available evidence would seem to overwhelmingly suggest that in the current era representations of strangers have taken on a harder quality and become more prolific. Not only is the stranger more prone to be negatively coded, but the sheer regularity of stories depicting this vision appears to be rising dramatically. If the qualitative content of the mass media has changed in response to a wider social shift, it follows that identifying 'media effects' should be possible. The limited work that is available suggests that this is indeed the case. A study of Finnish adolescents, for example, demonstrated that the regular viewing of reality crime television programmes seemed to reduce levels of trust (Salmi, Smolej and Kivivuori 2007).

With the literature we have been discussing marking a sort of intellectual horizon, in this chapter we set out to review wider social attitudes towards strangers and to map their social distribution. How do we feel about strangers in public places? Are they something or nothing to us? Do we view them in intrinsically positive or negative terms? Do we seek out opportunities to be around these strangers, or do we prefer to keep away from them as much as possible? Do people who consume a lot of popular culture and mass media products have a different view from the general population? Finally, do those who have recently encountered rude strangers differ from everybody else in the population? We begin our analysis looking at the social distribution of the two key psycho-social variables in the field. The first of these is 'fear'.

Fear

Earlier in this book we showed that fear was sometimes experienced in the specific encounter with the rude stranger. Here we are concerned with a more diffuse orientation. Over recent years 'fear of crime' has been a major topic of research in criminology. The concept itself is somewhat amorphous, capturing both a 'rational' or cognitive effort at individual risk assessment and an emotional response to a vague horizon of possibilities and victimization consequences.

Nevertheless, the research findings might be described as robust cross-nationally, and they represent one of our best sources of information on feelings about life in a world of strangers. In Australia, as elsewhere, fear of crime is strongest among the elderly and women. Nevertheless, levels of fear are in general quite low. Some 72 per cent of respondents to a 2004 Australian crime victimization survey said that they felt 'very safe' or 'fairly safe' when walking alone in their area after dark. The situation is somewhat more equivocal once gender is taken into account. Women were substantially more likely than men to say they felt 'a bit unsafe' (26 per cent versus 10 per cent) or 'very unsafe' (13 per cent versus 3 per cent). Those aged 16 to 24 and those over 60 were very modestly more likely to experience fear in the presented scenario than those in between these ages. It is thought that the fear of young people reflects a higher objective risk of victimization; women's concerns are oriented around sexual assault, while the elderly are concerned about the implications of crime, in particular being unable to run or fight back, and taking longer to heal. The same Australian results showed that having low income, being widowed/ divorced, being a crime victim and being non-English-speaking also predicted fear (Johnson 2005). All things considered, gender and a history of victimization were the strongest predictors of crime fear, the other factors having somewhat weaker effects. These findings, we note, are broadly consistent with those internationally, where Australia seems to be about middle of the pack for fear of crime (van Dijk, van Kesteren and Smit 2007).

In our survey respondents were asked: 'How safe or unsafe do you feel when out in public places by yourself during the day?' They were also asked about being out alone after dark in public places. It is important to notice that we phrased our question to refer to 'public places' rather than to 'where you live' or 'your neighbourhood'. Most crime victimization research looks for strong neighbourhood effects by making correlations of survey responses with census and police crime report data. Our measure is consistent with the more general interest this project has of circulations in public places populated by strangers. It also sets the bar somewhat lower for fear to be reported. Suburban residents from 'good areas' might be expected to experience no fear in their own perfectly ordinary street, but some fear in the central city or in entertainment zones. The results of this inquiry are shown in Figure 7.1.

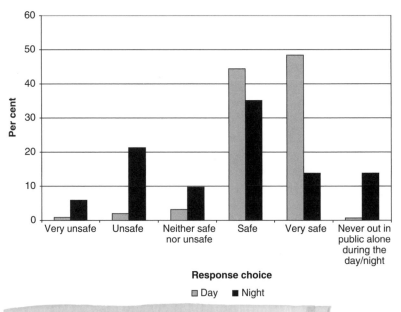

Figure 7.1 Fear of crime in public places during day and night

As we can see, consistent with other survey results levels of fear were generally quite low. Only 27 per cent of the respondents reported feeling 'unsafe' or 'very unsafe' in public places at night. Daytime was substantially unlikely to generate any fear at all – fewer than 3 per cent of respondents felt unsafe, while 93 per cent felt 'safe' or 'very safe'. The latter finding aligns with Liska and Baccaglini's (1990) assertion that fear of crime is largely a night-time phenomenon. The general picture we have, then, somewhat contradicts the relentless emphasis in the crime control industry, in urban criminology and in speculative social theory on fear-struck citizens. People generally feel pretty safe in public places. This empirical finding is broadly consistent with the more general theme in this book that fear should not necessarily be the emotion of greatest interest for incivility research.

Trust

Whereas criminologists are generally interested in 'fear' of strangers, studies of social capital often try to measure 'trust' in strangers. According to Putnam and others influenced by his work, trust is a crucial ingredient for quality of life, health, crime reduction and economic prosperity. Survey data provides some evidentiary support for Putnam's claim that levels of trust are declining. Although surveys exploring social capital often ask about trust in institutions (e.g., banks, churches), or in professions (e.g., journalists, doctors), of most relevance to this study are those asking about levels of trust in 'other people'. Surveys in the United States asking whether or not people in general can be trusted have shown long-term secular declines. Back in the 1960s around 55 per cent of Americans thought that others could be trusted, today only 41 per cent have this belief (Putnam 2000). The political scientist Clive Bean's work indicates that trust in others in Australia has generally hovered around the 45 per cent mark since the 1980s. Although men are slightly more trusting than women, and those in middle-age categories more trusting than the young and old, far larger effects are noted for status markers. Those with tertiary education, subjectively located in the middle class and objectively making more money tend to have more trust than less educated and working-class individuals (Bean 2005). The image one forms is of a relaxed and confident middle class and a cynical and suspicious working class.

In our survey 'trust' or attitudinal social capital was measured using three items derived from the longstanding World Values Survey (www.worldvaluessurvey.org). The first question asked if people try to take advantage or try to be fair. The second, whether people try to be helpful or are just looking out for themselves. The third asked if people can be trusted or whether one cannot be too careful in dealing with them. We see the last item as slightly flawed by virtue of its convoluted and negative wording. Including the two other more indirect items allows a slightly more nuanced picture to be developed of what we will call 'social faith'. We should also reflect on the fact that the measures we are using are abstract and de-contextualized. They do not ask about the respondent's own bank manager, nurse or crossing guard. To us this lack of specificity is an advantage. The items look to tap trust in a very 'generalized other', someone who the social theorist Bernard Barber (1983) has called the 'average person' who is neither a friend nor an acquaintance (see also Paxton 2007). The stranger in public is in a sense just such a person, and the rude stranger a person who violates some tacit set of norms about public behaviour. We also note that these indicators map onto what

George Gerbner and his colleagues (1980, p. 17) call the 'mean and dangerous world syndrome' or what Robert Putnam (2000) might label 'thin trust', and also indeed come close to capturing the 'onto-logical security' deemed by Giddens (1984) to be fundamental to social life (we discussed this at the start of Chapter 6). That is, they tap a general trust that we have in those with whom we share no personal history. In a sense they ask whether we are giving some-one the benefit of the doubt when we have only weak information about them; put another way, whether we have a strong sense of ontological security when it comes to faith in the tissue of fleeting social interaction. We can contrast this kind of sentiment with 'thick trust' – that which is afforded to our confidants, family and friends, the 'regulars' with whom we interact on a frequent basis. According to Putnam (2000), thin trust is consequential, perhaps especially so in a modern society where contact with strangers is an expected facet of daily life. He suggests that 'people who trust their fellow citizens volunteer more often, contribute more to charity, participate more often in politics and community organisations, serve more readily on juries, give blood more frequently, comply more fully with their tax obligations, are more tolerant of minority views, and display many other forms of civic virtue' (pp. 136–7). From this perspective, 'thin distrust' is a fairly nocuous societal condition, and thus worth our time to understand its precipitants.

Thankfully, this 'thin distrust' looks to be uncommon. Looking at Figure 7.2 we can see that for the most part people are trusting. The item specifically on trust itself showed that 41 per cent of respondents considered others 'almost always' or 'usually' trustworthy. This is slightly lower than Clive Bean's estimate, but it is also within the ball park for recent work in Australia using this measure of social capital. The items on helpfulness and fairness attempt to measure trust in an indirect way. These show that prosocial attitudes are quite common. Our respondents were much more likely to view others as generally helpful rather than as self-serving opportunists looking out for them-selves. The differences are even starker when asked whether people are generally fair or looking to take advantage of you (65 per cent versus 25 per cent). All things considered, these three items – like the 'fear' data we have just discussed – suggest that the prevalent image of rampant misanthropic, paranoid and individualistic attitudes is mis-taken. At the level of individual beliefs the picture is not so bleak for

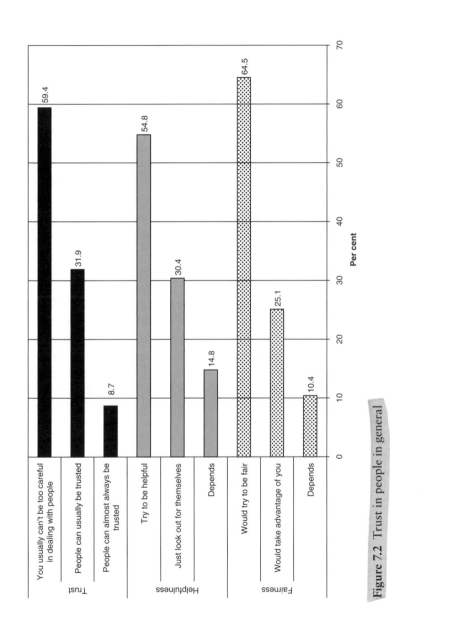

Figure 7.2 Trust in people in general

building social capital as Putnam, Bauman and the other theorists of a contemporary malaise might have it.

Predicting fear and trust

What exactly predicts the social distribution of fear and trust? The existing extensive research on social capital has indicated the role of various types of factors. First, there are the individual-level and demographic variables, such as age, education, religion and gender. Second, there are the comparative influences of macro-level factors influencing the nation, such as democracy, totalitarianism or democratic transition. Third, there has been a raft of work inspired by Putnam looking at social networks and group membership (Paxton 2007). While we acknowledge all these as significant, our major focus in this book is on the impact of individual-level experiences on attitudes, especially rude stranger encounters. This path looking at life events has been largely neglected in academic research, although there has been some research indicating that negative experiences like crime victimization can decrease trust (Salmi, Smolej and Kivivuori 2007). Further, experimental work with small groups would seem to suggest that individuals learn from the past, modifying their ongoing attitudes to take into account positive and negative outcomes from concrete experiences of trusting others (Boyle and Bonacich 1970). The hypothesis that rude stranger encounters might influence levels of trust can be further grounded theoretically in the set of ideas we raised in Chapter 6 concerning ontological security. In effect, disruptions to ontological security generated by any particular incivil individual will translate into a reduced trust in the generalized others on the streets. As the saying goes, once bitten twice shy.

Turning to Tables 7.1 and 7.2 we find a picture of the social factors driving fear in public places, and also the allocation of trust. Here we break down fear and trust with respect to a raft of familiar socio-demographic variables. We also include some further predictors that are of greater theoretical centrality to our project: exposure to the mass media; prior crime victimization; exposure to landscapes of mass culture (shopping malls, public transit, etc.); and a recent rude stranger encounter. These variables are of interest because they allow us to explore whether lifestyles and experiences modify structural and demographically-based predictors of trust and fear.

Let's first consider fear of crime as measured by respondent feelings of safety, or lack thereof, in public places at night.[1] The familiar gender difference in fear of crime is also reflected in the ELIAS Survey. Thirty-eight per cent of females in our survey felt unsafe compared with only 16 per cent of males. However, our findings differ from prior work with respect to fear of crime, age and area of residence. Whereas extant work often finds a positive correlation between age and fear, our data indicate that fear of crime at night *in public places* declines with age and does not significantly differ based on area of residence. Although it is difficult to say for certain why the present results for these variables differ in comparison with prior research, one likely reason is that we specifically ask about fear in public places. The elderly are less likely to spend time in public areas at night, which may moderate their perceptions of fear in such domains.[2] In a similar fashion, those residing outside metro-areas may generally feel safer in their immediate residential environments, but their perceptions of fear in public arenas are no different than metro-area residents. Beyond these demographic factors, we also see that crime victims and those spending more time in landscapes of mass culture exhibit higher levels of fear. The latter two correlations are quite sizeable. Fewer than 23 per cent of respondents who spend little time in public settings such as shopping centres, casinos and restaurants feel unsafe compared with about 31 per cent of those spending quite a lot of time in these areas. One interpretation of this association is that people who spend more time in the presence of strangers knowingly put themselves 'at risk' of victimization, which in turn influences perceptions of safety.

Two additional findings from Table 7.1 are noteworthy. First, we observe a rather intriguing finding with respect to mass media consumption. Prior research suggests that the amount of time viewing television increases fear of crime and perceived risk of victimization (Gerbner *et al.* 1980), presumably because couch potatoes witness crime and violence with some frequency on the evening news or popular programmes. Yet our results suggest a more nuanced interpretation.

[1] We do not present the correlations for fear during the daytime hours because so few respondents felt unsafe.
[2] The notion that older people spend less time in public settings is intuitive and is strongly confirmed by the ELIAS Survey data. For instance, the correlation between age (in the five categories shown in Table 7.1) and our composite measure of time spent in public places is −.40 ($p < .001$). See also Chapter 5.

Table 7.1 *Perceptions of danger at night by respondent characteristics*

	Percentage within each group saying unsafe or very unsafe
Gender	
Male	15.6***
Female	38.3
Age	
18–25	33.2**
26–35	31.5
36–55	28.7
56–65	22.4
Over 65	16.7
Education	
Less than 10 years	29.8
High school, trade, or certificate	29.1
Bachelor's degree	24.1
Area of residence	
Not in city	25.5
Outer metro	28.8
Metro	28.2
Victimization	
No	24.5***
Yes	35.1
Media consumption – entertainment and commercial	
Low	22.9*
Medium	28.0
High	30.1
Media consumption – news and talkback	
Low	30.5*
Medium	28.1
High	22.6
Time spent in landscapes of mass culture	
Low	22.6**
Medium	29.5
High	30.9

Table 7.1 (*cont.*)

	Percentage within each group saying unsafe or very unsafe
Rude stranger encounter	
No	25.8*
Yes	30.7

* $p < .05$
** $p < .01$
*** $p < .001$

Note: The wording of the question for perceptions of safety was as follows: 'How safe or unsafe do you feel when out in public places by yourself after dark?' Also, see the 'note' after Table 7.2 for descriptions of the variable coding. For this table the continuous variables were grouped based on the 33rd and 66th percentiles to have approximately equal numbers in each of the three groups (low, medium, high).

Respondents who view or listen to more entertainment shows, read the tabloids and watch more commercial programmes indeed report higher levels of fear, but the relationship is in the opposite direction for those who spend more time in front of the television or radio consuming more 'serious' news programmes or non-commercial talk-back radio. It appears from the bivariate statistics in Table 7.1 that we cannot simply associate mass media consumption with fear of crime. The type of media one consumes is consequential. Highbrow and less sensational programming tends to attenuate fear, while lowbrow and commercial media appear to exacerbate it. Second, we find a signifi-cant association between perceptions of safety in public places and recent encounters with a rude stranger. Respondents who reported a recent run-in with rudeness were more likely to say that they felt unsafe in public places at night, although the strength of this associ-ation is not particularly large (31 per cent versus 26 per cent). We shed more light on this correlation shortly.

Table 7.2 shows the bivariate associations for the same set of pre-dictor variables and social distrust. The latter is an index based on the three 'social faith' indicators described above. This index ranges from 0 to 3 with higher values indicating more distrust of others.

Table 7.2 *Bivariate correlations for social distrust and predictor variables*

	Social distrust
Male	.02
Age in five categories	– .10***
Education	– .14***
Reside in metro area	– .01
Prior victimization	.19***
Media consumption – entertainment and commercial (logged)	.09***
Media consumption – news and talkback (logged)	– .07**
Time spent in landscapes of mass culture	– .01
Rude stranger encounter	.01

   * *p* < .05
  ** *p* < .01
*** *p* < .001

Notes: Correlations are based on the full sample of 1,621 respondents. Variables in the table had few, if any, missing cases (largest number of missing cases was for time in landscapes of mass culture [N = 1,592]). *Prior victimization* is an index based on responses to five survey items that asked about the frequency of victimization (none, once, twice, three or more than three times). The five indicators referred to the number of times anyone (1) stole something from you, (2) attacked or assaulted you, (3) deliberately damaged your property, (4) threatened to attack you, or (5) subjected you to personal vilification. *Media consumption of entertainment and commercial programming* was the sum of hours each day spent on the following: watching commercial television news (including SKY news); watching crime and investigations drama series; reading tabloids (e.g., *Herald Sun*), and listening to commercial talkback radio. *Media consumption of news and talkback programmes* was calculated as the sum of hours each day spent on the following: watching ABC/SBS television news; watching documentaries about real crimes and investigations; reading broadsheet newspapers (e.g., *The Australian*, *The Age*); and listening to ABC talkback radio. The latter two indices were logged to reduce skew. *Time spent in landscapes of mass culture* is an index based on the frequency with which respondents visit fourteen types of public places. For each indicator respondents reported the amount of time according to a seven-point ordinal scale ranging from 'almost every day' to 'never' (see Chapter 5).

Consonant with other work in this area (Bean 2005), we see that distrust declines as education increases. Age is also inversely correlated with distrust. Older respondents generally have more faith in other people than younger respondents. This most likely indicates a cohort effect: respondents growing up in the 1940s and 1950s are generally more trusting. This finding is consistent with a more general claim in the social capital literature that has received empirical support. The worldview of the 'greatest generation' persists into the golden years, the baby boomers are less trusting (cf. Putnam 2000, ch. 8), and 'Generations X and Y' have been infected with postmodern irony and cynicism (Jennings and Stoker 2004).

We also find significant bivariate correlations between our variables of theoretical interest and social distrust. As we might expect, distrust increases with the crime victimization. This is an intuitive association in that respondents who have been offended against or otherwise violated by others are less apt to put much trust or faith in strangers. Moreover, and similar to the findings for perceptions of safety in public places, we again see that the type of media consumption matters. Distrust in others appears to increase with the amount of commercial and entertainment media consumption. Conversely, those who consume more non-commercial television news and talkback radio are significantly less likely to be distrustful of others. Finally, we find no bivariate correlation between our measure of social distrust and two variables of theoretical interest: time spent in public places and recent encounters with rude strangers. The former is notable, especially when compared with the media effects noted above. Viewing crime dramas and commercial network news may increase perceptions of distrust, but actually spending time in places where strangers come and go with some frequency is less consequential. It appears that the reality of everyday life in public settings does not match the power of the vision of strangers produced in the mass media. Likewise, being on the receiving end of a rude stranger's conduct does not significantly influence one's outlook on others in general.

The latter finding might come as somewhat of a surprise. Are runins with rude strangers really so benign? Or are the circumstances related to the encounter rather than the event itself important? We might also ask whether the bivariate correlations noted in Tables 7.1 and 7.2 hold when we control for other factors. To examine the latter questions we turn to a set of regression models in Table 7.3. Model 1 in this table shows the partial regression coefficients for perceptions of safety in public places at night. We see that some of the bivariate correlations attenuate in the logistic regression model. We can confidently conclude that sex, age and prior victimization drive perceptions of safety. Net of these effects, however, time spent in landscapes of

Table 7.3 *Regression coefficients: predictors of fear of crime and distrust in others*

	1 Fear (logistic)	2 Distrust (ordered logit)	3 Fear (logistic)	4 Distrust (ordered logit)
Male	−1.274***	.093	−1.27***	.107
	(.127)	(.093)	(.127)	(.093)
Age	−.185**	−.182***	−.193**	−.188***
	(.062)	(.047)	(.062)	(.047)
Metro-area residence	.094	.065	.096	.044
	(.131)	(.102)	(.131)	(.102)
Education	−.145	−.307***	−.144	−.307***
	(.082)	(.063)	(.082)	(.063)
Victimization	.103**	.197***	.099**	.193***
	(.034)	(.030)	(.034)	(.030)
'Lowbrow' media	.140*	.195***	.153*	.198***
consumption (logged)	(.066)	(.051)	(.066)	(.051)
'Highbrow' media	−.035	−.114*	−.048	−.113*
consumption (logged)	(.065)	(.050)	(.065)	(.050)
Time spent in landscapes	.010	−.013*	.009	−.012*
of mass culture	(.007)	(.006)	(.007)	(.006)
Rude event	.056	−.030	—	—
	(.128)	(.103)		
Rude event entailing	—	—	.693**	—
bodily decorum			(.253)	
Rude event *not* entailing	—	—	−.073	—
bodily decorum			(.137)	
Intense anger immediately	—	—	—	.381*
after rude event				(.165)
Rude event without	—	—	—	−.200
intense anger				(.116)
Constant	−.315	—	−.268	—
	(.394)		(.396)	
N	1,613	1,621	1,613	1,621

  * $p < .05$
  ** $p < .01$
  *** $p < .001$

Note: Standard errors are in parentheses. See note below Table 7.2 for description of variable coding. For the models shown in this table the continuous variables are used in their true or logged form as indicated (as opposed to the categories used in Table 7.1). Since each variable in the model included a small number of missing cases we imputed mean values for missing data, and hence the valid N for each model is larger than that reported in previous tables. We also note that the test for proportional odds failed to meet this assumption for the ordered logit models (models 2 and 4 above). We, nonetheless, present the ordered logit coefficients for two reasons. First, it is simply a more parsimonious presentation than a multinomial model. Second, and more importantly, a partial proportional odds model (using gologit2 with the autofit command in Stata) showed that the majority of variables, including 'strong anger' in model 4, met the parallel lines assumption (see Long and Freese 2006). In addition, we point out that the results of a multinomial logistic regression model yielded the same substantive results.

mass culture and recent encounters with rude strangers are no longer statistically significant. The same can be said for the amount of time taking in news and talkback programmes, although consumption of commercial and entertainment programming remains positively and significantly correlated with fear. There are, of course, two ways to interpret this coefficient. On the one hand, we might conclude that exposure to crime dramas and coverage of heinous acts of violence on the evening news instil a general sense of fear. That is, we interpret these images as fair and accurate reflections of the real world, one in which strangers are understood as dangerous and eager to take advantage of you. This interpretation is consistent with extant research showing a positive correlation between coverage of violence in the media and fear (see Liska and Baccaglini 1990 on coverage of violence in newspapers). On the other hand, it is entirely tenable that those who already see others as self-serving and distrustful are attracted to this type of programming. It resonates and simply feeds into a pre-existing set of beliefs about people in general. These respective interpretations are symptomatic of the classic chicken-and-egg problem inherent to much social science research. We are unable to definitively adjudicate between these competing interpretations with the ELIAS data, although we note that prior research based on longitudinal data finds empirical support for the first of the two possibilities (Gerbner *et al.* 1980).

The lack of an effect for encounters with rude strangers in model 1 of Table 7.3 is revealing and important. As we have discussed in previous chapters, the literature on incivility gives considerable attention to fear. The prevailing wisdom is that incivil encounters have disproportionate impacts – when people should read them as trivial they instead interpret them through the lens of fear. This does not seem to be going on here. To be fair, we did find in Chapter 4 that a small proportion of people were fearful after run-ins with rudeness, even if these feelings decayed rather quickly. Yet the results in model 1 of Table 7.3 further suggest that fear might not be the overriding emotion with respect to incivility. We assume that one would rather not be on the receiving end of another's rude behaviour, but to the extent that this transpires these events have little impact on victims' general sense of fear in public places.

Model 2 in Table 7.3 shows the ordered logit coefficients for our measure of social distrust. These coefficients are much in line with the bivariate associations noted above and can be described quite summarily. Distrust of others is lower among older respondents and those with more education. Distrust is also lower for those who consume more non-commercial news programming and for respondents spending more time in public places. Yet distrust is higher among crime victims and those who consume more entertainment and commercial media programming. Net of these effects, encounters with rude strangers have no effect on distrust.

Models 1 and 2 of Table 7.3 thus indicate that rude events have no association with fear or trust. But is the *nature* of the rude encounter consequential? In Chapter 6 we saw that some types of behaviour, namely bodily management, affected the subsequent behaviours and attitudes of respondents more than other types of rude behaviour, such as foul language, annoying sounds or bumping shoulders. In addition, we described how the processing of these events is important for determining how they influence subsequent behaviour and attitudes. Anger, for instance, was a common and consequential emotion. In light of these findings we investigate whether the nature of rude events and the emotional reactions of victims have any discernable effects on fear and distrust.

The coefficients in models 3 and 4 of Table 7.3 indeed suggest that the nature of the stranger's conduct and the victim's emotional processing are important. For instance, respondents who described a recent encounter with a rude person that entailed poor bodily management or obscene bodily gestures are more likely to feel unsafe at night ($b = .693$, $p < .01$; see model 3), while respondents encountering other types of rude behaviour report levels of fear that are not significantly

different from non-victims.[3] At first glance this may seem like a pecu-
liar finding. Why, we might ask, is the bodily management of a rude
stranger significant for perceptions of safety in public places? One
possibility is that this type of behaviour can be interpreted as threatening. As described in Chapter 2, we measure bodily management
with reference to five types of behaviour by the rude stranger: spitting; picking or scratching orifices; bodily gestures such as dirty or
lewd looks; waste disposal; or acting in poor taste, for instance by
reading porn in a public setting. By far the most common of these acts
was the dirty or lewd look.[4] Such communicative rudeness differs in
kind from others which indicate simply selfishness or lack of sensitivity to others (e.g., loud mobile phone use, dog mess). The dirty look
can create a sense of uneasiness that might put one on edge – it signals
personally and cuts directly to the question of ontological security.
We are speculating here, but the scenario seems plausible.

Model 4 indicates that the emotion of anger is also significant with
respect to perceptions of social distrust. In this model we compare
respondents who reported no rude event in the last month (omitted
as the reference category in model 4) with two groups – those who
encountered a rude stranger and felt an intense sense of anger, and
respondents who recently had a bout with rudeness but did not report
intense feelings of anger. It is worth noting that a sizeable number
of respondents (N = 145) reported strong or very strong feelings of
anger immediately after the rude event. The coefficients in model 4
indicate that angry victims were significantly more likely to report
higher levels of distrust in others than those who did not experience
a rude event ($b = .381$, $p < .05$). Interestingly, victims of rude events
that did not lead to intense anger were actually less distrustful than
non-victims, although this coefficient is only statistically significant at
a rather modest alpha level ($b = -.200$, $p < .10$, two-tailed test). As in
Chapter 6, then, we see that emotions play a significant role in shaping general attitudes about strangers.

[3] We created three dummy variables for the regression model: rude encounters
entailing bodily management; rude encounters that did not entail bodily
management; and no rude encounter at all. The categories are mutually
exclusive and the latter (no encounter at all) is the reference category in the
regression model.
[4] Specifically, 79 respondents described a rude event that entailed bodily
management. Sixty-seven of these respondents made reference to bodily
gestures such as dirty or lewd looks.

Trust, fear and the media

In some of the data analysis earlier in this chapter we touched on the role of the media, noting that there appeared to be robust effects to media consumption. We put these aside so that we could complete our investigation of the impact of the rude stranger encounter on attitudes. We can now return to the oft-debated concerns about the role of the media in forming wider social attitudes and beliefs about the 'Other'. Painting with a broad brush, we might say that the majority opinion in academic fields has been to take a fairly dim view of the media as a social institution. The argument has been overwhelmingly that they erode the social, whether by: actively spreading fear and loathing; reinforcing conventional social roles and stereotypes; dragging people away from the plazas, piazzas and town meetings so that they morph into isolated consumerist couch potatoes; distracting with bubblegum entertainment; or by trivializing and dumbing down complex social and political issues. This meta-myth of a pernicious and powerful media can be traced back to the mass society hypotheses of the mid-twentieth century with their vision of impressionable publics, and forwards from there through models of agenda setting. More recently research in the cultural studies field has continued this trend, decoding programmes using semiotic methods in order to uncover narrative and visual techniques that subvert possibilities for critical rationality or collective solidarity.

This general image of a poisonous media finds a specification in the research fields central to this chapter. For Robert Putnam (1995, 2000), most famously, television is one of the chief villains in his narrative of declining civility and waning social capital. Watching television, he says, takes people out of the public sphere. Whereas citizens used to spend their leisure time in voluntary associations, clubs and hobby groups, now they spend it in their homes. The 'real' social ties that build trust are replaced, in his view, by synthetic and familial ones or simply dropped altogether. The influential psychological research of George Gerbner and his associates on 'cultivation theory' shares this negative perspective. Working in the 1970s and 1980s, his team repeatedly found strong correlations between viewing television and having a more general vision of the world as dangerous and hostile (Gerbner *et al.* 1980). If Gerbner was a pioneer, in the literature of criminology there has been ongoing dismay at the content of crime and policing programming. Analysts have repeatedly argued, for example, that the crime news is driven by sensationalism. They note that crime dramas focus on highly unlikely forms of random predation perpetrated by evil characters of above-average intelligence, and that prudence and aversive behaviour are represented as a sensible way to respond to an unpredictable world. For example, a study of coverage of the 2002 Washington Sniper by Stephen Muzzatti and Richard Featherstone (2007) indicated the prevalence of themes of fear, uncertainty and vulnerability (the sniper was randomly targeting ordinary people). The voices of those saying they were not too worried or would not change their daily habits were marginalized or dismissed in reporting. The point that authors like Muzzatti and Featherstone make is not only that such representations are misleading because the media ignore the ugly and pathetic aspects of quotidian offending (e.g., domestic violence) or crime's structural roots (e.g., the ties of drug culture to poverty), but also that they spread a diffuse anxiety and distrust. When the media repeatedly offer up the unrealistic and stereotyped image of streets filled with serial killers, rapists, hoodlums and snipers waiting for innocent, middle-class victims, then even those in the leafy suburbs will start to feel uneasy. Aside from reducing quality of life and the depth of civic participation, this media-driven fear has in turn been linked to collective social and political outcomes. We might point to the groundswells of penal populism that can support mass incarceration or harsh and humiliating punishments (Pratt 2008) as possible outcomes of the deep influence of the media on crime control policy.

If intuitively persuasive, the vision of a powerful crime media with a strong influence on opinion and emotion can be challenged on theoretical grounds. As far back as the 1950s authors like Elihu Katz and Paul Lazarsfeld (1955) noted that interpersonal networks modified the reception of messages. In effect 'opinion leaders' shaped the interpretations of their peers as they listened to political broadcasts. More recently the field of 'audience ethnography' has highlighted the existence of an 'active audience' with possibilities for multiple, pleasurable, paradoxical and ironic readings of print and visual media. Put another way, those who watch CSI or Dirty Harry do not necessarily fear abduction by a serial killer or endorse authoritarian policing. Sometimes a film is just a film – it might even be fun. We might also note a third reason for doubt about the dominant perspective. This comes from the minority body of work suggesting that the mass media *build* sociability. As Jeffrey Alexander and Ronald N. Jacobs (1998) suggest, the mass media *are* the public sphere – or at least a substantial part of it. It is not easy to imagine a functional substitute for the mass media when it comes to society-building cultural activity in the condition of modernity. By offering a forum for debate on vital concerns and connecting events to shared sacred symbols, by consecrating and relaying integrative civic rituals like coronations or elections, by implicitly suggesting that society is more than just a collection of atomized individuals the mass media might be thought of as fundamental to, rather than antithetical towards, trust and solidarity.

Sustaining this position empirically we might cite the work of Benedict Anderson (1991) looking to print media as pivotal to the emergence of national 'imagined communities' in the nineteenth century, and that of Daniel Dayan and Elihu Katz (1992) on 'media events' as among the core integrative rituals of modernity. During the moon landings, Olympic Games or state funerals people come together and share in the wider experience of belonging to a collectivity. The recent trend for big screen presentations of sporting events, such as the soccer World Cup, to mass audiences in public parks would seem to confirm the validity of this perspective. Such gatherings of perfect strangers are largely peaceful and solidaristic. In the case of Germany, for example, the open-air festive watching seemed to help heal division between the former East and West by allowing for shared participation in a more general festive event (Spiegel Online 2006).

So diverse theoretical positions can be built: but what do we really know about media effects upon trust in, and fear of, strangers in public? Concrete investigations dedicated to this question – whether qualitative or quantitative – are surprisingly hard to find. As with all media research, we generally discover that the higher the quality of the project and the more control variables that are introduced, the weaker and more complicated or compromised the impact of media consumption seems to be. What looked like a sure-fire bet turns out to be something of a damp squib, as results become scattered and inconclusive. For example, some scholars have experienced curious difficulties replicating George Gerbner's powerful results, and have suggested that contexts such as the real neighbourhood where one lives might be far more salient as predictors of fear of crime than what one sees on television (Wober 1979). Yet a Finnish team did recently find that watching reality crime programmes reduced trust (Salmi, Smolej and Kivivuori 2007). Further, in a controlled regression analysis with a host of variables Kenneth Dowler (2003) found a positive effect to fear arising from watching crime drama, albeit an effect much weaker than those relating to familiar demographic variables. Another study in Orange County discovered that newspaper reading reduced fear of crime among whites, but had no effect on Latinos. Watching television, by contrast, increased fear in Latinos but had no impact on whites (Lane and Meeker 2003). Other work suggests an even more nuanced association between the media and crime. Heath (1984), for instance, showed that newspaper coverage of crime did not necessarily translate into higher levels of fear. Crime stories increased fear only when the content largely referenced local crime stories that entailed apparently random acts and sensational offences. Liska and Baccaglini (1990) also find different effects for coverage of local as opposed to non-local criminal offences.

When it comes to 'trust' or social capital there are similarly mixed messages documenting relatively feeble impacts. A study of political participation in the United Kingdom based upon a national survey suggested that listening to the radio and actively engaging with the news predicted higher levels of voting and taking political action. Fewer political actions were taken by those who watched television. Looking at these findings Sonia Livingstone and Tim Markham (2008) suggest that the news operates as a means of engaging public interest, or put another way to increase social capital. Another quantitative effort found that higher levels of interpersonal trust were associated with listening to political talk radio and reading newspapers (Lee, Cappella and Southwell 2003). Yet, by contrast, Patricia Moy and Dietram Scheufele (2000) report using data from the 1996 American National Election Study that watching television news reduced rather than increased trust.

If you found the previous two paragraphs annoying, distracting and unfocused, this is not accidental. We wrote them as a textual analogue to the state of the field. The story from the data is all over the place, with bits and pieces of finding and non-finding heading off in various directions. The slim published record and the contradictory results, we feel, might very well indicate weak media impacts. They could also be driven by a lack of appropriate specificity in measures. Broadly cast survey items on media use might capture contradictory trends, with any effects thus bleached out in the wash. Asking 'How much crime television do you watch?' might lump together the viewer of PBS who looks at programmes hosted by Bill Moyers on issues such as racial sentencing disparities, and those who dial in to America's Most Wanted. The more liberal views of one will be cancelled out by the populist views of the other. Pippa Norris (1996) of Harvard University makes this argument for the case of television and political involvement. Her research indeed shows that at a superficial level one can accurately say that 'tuning in' often means tuning out of political participation. Yet the content of television viewing is critical. For instance, those who spend more time watching current affairs programmes remained heavily engaged in voting, community engagement and other measures of social capital.

More directly pertinent to our argument, an investigation into Australian national identity conducted by two of the authors of this book has already suggested that scholars need to break down the familiar technology and exposure variables to take account of the precise genre or cultural code within which information is packaged. We concluded there that consumers of 'highbrow' media genres (such as broadsheets and public television) were more likely than consumers of 'lowbrow' media genres (tabloids, commercial television, talkback) to have an open and inclusive sense of Australian citizenship and identity (Phillips and Smith 2006b). These results would have been missed had we just asked about 'reading newspapers' or 'watching television'. Importantly, these effects were of similar magnitude to the usual demographic suspects that were introduced as statistical controls. Further, given that beliefs about who should be 'within' or kept 'outside' the nation run close to those on fear and trust of strangers, we see this lesson as instructive for the task of this chapter. Taken together this research suggests that trust and fear might be generated by involvement with very particular product types: the scary television drama, populist commercial talkback radio and so forth.

The ELIAS Survey was not dedicated to exploring media consumption. It does, however, contain a reasonably detailed inventory of media formats, one that we believe is perhaps stronger than any used to date to explore media impacts on fear and trust. The survey inquired about the number of hours respondents spent on four general types of media consumption: watching television news; watching entertainment programmes about crime; reading newspapers; and listening to talkback radio. Within each of these four categories we further specified highbrow and lowbrow types of media usage for a total of eight types of media consumption. The data thus permit us to compare respondents who spend more hours watching Australian Broadcasting Corporation (ABC – broadly equivalent to BBC or PBS) and Special Broadcasting Service (SBS – basically an upscale multi-cultural free-to-air channel) television news (highbrow) with those watching more commercial television news (lowbrow). Similar comparisons can be made for time spent watching crime documentaries versus crime dramas; reading broadsheet newspapers versus tabloids; listening to ABC versus commercial talkback radio.

Consistent with our earlier analysis of fear and distrust, we again employ a set of logistic regression models to assess the unique effects of each type of media usage, controlling for gender, age, area of residence, education and criminal victimization (the control variables are not shown in the tables). Table 7.4 reports the coefficients for our analysis of fear of crime. The table includes four models, each comparing genres within a given media format. For instance, model 1 shows that the number of hours spent viewing commercial television news, which we treat as an indicator of lowbrow news consumption, is positively associated with fear of crime. However, time spent on highbrow news consumption (e.g., ABC/SBS news) is not significantly associated with fear. In the latter case the coefficient is actually negative, albeit not statistically significant. Model 2 reports the results for television entertainment programmes. Here we see a rather strong correlation between the amount of time dedicated to television documentaries about real criminal events and fear of crime ($b = .396, p < .001$). In addition, it initially seems evident from model 2 that time spent watching crime dramas is unrelated to fear of crime, although we are reluctant to make this conclusion. Watching crime dramas is actually positively and significantly associated with fear when the variable measuring time spent viewing crime documentaries is omitted from the model. The two variables are fairly highly correlated ($r = .40$), which indicates that those interested in crime stories gravitate towards 'true crime' documentaries as well as crime and investigation drama series. We might more accurately conclude that the amount of time spent consuming crime stories on television tends to increase one's sense of fear in public places. Turning to print and

Table 7.4 *Logistic regression coefficients: fear of crime at night on media consumption*

	Model 1	Model 2	Model 3	Model 4
Watching ABC/SBS television news	– .047 (.071)			
Watching commercial television news (including SKY news)	.243*** (.069)			
Watching documentaries about real crimes and investigations		.396** (.099)		
Watching crime and investigations drama series		.065 (.094)		
Reading broadsheet newspapers (*The Australian, The Age*)			– .012 (.078)	
Reading tabloids (*Herald Sun*)			.068 (.083)	
Listening to ABC talkback radio				– .116 (.067)
Listening to commercial talkback radio				.032 (.057)

N = 1,613
* *p* < .05
** *p* < .01
*** *p* < .001

Note: Standard errors are in parentheses. To reduce skew in the variables, we added a constant of 1 to each media indicator and then calculated the natural log. Thus, the media consumption variables represent logged hours spent on each type. All models control for gender, age, metro-area residence, education and criminal victimization (measurement of control variables was discussed earlier). These coefficients are not shown in the table because they do not change appreciably across models and they are entirely consistent with the coefficients shown in Table 7.3 above. As with the models in Table 7.3, we used mean substitution for missing cases in the regression models, although models without mean substitution yielded the same substantive results.

radio mediums (models 4 and 5), we find no significant association between either highbrow or lowbrow formats and fear of crime.

In the light of this discussion what do we make of the results in Table 7.4? Two notable findings stand out. First, three of the four indicators of television viewing were significantly and positively correlated with fear, while the measures of print and radio consumption were insignificant. To the extent that fear of crime in public places is driven by the media, it seems that television is particularly capable of raising questions about personal safety. One plausible explanation is that television is replete with dramatic images that can feed into emotions of fear. News broadcasts might include on-screen blood and ambulances, police putting up crime scene tape, offender mug shots and news anchors might emphasize that the perpetrator is 'still out there'. One does not get the same immediate and iconic effect from reading cooler newspaper articles which might, at most, include a still photo along with a descriptive account of a crime. To the extent that visual depictions of crimes and criminal events are influential, radio might be equally unlikely to rouse personal anxiety. A second point that we can glean from Table 7.4 is that genre does not matter *if* the television topic of the programme is criminality. That is, tuning into a real life crime documentary or a fictitious episode of Criminal Minds can both increase perceptions of fear in public. By contrast, only more sensational types of news coverage are associated with fear. Taken together, we might say that television *can* increase perceptions of fear, but this is likely only if the coverage is sensational or if programming is focused on crime itself.

Turning to social distrust of strangers, a related set of ordered logit models is presented in Table 7.5. One pattern worth noting at the outset is that the genre effects are more pronounced for distrust than for fear. For instance, we see that time spent watching commercial news is strongly and positively associated with social distrust, yet the effect is negative (but not significant) for our indicator of highbrow news consumption (model 1). The coefficients in model 2 are exceptional in that the true crime stories are associated with distrust, while crime dramas are not. Considered in tandem with the analysis of fear above, it appears that true crime documentaries leave an impression. They are not only associated with more fear among regular viewers, but they may also leave a cynical aftertaste. This may have to do with the reality of the programme. It's a *real* story about a *real* victim

Table 7.5 Ordered logit coefficients: distrust on media consumption

	Model 1	Model 2	Model 3	Model 4
Watching ABC/SBS television news	−.018 (.055)			
Watching commercial television news (including SKY news)	.234*** (.053)			
Watching documentaries about real crimes and investigations		.393*** (.079)		
Watching crime and investigations drama series		−.094 (.074)		
Reading broadsheet newspapers (*The Australian*, *The Age*)			−.251*** (.060)	
Reading tabloids (*Herald Sun*)			.003 (.064)	
Listening to ABC talkback radio				−.179*** (.049)
Listening to commercial talkback radio				.101* (.044)

N = 1,621
* $p < .05$
** $p < .01$
*** $p < .001$

Note: Standard errors are in parentheses. To reduce skew in the variables, we added a constant of 1 to each media indicator and then calculated the natural log. Thus, the media consumption variables represent logged hours spent on each type. All models control for gender, age, metro-area residence, education and criminal victimization (measurement of control variables was discussed earlier). These coefficients are not shown in the table because they do not change appreciably across models and they are entirely consistent with the coefficients shown in Table 7.3 above. As with the models in Table 7.3, we used mean substitution for missing cases in the regression models, although models without mean substitution yielded the same substantive results.

of a *real* offender. This dimension of crime documentaries may render them particularly influential with respect to viewers' beliefs and inclinations about strangers in public. But again, model 2 is exceptional, and models 3 and 4 are more in line with our prediction that lowbrow media propel distrust, while highbrow media attenuate it. For instance, time spent reading broadsheet newspapers is negatively associated with distrust. In contrast, reading the tabloids has no apparent association with distrust (model 3). The results for radio are also quite compelling. The amount of time listening to highbrow talkback radio (ABC talkback) is rather strongly and negatively associated with distrust ($-.179$, $p < .001$; see model 4). However, we find just the opposite for lowbrow talkback radio. More time consuming commercial talkback radio is associated with stronger feelings of distrust in others ($.101$, $p < .05$). To give a better idea of the magnitude of these effects we graph the expected probabilities of falling into the highest category of mistrust, i.e., choosing the 'distrustful' category for all three indicators described above. Figure 7.3 indicates about a 4 per cent swing in attitudes as one moves from no consumption to high consumption (about 1 standard deviation above the mean) of a given genre-medium.

We close by highlighting three points with respect to media consumption, trust and fear. First, the general picture that emerges from our analysis is that electronic media, television in particular, are more strongly associated with generating fear and trust in unknown others than print media. In this respect our results for fear and social distrust are congruent with earlier work by the first two authors of this book on identity and national attachment (Phillips and Smith 2006b). Television appears particularly salient for fear of crime, presumably because it allows for the presentation of graphic images (unlike radio) and spoken emphasis on particular words or urgent phrases such as 'dangerous' or 'still on the loose' (unlike newsprint). To some extent, then, the medium is indeed the message. However, and as a second point of emphasis, genre proves to be an even more salient concept than the type of medium for understanding the association between media and social attitudes about strangers in public places. It seems that television watching may not be as harmful as Putnam and others have suggested. Rather, the nocuous side effects of 'tuning in too often' are contingent on the nature of the programming. We find no evidence that highbrow television programming increases distrust or

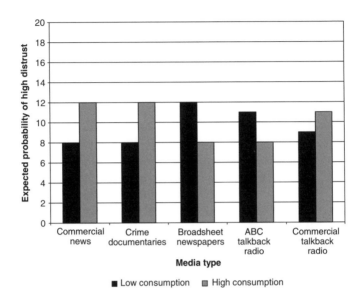

■ Low consumption   ▥ High consumption

Note: The figure shows the expected probabilities of falling into the highest category of social distrust. Expected probabilities are generated based on models 1–4 in Table 7.5. All control variables are held at their mean values when generating expected values. A value of zero indicated 'low consumption', as this value was generally around one standard deviation below the mean. 'High consumption' refers to values equalling one standard deviation above the mean. Expected probabilities were estimated using the 'clarify' procedure in Stata (King, Tomz, and Wittenberg 2000). Genre-medium combinations that were not statistically significant in Table 7.5 are not shown in the figure.

Figure 7.3 Expected probability of high distrust by type of media consumption

fear, although time spent viewing programmes about crime on commercial television may leave viewers more fearful or cynical. We find similar effects for newspaper reading and talkback radio in our analysis of social distrust. Finally, we again acknowledge that our data do not enable us to make absolute claims about causality. Respondents who prefer ABC talkback radio likely differ in meaningful ways from those who listen to commercial radio with its assortment of flamboyant, populist personalities. One could argue that distrustful people seek out sensational coverage because it resonates with their pre-existing views and personality. Or, perhaps another attribute of respondents' personalities – for instance, an ingrained, old-school, conservative mentality – explains both media consumption patterns and trust. If this is the case, our causal arrows might point in different directions. We have tried to minimize this possibility by controlling for potential confounding variables – education, experience with incivility and crime victimization – and our findings did not wash away when accounting for these and other factors. We can thus say with confidence, although not complete certainty, that exposure to particular genre-medium combinations is conducive to, or has an elective affinity with, the distribution of fear and trust in strangers.

The main findings of this chapter are:

- The image of catastrophically falling trust and steeply rising fear made by many criminologists and social commentators is over-drawn. Our respondents had reasonably high levels of 'thin trust' in the stranger, generally low levels of 'fear' in public places.
- Feelings of safety in public places were higher for older people and for men.
- The older and better educated also had more thin trust.
- Crime victimization decreased trust and increased fear.
- Rude stranger victimizations had surprisingly little impact on trust and fear. Those involving body display and generating anger seemed to be the most potent.
- The mass media would appear to play a significant role in shaping or reproducing worldviews. In particular, we note that watching crime documentaries and commercial news were associated with reduced trust in the stranger.

Week #5 Readings (end)

8 | *How to confront incivility*

Before rushing into this rather lengthy chapter we should first note that a question has been begged by our title: should we confront everyday incivility? Common sense says yes. Opinion polls show that people see rudeness as a problem worthy of remedy (Public Agenda 2002). Moreover our own book has uncovered a realm of reasonably frequent events that usually produce unwanted emotions. These generally require coping, may generate fear and aversive behaviour, and can lead to less sociable attitudes. Here, then, we have a social problem. Yet a little reflection might be in order before we move forward to propose some fixes. We might start with the sociologist Emile Durkheim's (2006 [1897]) observation, one famous among sociologists, that norm violation was often a precursor to positive social change or creative renewal. He cites the example of Socrates, a man subject to vilification, yet whose thinking was more progressive and acute than that of the Athenian state which condemned him. Perhaps a society without such 'antisocial' behaviour would be stagnant. Certainly, it might be rather unexciting and without grit or edge. The overwhelming comment one hears from people who have been to Singapore – even more so those who have lived there – is that it is clean, safe and boring (e.g., Singapore Expats 2007). Nobody says this about Manhattan. There is a price to be paid, it would seem, for banning chewing gum or Monty Python's irreverent and provocative *Life of Brian*.

We would also do well to remember that 'rude' and 'incivil' are labels that have been applied throughout history to discredit the marginal and disempowered. At one time African-Americans who tried to behave with dignity or to achieve socially were described as 'uppity'. The suffragettes were understood too as rude women who did not understand the obligations of polite society. Gandhi was a nuisance to the British. So efforts to eliminate what is considered to be 'rude' behaviour might be forms of political control. Certainly, incivility has had a long history in the annals of organized civil disobedience. Blocking buildings and doors, ridiculing and mocking leaders, shouting them down, throwing flour or eggs – these are all techniques of broadly legitimate political protest which can easily be thought of as rude. Yet looked at in a positive light one might say they form an attractive alternative to terrorism. There is also the question of style policing. As Mark Caldwell (1999) argues, rules of decorum have historically functioned as status markers, working to exclude and degrade outsiders. There is a need to be careful not to rush in to persecute pointless breaches of etiquette, rather than failures of public manners or mutual respect. If we get the judgement wrong, then efforts towards improved regulation and control might simply assist the reproduction of social hierarchy. Yet drawing a line between harmless bad taste and antisocial rudeness might prove empirically difficult. As Ian Woodward and Mike Emmison (2001) showed in an interview study of middle-class Australians, these are conjoined in everyday reason and talk. For example, wearing socially appropriate clothing is understood as an indicator of good taste and also of respect for public norms. The questions inevitably emerge: whose rules? Whose boundaries?

Our focus in this book has been on the non-political, non-progressive aspects of rudeness, but these cautionary notes suggest it is worth keeping an eye open for policy over-reach. They indicate the work that might need to be done to separate out legitimate forms of political protest and self-expression from other forms of 'rude' behaviour. Still, some modes of rudeness clearly deserve to be eliminated. Would anyone care to defend queue jumping, or sexual grabbing and groping? Further, we believe that all social parties – including perpetrators – would like to eliminate unintended, non-communicative, apolitical actions such as bumps and knocks. The desire for such a reduction in rudeness can be seen as a component of the wider, more positive quest for a civic or civil culture. This has been a preoccupation for thousands of years. Scholars such as Aristotle, de Tocqueville, Hegel, Locke and Adam Smith made this a central concern of their thinking. Civility has been variously understood as the product of virtue in the self, as the outcome of voluntary associational life in churches, clubs and schools, as a sphere of disinterested discourse and moral evaluation sustained by a set of communicative institutions. Another approach, one advanced most analytically by Erving

Goffman and Richard Sennett, but also present in books of etiquette for ladies and gentlemen from other centuries, is to see civility very concretely as the cumulative outcome of positively valued interpersonal encounters with unknown others in public settings. Closer to a cosmopolitan ethic, our focus in this context might be on respect, tolerance and dignity for the 'Other'; on the micro-rituals of deference and demeanour; and on subjective feelings of safety and wellbeing in public spaces. We might perhaps define this kind of civil environment using the archaic term of the 'polite society'. Found, for example, in the novels of Jane Austen it is characterized by individuals who are measured and who, for the most part, take great pains not to offend others as they meet them at formal dances or sit beside them during interminable coach journeys. We have moved a long way since the early nineteenth century. Yet the nostalgia for Austen films and books attests to the continuing appeal of such a way of living. We might think of it as the unrealizable fantasy against which experience comes to be judged.

In a sense this book has explored when and how this dimension of embodied and spatially proximate interpersonal civility is found wanting, but by today's standards. Put another way, it tells us what happens when things go wrong as people encounter each other. We have diagnosed and sketched the problem. We have uncovered a realm of reasonably common, low-level incivility. How might our findings allow us to assess the merits of various potential rudeness reduction strategies? Here in our last chapter we try to suggest and evaluate some candidate remedies and cures. We argue that there are five available strategies: self-help; legislation; diversion; education; and design.

- *Self-help* is all about individuals making their own choices in an ongoing and flexible way. Generally speaking this is a matter of changing routines, habits and interpersonal behaviours.
- *Legislation* works alongside enforcement as a solution. It tries to make possible the intervention of the formal criminal justice system. The basic principle is to expand the downward reach of statute into areas traditionally governed by customs, norms and informal social control.
- *Diversion* seeks to distract, re-route or otherwise take out of circulation potentially incivil people. This strategy can relate to

time–space dynamics, but also it can simply involve changing the mood or focus of attention in a setting.

- *Education* involves efforts at sharing knowledge about social norms for behaviour in public. This can have both cognitive and moral dimensions. We can focus on making people aware of how they should behave, or make them more ashamed of how they do behave.
- *Design* strategies focus on transforming the built environment such that stress levels are reduced, human movements facilitated and more civic spaces emerge. This strategy is similar to diversion, but requires more permanent infrastructural innovations.

Self-help

One option for dealing with the rude stranger is self-help. A do-it-yourself strategy has several advantages. It does not require committees or budgets. It is consistent with libertarian sensibilities. Each can make their own choices, these to suit their own moral preferences and personalities. Flexible, practical decisions can result. One can live with rudeness, avoid it or confront it. For some, the first of these options is an ongoing reality. Living with a measure of rudeness is an acceptable trade-off for some other pleasure or amenity. Consider the case of driving a Hummer. These are the huge, military-style vehicles that are considered by many to be environmentally damaging, dangerous and aggressive. Hummer drivers say they are continually subject to abuse from strangers (Jain 2007). This includes:

- people giving the finger;
- rude notes in the car park with comments like 'Stick your Hummer ...;
- people shouting and screaming at stoplights;
- angry and aggressive driving;
- dirty looks and rolling eyes at the petrol pump;
- having to justify to others why they drive a Hummer.

The Hummer drivers are not making this up. The website FUH2.com is a forum for anti-Hummer activism and vitriol. A visit will show hundreds of photos of Hummer haters proudly giving the finger or 'flipping off' the Hummer. To stop this sort of abuse Hummer owners can simply trade in their cars, perhaps for a less conspicuous SUV.

This would be the path of avoidance. Most, however, choose to live with the abuse, often citing freedom of expression, their own individualism, resistance to bullying by liberals, or their practical need for the Hummer as reasons for not changing. This is a choice to live with the ongoing risk of exposure to rudeness.

Driving a Hummer is an extreme and emotive example. But the same logic holds elsewhere. Often in our lives we can engage in a sort of calculus. Should we change something about our routine behaviour or is it better to put up with some quantum of antisocial experience? For example, should one adjust one's daily walk to work so as to avoid a location plagued by rude and abusive people? We see two problems emerging here. One is that people are being forced to make choices that are not of their choosing. The rude people, in effect, are calling the shots not just by setting the quantum of displeasure in the decision-making matrix, but also by leading us to make a choice in the first place that we would rather not make. We should decide whether or not to drive a Hummer based upon need, upon informed decisions about the environment and so forth, not on how much abuse we will receive. We should be able to decide whether or not to walk through the park based on the weather or our wish for exercise, not the presence or absence of loitering drunks at the rotunda. To clarify this normative point it is helpful to look at an extreme example. In the American Deep South during the days of segregation African-Americans developed routines and ways of interacting that minimized the chances of experiencing racist abuse or more subtle forms of discrimination and rude behaviour. Not using the public drinking fountain, crossing the street to avoid whites of the opposite sex, not trying on clothes in stores: through such self-censored actions individuals could minimize their chances of having negative social experiences. African-Americans would 'learn what the taboos are and how to avoid them' (Hindman 1953, p. 123). Is it right or fair that people should have to live thus, that the victim should have the potentially rude stranger control their choices and movements?

The second problem with the 'live with it' versus 'avoid it' logic is that it fits with environments where there are stable, predictable and frequent encounters with rudeness, such as driving a Hummer (or, indeed, being black in the Jim Crow Deep South). Yet what we discovered in this project was that for the most part rudeness was predictable only *in the aggregate*. We can be fairly certain there will be a horrific shooting spree in a high school or college somewhere in the United States in any given year. We cannot predict just where or when this will take place. So we send our kids to school or show up in class ourselves to teach. Likewise we can predict from the findings of this book concerning transportation nodes and dromology (Chapters 2, 3) that Grand Central Station in Manhattan will generate or host a large number of rude encounters every day. Yet the odds that any one of these incidents will happen to any one person who passes through are quite small. No Manhattan commuters will change their routine. Our respondents experienced a rude encounter every three or four months. This episode was often severe enough to require some coping activity. Yet such infrequent, unpredictable events as experienced by the individual do not lend themselves well to aversion. We can avoid the drunks who are always in the park, but we cannot predict just when the respectable-looking middle-aged man in a suit, our ideal type of the rude stranger, will crash into us on the railway platform. Like asteroid collisions with planet earth, the probabilities on any given day are quite small, the costs to precautionary measures quite large: most of the time we are going to opt to 'live with it'. The existence of a choice 'to avoid' is purely nominal.

Of course, when the asteroidal rude event eventually takes place there is also the self-help option of doing something to reduce it in future, perhaps with the assistance of the market. The small business CrazyHappy (2008) offers eight 'Rude Stranger Cards' for sale on the Internet, each intended to let offenders know of their offence. Purchasers are to carry these around in their purses or wallets. Then 'instead of causing a huge scene, throwing your drink or taking a hissy fit in the returns department of Sears' they can simply hand over the card. Sounds like a good idea? In fact, the Rude Stranger Cards are confrontational and likely to erode rather than to build civil relations in public. Consider being handed the following: 'Nice parking job buddy. Next time maybe try pulling your head out of your ass before pulling in.' How would you feel: angry, or perhaps frightened? Aggressive self-help is also recommended by the *Village Voice* (2008), New York's would-be-hip newspaper and website, as it gives its Best Reason to Be Rude to a Stranger:

You've all been there: rushing toward the subway stairs, clutching your *Times* or *Savage Detective* on your hurried way to work, part of the ever-flowing crowd that is New York City. Ever-flowing, that is, until you reach that person – **the man or woman, cellphone to ear** – who has decided it's perfectly acceptable to stop on the subway stairs in order to finish their call, impeding all the rest of us, damming up the crowd like one of those Chinese quake lakes. Citizens: Do not accept this selfishness! Berate these oblivious yappers! Use pointed, intemperate language – sarcasm, if necessary – to assail their breach of the commuters' social contract. For, indeed, upbraiding subway-stair blockers is the best reason to be rude to a stranger.

We might suggest that if this is the response, then the net total of rudeness in our society is simply increased. We have a recipe for dispute escalation. Of course, more conciliatory ways of letting the rude stranger know what they have done are possible. Or one might just say 'excuse me' with irony. As we saw in Chapter 4, many times our victims signalled their disapproval through the self-help strategy of grunts, sighs and other communicative noises. Still, although appealing in the abstract and as a form of therapeutic mental fantasy, more confrontational, ironic or assertive self-help solutions favour the quick thinking, the socially confident, the risk taker and the physically large. They are scattered and individual responses. For them to be effective as a cure they also assume a rude stranger who is somewhat sensitive to the norms of public life and shamed by critique. This is a tall order – even when they were not read as deliberately rude, our respondents often rated the rude strangers they encountered as self-centred or self-absorbed 'bubble people'. Further, we must be mindful that accosting rude strangers is increasingly risky when they are in a group. Conflicts more often escalate to violence when groups are involved (Phillips and Cooney 2005). Hence, Lynne Truss (2005, p. 104) admits to a constraint on her own ardent litter bug vigilantism 'If the person is bigger than me, or is (a very important consideration) accompanied by someone bigger than me, I walk away.'

Cures follow from theories of disease. Incivil behaviour, as we have argued, arises not from personalities, but rather from the organization of society as it distributes bodies through time and space. A collective problem requires a collective solution. The idea of looking for public and shared solutions to the fundamental issue of civility is not new. Civic education in schools, for example, has been proposed as a way to build virtue. Social capital, some have argued, can be constructed. We might support community associations with tax breaks, organizational resources or facilities. Where free and fair discourse is not possible, then steps to support independent media or to bring in excluded voices have been advocated. Here we avoid such indirect and long-term suggestions which focus on amplifying social capital and boosting civil society. We identify in their place some collective solutions that go more directly to the matter of regulating and shaping interpersonal conduct.

Legislation

As we argued in Chapter 1, when reading newspapers, political speeches and the criminology journals the impression one gets is of rude strangers as a particular type of social problem. There are groups of drunken youths who come out of the pub on a Friday night and shout obscenities; the homeless sitting around the town square waving their bottles at the Volvo-driving classes; the mentally-ill losers staggering around our high streets screaming that God is dead (or alive); the truculent skateboarder and so forth. These are the cast of characters, the stereotyped outsiders who invade public spaces and intimidate others. The silent majority in its turn is indignant and fearful and calls on authority to 'do something'. New legal regulation, especially at the local level, is one quick and sometimes popular fix to this 'do something' cry. The more urgent enforcement of existing laws, say against public drinking or noise, is another possibility. The strategy seems vaguely plausible when there is a defined group of 'troublemakers' engaged in a high visibility incivil action in a predictable location: skateboarding in the mall, drinking on the library steps and so forth. In such situations resources can be concentrated and the force of the law brought to bear. Usually, of course, displacement is the result. The so-called 'troublemakers' move elsewhere, only to return when police attention is removed.

The portrait we have given in this book is of fleeting and annoying encounters among people of all ages and social backgrounds. These are often invisible to onlookers and they take place everywhere. What of the kinds of commonplace incivility that we have uncovered: the invasion of personal space in front of a supermarket freezer; queue jumping; sidewalk collisions and so forth? In such situations there are rarely impartial witnesses, on-looking police officers ready to arrest, or rude strangers kind enough to stick around until they are ticketed. More important still, the exact interpretation of 'what happened' and whether or not something was really rude or incivil is relentlessly contestable. If there is a new law, how are we to determine whether this law really was broken? Even offences where there is some consensus on who is responsible can be hard to prosecute if the offender is mobile. Consider the case of 'Boom cars'. These are generally considered highly incivil. Kitted out with very expensive stereo systems, special speakers and amplifiers they impose what is interpreted as noise pollution on the wider community. Their users like to play rhythmic music very loud, sometimes to the point where it will shake and rattle objects in adjacent houses. If the offender is parked in a car park, some possibility exists for the imposition of ordinances. The police officer might be able to creep around with a decibel meter or apply some common sense, but legally valid metric for 'noise disturbance'. When the boom car is mobile there is almost nothing the police can do (The Quiet Zone 2002). Being caught in the act is key, and mobile offending makes this difficult to accomplish.

Other than problems of enforcement, a further worry about the regulation of incivility is that it can constitute an over-reach of the law, what the neoFoucaultians refer to as 'net widening' or 'mesh thinning' and the civil libertarians see as an attack on basic rights and freedoms. In December 2008, for example, the city of Brighton, Michigan, passed an ordinance as follows:

It shall be unlawful for any person in the city to insult, accost, molest or otherwise annoy, either by word of mouth, sign or motions any person in any public place (Totten and Karol 2008).

This sounds reasonable enough. Who would not want to deal with repeated acts of harassment in public places? Objectors voiced legitimate concerns over civil liberties. The police and courts would have to engage in overly subjective judgements on what was 'annoying'. The dangers of the law were greater than its possible benefits. Such ordinances are easy prey to legal appeals. Since *Kolender* v. *Lawson*,[1] where the Supreme Court struck down a California law that required persons loitering or wandering to account for their presence to police

[1] 461 U.S. 352 (1983).

(one recalls the anti-racist comedy sketch in which the accusation was 'loitering with intent to use a pedestrian crossing'), the United States appellate courts have been rather unsympathetic to vaguely defined ordinances concerning disorderly behaviour. City ordinances such as Brighton's have already received setbacks. For instance, a city of Las Vegas statute was deemed unconstitutional by a state appellate court when a man was charged with 'annoying a minor'.[2] One man's annoyance, it seems, is another's free speech, and the courts have largely privileged the latter. To the extent that such statutes remain in legal limbo, everyone's time and energy is potentially wasted. In 2007, for example, a Louisiana town was sued after it threatened to arrest an 'annoying' man who stood outside a bar and spoke on religious themes (Totten and Karol 2008). In addition, provoking legal action can be used as a way to gain free publicity or martyrdom. In such cases invoking the law gives perpetrators of deliberate incivility exactly what they want. The Gay Pride festival in Philadelphia of 2004 was disrupted by the group 'Repent America', who quoted Bible verses with bull horns and generally got in the way. According to gay rights activists, the protestors were hoping to be arrested so as to challenge legal precedent on hate speech, invoke free speech amendments and generally have an opportunity to air their homophobic views (David 2007). Here the law leads to dispute escalation, not resolution.

Beyond the constitutional quandaries, frontline police officers are not always eager to enforce these annoyance statutes and related municipal codes. Consider, for instance, police officers' reactions to a city code and related department policy to investigate incidents that are 'malicious or offensive' and motivated by 'race, religion, ethnic background, culture or lifestyle, including criminal and non-criminal acts', the latter of which include activities that might make others feel intimidated (Boyd, Berk and Hamner 1996). Although some officers embraced the policy, many were unimpressed. As one officer lamented, 'A couple of fruits get bashed – that's not a crime. That's normal. There are just two kinds of crime – dope and cars. The rest is just stupidity' (p. 827). Even in New York City, where the top brass has long advocated order maintenance initiatives, support for these efforts among the rank and file has been mixed (Vitale 2008). Officers

---

[2] *City of Las Vegas* v. *Dist. Ct.* 118 Nev. Adv. Op. No. 87, 20 December 2002.

frequently shun such assignments and see them as distinct from 'real police work'. Some even fear being sued.

Finally, we remark that legislative efforts at control and regulation can confirm and reinforce ongoing stereotypes and social divisions. Consider, for instance, the case of 'boom cars' discussed above. A study of one zero-tolerance policy in Kalamazoo, Michigan found that black motorists who violated the noise ordinance were almost three times as likely to be arrested as whites (Crawford 2006). Not surprisingly, many in historically marginalized communities are often sceptical of such efforts (Spitzer 1999, ch. 4). The legislation is often a response to public protest by organized constituencies. Enforcement is frequently selective, with the police dealing for the most part with those highly visible problems that confront established interests, such as shopkeepers, civic boosters and busybodies with nothing better to do with their time. According to the criminological literature, noted targets of such 'police–community partnerships' are skateboarders, failed consumers in the mall, the homeless mentally ill and young people of colour hanging out. In its turn, the very act of legislating and enforcing can reinforce perceptions of second-class citizen status, generate animosity and a sense of injustice (Spitzer 1999). Further schism and resentment can result. Is there another way forward?

Diversion, distraction, choice

We believe that responses oriented around distraction and diversion can be more effective than legislation or self-help, but for the most part again when a defined 'problem group' can be identified in a 'problem space'. Initiatives can then come into place to distract and divert away from risky situations. This approach is less confrontational and con-stitutionally problematic than trying to legislate against and punish offenders. It does not make incivility illegal, but rather tries to head it off at the pass by manipulating the qualities of situations and set-tings. A common response is to better organize the physical congrega-tion of problem people at problematic times, not through enforcement or even 'move-on' powers, but rather by making it easier for them to exit an area. This path has been popular in the field of 'Problem Oriented Policing', where the aim is to identify hotspots and deal with the conditions that enable the problem rather than simply relying on deterrence or traditional law enforcement (Goldstein 1990). Perhaps the most common strategy here is oriented towards dispersal. At the end of soccer games in Europe, for example, there is frequently a history of persistent incivility or worse as fans express old rivalries. The police often take care to route opposing fans in different directions as they leave the stadium. Similarly, school closing hours have been staggered so that sidewalks are not clogged with excited teenagers; improved or free public transport might be laid on outside nightclubs and entertainment zones so as to get people out of the area quickly; alternative entertainment spaces are opened up, such as skateboard parks, night sports leagues or youth clubs (Scott 2001).

If identifiable situations create rudeness, then we can try to eliminate those situations. Here is another example: in a *Guardian* column that generated over two hundred online comments, Madeleine Bunting (2008a) observes the horror of the London bus ride:

A grey weekday morning at 7.40 am in Edmonton bus station in north London, and it's teeming with schoolchildren. As the bus arrives, a crowd surges forward to squeeze their way on. People get knocked over. The children, screaming and pushing panic ... The ones with the sharpest elbows make it. Where are the buses, the stewards or bus conductors they need? Why are transport services in poorer areas so under-resourced? Every morning these kids are getting a crash-course in how aggressive self-assertion is your passport in life.

From our perspective the rhetorical questions Bunting asks here are pertinent. The children are not innately incivil. They perhaps do not have a fixed antisocial predisposition. Rather the immediate environment for incivility is generated by a scarce resource – space on the bus. A solution also is possible. Perhaps all that is needed is to creatively adjust the bus timetable to better suit peak hour needs, a simple organizational fix to the problem of dispersal.

Another, more dramaturgical option is to change the culture of public spaces by giving potentially rude – or as we would have it 'high visibility rude' – people something to do other than engaging in their usual problem behaviours. The aim here is not so much to move people on as to change how they interact *in situ*. In Newcastle-under-Lyme, United Kingdom, the incivility problem was understood to be the product of excessive drinking behaviour. The city hired stilt-walkers, jugglers and fire-eaters around Christmas. The 'binge drinking youth' leaving nightclubs were treated to a carnivalesque revelry – all this an intended thematic distraction from the usual self-produced tableau of name-calling and brawling. Now the high-spirited could talk about the amazing performances they were seeing, not trade insults (Levy 2008). Strategies here are somewhat close to those seeking to adjust the 'choice architecture' of situations so as to make it less likely that emotive people will do things that are not in their own best interests – in the case of Newcastle-under-Lyme's youth, fighting rather than talking or laughing. Often we act in haste, repent at leisure. One parallel idea, advanced by University of Chicago Professor Richard H. Thaler and Harvard's Cass R. Sunstein (2008), is the so-called 'civility check' on e-mails. Based on the premise of the spell check, this can quickly scan a document for problematic content (e.g., swear words) and then ask the writer 'Do you really want to send this potentially offensive e-mail?' A further option might be to put in an enforced delay. The author might have to hit the send button an hour or more after the e-mail is written. This much touted idea is designed to stop angry, drunken or late-night e-mails to bosses, ex-partners and friends. An intriguing variant asks people to complete maths questions. Again, the point here is not to ban behaviour or even to check for intoxication, but rather to encourage emotional cooling by shifting the mood. The mathematics works in the same way as the circus performance – it shifts and displaces mental energies.

Fire-eating and stilt-walking represent innovative and potentially effective options for distracting inebriated youths as they exit the bars, a maths quiz chills the intemperate e-mailer. However, our data show that a healthy sum of impolite behaviour takes place in tighter unpredictable quarters, such as crowded buses or narrow supermarket aisles. Yet even here there are less extravagant ways to alter the atmosphere and perhaps limit incivility. Mayor Bob Harvey of Waitakere City, New Zealand, simply played a steady stream of classical music around a concourse near the city's transportation centre to keep trouble-hungry kids away. Piping Mozart, Vivaldi and other classics through the centre's speakers is designed to annoy unruly adolescents to the point that they will avoid the area altogether. As the mayor puts it, classical music to teenagers is 'like us being locked in a room with hip-hop. It would be enough to drive you crazy' (Booker 2009). At first glance the idea of using classical music to deter unruly teens or prowling taggers seems a bit far-fetched, even if Mayor Harvey would argue that his plan has effectively kept vandals at bay for years. But in this case the Mayor might be on to something. Experimental research in the field of behavioural psychology suggests that music affects atmosphere, which in turn influences behaviour. For instance, a study of consumer behaviour finds that shoppers move at a slower pace when slow tempo background music is played in the supermarket (Milliman 1982). The notion that musical tempo dictates the pace of movement in confined areas is certainly relevant in the present context because much incivility is related to movement, speed and use of space. Another experiment found that slow tempo background music decreased the likelihood of traffic violations such as speeding, running red lights and blocking lane crossings (Brodsky 2002). Moreover, music helps us relax and manage stress (Scheufele 2000), thus potentially lessening the likelihood of a prolonged and heated argument with an unruly stranger. Some light music, it seems, helps us chill.

If all this sounds promising, there are some problems with diversion and distraction strategies. One, mentioned at the outset of this section, is that such interventions seem to work best when a clear group (youths, football fans, bus passengers) and hotspots (closing time, final whistle, morning bus station) can be identified. Taking back the streets on Friday night or clearing the transportation concourse of desperate commuting school children through diversion and distraction is one thing; eliminating the perpetual, ongoing, low-key, bell curve-distributed everyday incivility we have discovered in this book is another. We are also concerned that these diversion and distraction initiatives seem to prejudge guilt, and so stigmatize widely. They tend to be disproportionately aimed at the 'usual suspects'. Mayor Harvey's initiative disadvantages *all* young people who do not like classical music. It drives them out of civic spaces even before they have done anything wrong. Can such efforts centred around performance and carnival work more widely? Can they do so not merely as a diversion, but as a way of permanently changing norms at street level? Can they be applied without prejudging who is responsible? An innovative educational experiment in Bogota, Colombia suggests that this might be possible.

Education

Educating people to be civil sounds like a good idea. But just who is going to volunteer for those evening classes? In the United States, some 80 per cent of people consider rudeness to be a serious problem. Yet 99 per cent think that they are not themselves rude (Are You Rude? 2008). Still, popular opinion is quick to point to the need for an educational fix. The Public Agenda (2002) survey found 84 per cent of respondents agreeing with the statement that 'too many parents are failing to teach respect to their kids'. In his substantial and more academic analysis of the problem, Stephen L. Carter (1998) argues that civility education should be part of routine formal schooling, this to be backed up by intensive modelling and supervision behaviours by parents. Yet who now listens to teachers or parents? The argument has been widely made that children are far more influenced by their peers or by antisocial distant role models (such as gangsters, rappers, badly behaved rock and sports stars) than their elders. Besides, if the problem is urgent, do we really want to wait until the kids have grown up?

Better would be a system of instruction or policy that does not take the form of preaching, or blaming. Perhaps this could even be entertaining and take place at the spatial locus of real civic encounters rather than in the schoolroom. Once elected Mayor of Bogota in the 1990s, the mathematician and philosopher Antanas Mockus implemented an initiative along these lines. The aim was to improve life on the streets, or basic civic culture. This was no easy task in a city known for chaotic public life, poor infrastructure and a history of violence. According to Mockus: 'If people know the rules, and are sensitized by art, humour and creativity, they are much more likely to change' (Caballero 2004). Put another way, the vision here is of teaching the rules of civility informally rather than invoking sanctions or issuing droning homilies about virtue. For Mockus the aim was to shift the culture of citizenship; defined as 'the sum of habits, behaviours, actions and minimum common rules that generate a sense of belonging, facilitate harmony among citizens, and lead to respect for shared property and heritage and the recognition of citizens' rights and duties' (quoted in Montezuma 2005). This sounds just a little like a tedious and conservative agenda. Not so the implementation. Mockus himself put on a Lycra suit and paraded the streets as 'Supercitizen', a kind of civil-minded counterpart of Superman. He deployed 420 grease-painted, white-gloved mimes to ridicule jaywalkers and to interact with drivers who were impolite, aggressive, or who violated minor ordinances. For example, if drivers stopped their cars on the zebra-striped pedestrian crossing and blocked the foot traffic they were mimicked and requested to move back. All this took place without a word being spoken. Seeking social reinforcement, the mimes would look to the surrounding crowd for support and to applaud the decision to reverse. The mimes also tackled littering. In another dramatic gesture stars were painted on the road at spots where pedestrians were killed, this to instruct both drivers and would-be jaywalkers. The Mockus administration distributed cards with red on one side and white on the other that citizens could use to signal displeasure at the activities of others in the manner of a soccer referee. Mockus asked people to nominate kind and helpful taxi drivers to the city administration for special awards. He implemented a women's only night in which men were asked to stay at home so that women could enjoy civic spaces. Actors in monks' habits sought to combat noise pollution. The list goes on (Beckett and Godoy 2010).

All very creative: but did any of this work? We have only indirect indicators of an improvement in face-to-face manners, but strong markers of a shift in the wider quality of public life. Traffic fatalities halved. The murder rate decreased to a third of its prior level. Some 63,000 people paid an extra 10 per cent in voluntary taxes when asked by the mayor. One per cent of the city's guns were given in during a 'voluntary disarmament day'. Some 61 per cent of residents considered the civic culture initiative the most important for the administration, 96 per cent wanted it to continue, and the programmes were given an overall rating of 7 out of 10 by Bogota's citizens (Montezuma 2005, p. 3). Anecdotal evidence suggests that Mockus managed to change the feel of everyday life and to give people a belief in the possibility of wider civility among strangers.

Bogota's inventive approach to curtailing incivility clearly departs from the punitive actions taken in many US cities. Mockus appealed to the power of morality, instructive shaming and informal social control, albeit with a little help from the state. Among his goals was for citizens to feel a sense of obligation to clean up their act and minimize incivility; to solicit compliance by awakening their sense of duty. The juxtaposition between, for instance, the Bogota and Brighton cases described above is a microcosm of a long-standing philosophical debate about how to best maintain order and enlist compliance from citizens – through the threat of sanctions or via appeals to our moral obligations (Tyler 1990)? This deep question remains unresolved, although research on another type of behaviour that is not easily detected – cheating on taxes – might provide some guidance for the current case of incivility. In a classic experimental study, legal scholars Richard Schwartz and Sonya Orleans (1967) investigated whether informing citizens of the penalties for non-compliance or giving a reminder of one's obligation as a citizen to pay taxes better compels people to do the right thing. Those subjected to the moral appeal were significantly more likely to pay what they owed. Whether this response also holds in the case of incivility remains an open question, but as described above, there are reasons to doubt the efficacy of the law-and-order approach, while some of the less punitive approaches seem promising.

Might there be still simpler, more efficient ways of curtailing incivility than law, education and displacement alike? Perhaps so. To draw another analogy with the literature on tax compliance, sometimes it is just the simplicity of the tax form itself that makes people less apt to cheat (Clotfelter 1983, p. 368). A key theme of our book (Chapters 2 and 3) has been that incivility occurs in places and along vectors. What happens if we think of these as being analogous to that tax form?

Design

Aside from theatre, music and dedicated pro-civic initiatives, another option that might work to improve life on the streets themselves is simply to improve civic design and the provision of amenities. Importantly, and unlike most distraction and displacement strategies, such a 'design fix' targets nobody in particular. It applies to all indiscriminately and so fits well with our finding (Chapter 2) that rude strangers have a scattered demography. The idea that rudeness can be eliminated by means of architecture and urban planning has a strong precedent in the movement to 'design out crime'. With roots in Jane Jacobs' (1961) classic work on modern urban planning, the idea here is that the very architecture and layout of an urban space has implications for informal social control, incivility and ultimately crime and violence. The architect Oscar Newman advanced a related agenda with his notion of 'defensible space'. Newman (1972) advocated architectural design that encouraged residents, even residents in public housing facilities, to take ownership and responsibility for public areas. For Jacobs, Newman and others writing in this tradition the physical environment and social behaviour are seen as intertwined. Criminologists would later use these ideas as the foundation for a new means of crime prevention that de-emphasized criminal motivation in favour of manipulating the immediate physical environment – what is now commonly known as 'crime prevention through environmental design' (CPTED), or the related and more pointed concept of 'situational crime prevention'. From the latter perspective, forestalling the crime supersedes sanctioning the criminal as the objective of policy (see Clarke 1997, p. 2).

This prevention-oriented approach has captured the attention of local authorities and police departments in the United States, the United Kingdom and elsewhere. The push here is to modify or to build infrastructures and built environments such that crime becomes harder for motivated offenders. Although some means of implementation require substantial investment, such as redesigning public housing to increase defensible space and surveillance, other applications are deceptively simple. For example, the LAPD launched 'Operation Cul-de-Sac' in response to a spree of drive-by shootings in a crime-plagued area of Los Angeles in the early 1990s. The police simply placed concrete barriers at the ends of streets that led to major thoroughfares, essentially converting these streets into dead ends. The barriers precluded access to convenient escape routes, and shootings significantly declined in the following weeks (Lasley 1998). It is hard to shoot someone and then execute a three-point turn without facing some payback.

This type of initiative is consistent with one of the findings of this book that incivilities can be understood as the products of situations rather than individuals. Rather than looking to dispositions and enforcing sanctions as a path towards building a civil society, we might simply adjust the contexts in which people meet each other. If the context can be changed, perhaps the quality of the interaction might change too. The trick is to do this in a way that does not create an ugly city, one that deters civil life by virtue of its anonymity or sterility. Much work that 'designs out crime' has resulted in dystopian and prison-like outcomes. The barriers mentioned above might reduce drive-by shootings in the short term, but they were also eyesores and only served as a temporary fix. We might also cite unattractive bunker architecture, those nasty blue lights in public toilets (so drug users cannot find a vein to inject), the scratched stainless steel mirrors that go with those nasty blue lights (they are harder to damage), impertinent CCTV and window bars. Such responses, we would argue, increase fear of crime and decrease civic amenity (*cf.* Craik and Appleyard 1980, p. 80). They might even give tacit permission for incivil conduct or be read as a kind of incivil gesture themselves. An ugly landscape will change expectations about appropriate or expected behaviour. What are required are aesthetic surfaces that promote relaxed behaviour and signal civilization. In a sense this is a move that is consistent with the spirit of 'broken windows' theory itself, but without the spiteful aftertaste of 'zero-tolerance' policy. The narrative is romantic, not confrontational.

Sometimes aesthetically acceptable crime-reducing design adjustments can be found. Along with theme parks and airports, retailers and other commercial ventures suggest a way forward. These are faced with the problem of deterring offenders without driving away customers. Nobody wishes to shop in a prison. Solutions can be found, and sometimes they border on the obvious. Tesco, the largest supermarket chain in the United Kingdom, managed to reduce shoplifting by improving sightlines and lowering the stacks of goods on shelves. Potential offenders were now in sight of security cameras and other shoppers. Meanwhile, shoppers have returned to the stores, lured by the more attractive and open ambience (Design Council 2003). Curbside merchants have similarly reduced clothing thefts by simply alternating the direction of hangers so that they lock if a thief attempts to grab more than one hanger (Felson 2007, p. 302). Other solutions have been implemented by local authorities in residential and mixed-use areas. These include the use of landscaping to define public and private space, improving sightlines from homes into the street ('unseen eyes'; see Loukaitou-Sideris 1999 on bus stops), the use of garden fences and plantings that are permeable rather than offering a screen for wrongdoers, and improving human flows through the provision of seats, lighted walkways and sidewalk cafes (e.g., Western Australia Planning Commission 2006).

Such initiatives from the world of crime fighting are valuable for thinking about how to reduce low-key incivility, but their adoption needs to be thought about carefully. A number of assumptions are made that do not translate very well to the world that we have investigated in this book. They assume a predatory, motivated and somewhat rational criminal (Clarke 1997, p. 9; Cornish and Clarke 1986). This person is on the lookout for crime opportunities. They act purposively, weighing up costs and benefits, thinking about risks and likely rewards and acting accordingly. Against the criminal stand the law-abiding upright citizens with an interest in keeping their bodies and property safe, pushing up housing values in their neighbourhood and maintaining a civil society. This is a morality play. We have seen that everyday incivility is driven by a less remarkable cast of characters. Victims and offenders are often 'respectable', and acts are interpreted as accidental, selfish and insensitive rather than as wilful, malicious and threatening (Chapter 2). The problem is perhaps better defined in another way. It is not so much to deter potential offenders, but rather to create an environment in which well-meaning people can act without annoying others. Spaces and places need to be thought out so that tempers do not snap, people do not collide, those with baggage can get out of the way or are somewhere else, interpersonal space is maintained and behavioural externalities, such as smoking or talking on mobile phones, do not bother other people.

Some lessons for how to do this come from an unlikely source. Consider theme parks: places like Disney World are potential hotbeds for rudeness. In peak seasons there are long queues, big crowds, weary adults and overly-excited children. The sun is beating down – or perhaps it is raining – and the ticket prices are quite steep. Somehow such institutions have mastered the art of keeping large numbers of moving bodies interacting peacefully. Much of this is done with subtle environmental cues, such as water features and plantings. Other positives include wide walkways, distractions in queue zones (a waterfall, a view, a fish tank perhaps), plentiful toilets, free water fountains and signage. Criminologists and critical theorists generally take a dim view of Disneyland, seeing it as an example of insidious and subtle social control (e.g., Shearing and Stenning 1984). The argument there is that the landscape and experiential design subvert human rationality. Drawing on the work of the French theorist Michel Foucault, the case is made that the space is an aspect of power. It not only moulds human behaviour insidiously, but it also does so under the radar of consciousness. A Disneyfied happy-clappy consensus full of consumerist zombies follows. The argument we would take here is pragmatic rather than theoretical. Like most professional architects, we see no contradiction between well-designed civic spaces and the formation of a dynamic, attractive and interpersonally respectful public sphere where real bodies and minds can interact (Woodward 1998). Indeed, far from creating zombies, keeping people on an even keel might enhance the net volume of considered and rational human action.

Space is one key to relaxed mixing. If you look back to the *Village Voice* quotation near the start of this chapter you can see that room to move is really important. The immobile and insensitive mobile phone user is blocking the crowd trying to get into the subway. The history of the forum and the piazza strongly suggests that successful places which build face-to-face civility do not impede mobility: some can move and others stay put. Diverse trajectories and vectors can be accommodated. The Spanish Steps in Rome, or those of the New York Public Library, are often crowded with readers, lovers and picnicking office workers. Yet there always seems to be room to move, or sit. The Piazza San Marco in Venice is a notably civic environment, again one marked by space. It is no accident that such picky and neurotic aesthetes as Ruskin, Wagner and Proust could feel at home there. The lessons from such grand civic designs and theme parks are reinforced in certain mundane settings, such as Philadelphia's Reading Street Market, where there is somehow room to stroll, to sit at a lunch counter and to converse across racial lines (Anderson 2004).

Airports also provide instructive clues. Like Disneyland they point to the ancillary role of little things in improving our situational experience. Air travel is a major stressor, involving struggles with baggage, worries about paperwork and the clock, fussy security checkpoints and en route traffic. Travel workers themselves recognize this (Public Agenda 2003). It is no accident that the term 'air rage' emerged in the 1990s; nor that efforts to improve passenger experience have been relentlessly researched by organizations such as the Transport Security Administration (TSA) which is charged with a lot of the screening activities at major US airports. This attention is not purely disinterested. A relaxed flyer is more likely to spend money in airport shops. Further, antisocial individuals can generate bottlenecks when they take up the time of key staff or when they trigger security alerts. These can lead in turn to delayed flights. Sometimes a quick fix can be engineered. The TSA suggested that the introduction of a 'composure bench', for example, would allow people to put their shoes back on with more dignity and comfort and speed after going through the metal detector. At Vienna airport one of the authors of this book was offered a shoe horn by a security officer – a civil touch indeed. Subtle adjustments of light and music could also make cueing a less formal, more relaxed activity (and allow the suspicious to stand out from the stressed) (Airport International 2008).

Other adjustments in airports are harder to retrofit and involve a more comprehensive and costly attention to landscape management. Research suggests that the recipe for a stress free, rage free airport seems to be expensive, but it is consistent with our message that crowds need space. According to one report 'parking should be plentiful and connections to terminals efficient'; there might also be 'clear way-finding signs, good retail outlets, well-lit gate locations, clean restrooms and even High Street prices' (Chivers 2008). Another mentions the need for 'space, daylight and views' in contrast to 'corridors and enclosed areas' (Geoghegan 2008). It is no accident that the most highly regarded airports in traveller surveys such as Incheon, Zurich and Hong Kong tend to be larger, newer and have quicker throughput times. Overburdened older structures such as Heathrow and JFK are less popular and are plagued by word-of-mouth horror stories. True enough, airports have the advantage of a visible authority structure and the consequent possibilities for sanctioning the truly antisocial. Nevertheless, the best of them might well serve as a model for designing the privately-owned public spaces in which a good deal of incivility takes place.

Much the same story about good infrastructural design can be said for roads. Where there is crowding and competition for space resulting from poor planning, then incivil driving or road rage can result. The economist Steven Levitt writes of an off ramp as follows:

When I used to commute, there was one particular interchange where incivility ruled ... There are two lanes when you exit the highway. One lane goes to another highway, the other goes to a surface street. Hardly anyone ever wants to go to that surface street. There can be a half-mile backup of cars waiting patiently to get on the highway, and about 20% of the drivers rudely and illegally cut in at the last second after pretending they are heading toward the surface street. Every honest person that waits in line is delayed 15 minutes or more because of the cheaters. (Levitt 2005)

Levitt's analysis is consistent with our argument that designing-out crowding and queuing will often reduce rudeness. If we were serious about eliminating this rude driving hotspot, the solution could be a re-engineering of the ramps and merging zone such that they can realistically accommodate the volume of traffic moving from one expressway to the next. Such an improvement in the infrastructure would shrink the currently substantial payoff to queue jumping relative to following in line.

Something as simple as a wide, high quality sidewalk can make a big difference to the risk of commonplace rude collisions and bumps. We saw in Chapter 2 that the third most common location for incivil encounters was the outdoor walkway, and that many typically involved problems of space management or body movement. Nowhere better illustrates the need for space. The minimum design standard has generally been for an approximately 5-foot (1.5-m) sidewalk. Yet the usable area of such a sidewalk is in fact much smaller than we might think. As the Federal Highway Administration (1999) writes, pedestrians prefer to use the centre of the sidewalk. They avoid the 2 feet (60 cm) nearest to the road where there is automotive traffic, and also the 2 feet nearest to the walls, fences and doorways on the other side. In the trade this is known as the 'shy distance'. Thanks to this shy distance, our seemingly generous sidewalk actually has only 1 foot (30 cm) of usable space. Likewise a 10-foot-wide (3-m) sidewalk has only 6 feet (1.8 m) of usable space. If we throw in a lamp-post, a mail box, crowds of people front and back, a bus stop, someone coming out of a store and a person pushing a baby stroller who is closing fast from the other direction, then the possibilities for accidental and anti-social collisions increase rapidly.

Even this imperfect 10-foot sidewalk might be unattainable. In established urban environments, such as the medieval centres of many European cities, there is simply nowhere for the width to come from. As the old saying goes, land – they don't make it any more. Times Square in New York is a fine example of the chaos that can result when demand for space outstrips supply. Here we have a volatile mix of destination-focused locals, relaxed theatre-goers, dawdling map-reading tourists, unlicensed vendors and construction scaffolding. This is one of the busiest places on earth. Yet the sidewalk width is just 14 to 20 feet (4.23 m to 6 m). It is hardly surprising that a survey by the Times Square Alliance (2005) revealed that overcrowding was the number one complaint. Some 16,817 people per hour passed along some sidewalks, and over 1,000 per hour used the street, thus exposing themselves to risks of automotive collision. Times Square and the streets around it from West 42nd to West 47th are right now characterized by a Level D quality of pedestrian service. Level D is defined by the Alliance as 'Restricted freedom to select pace and a high probability of conflict'. Projections by the Times Square Alliance suggest a continuing upward trend in pedestrian volumes. It creatively dubs the ongoing situation as 'pedlock' and advocates expensive design solutions to generate more pedestrian space, such as an elevated island in the middle of the square. Building up always was the Manhattan fix. Although at the time of writing some experimental closures of Times Square to traffic have been made, a bright future might still be a long way off. For the most part the current environment is one that simply generates rudeness. Mixed trajectories, mixed speeds and crowds in motion, as we know from our study (Chapter 3), are a toxic combination. As one blogger writes:

Lately I've been freelancing out of the house, and my commute takes me from a busy part of New York smack into the busiest part of New York – Times Square. I have three blocks where I run the tourist gauntlet (within one crosswalk I veered around a guy on a skateboard and a pair of grannies with walkers). It's really easy for strangers to be rude when you're packed in together like that ... (Hawkins 2007)

Even if lack of space is at the root of much incivility, solutions need not focus on space management alone. We might look to time as well. Time has a direct impact on how we move through space. We might be less inclined to fight through a crowd if we're not in a hurry. We may skip the overcrowded bus if we know the next one is only two minutes behind. And when rude strangers cross our path, we may see them as less of an annoyance if we are not stressed about being late at our destination. In short, people are less likely to expose themselves to hotbeds of rudeness and incivility when they are not racing the clock. Moreover, when not pressed for time people are more apt to keep their cool and brush off encounters with discourteous or uncouth strangers in public settings.

This latter assertion with respect to keeping one's cool in the wake of incivility finds some support in the ELIAS data. For instance, feelings of anger were reported by 58 per cent of respondents who felt only a 'little rushed' or 'not at all rushed' at the time of the encounter.

By comparison, 73 per cent of respondents who were 'quite' or 'very' rushed at the time of the incident felt angry. Victims also reported more coping behaviours after the incident if they were in a hurry at the time of the encounter. Hence, victims remain more impassive in the midst of rude behaviour if they are not pressed. Stoicism and time are natural allies.

Certainly, it would be naive to suggest that everyone adopt the self-help solution of slowing down or leaving a bit earlier for their destination. So what can the urban architect or the city planner with an eye on curtailing incivility do? One option is to simply increase information about time. Consider public transportation, which was the locus of many rude encounters reported by ELIAS respondents. Travellers feel a greater sense of security and report less anxiety when travel information such as the departure time is clearly displayed for them (Dziekan and Kottenhoff 2006). For instance, the Transit Tracker system in Portland, Oregon (2003) uses GPS technology to estimate the time until the next bus arrives. This information is conveyed in real-time to passengers via an electronic display at the bus stop. Comparisons of survey data before and after the implementation of the programme showed an increase in riders' perceptions of personal security after implementation. As one respondent commented, 'It [Transit Tracker Online] allows me to be safer, [which is] important to me as I am a woman usually travelling alone.' Dziekan and Kottenhoff (2006) add that knowing the departure time, or even better the time remaining until departure, limits uncertainty and could reduce stress. Whether real-time information would substantially reduce the actual incidence of incivility remains an empirical question, but prior work suggests that people are less antsy and stressed when they know what to expect and feel a sense of control (Thompson 1981). This, at a minimum, may limit the intensity of conflicts and minimize the amount of coping should a bout with rudeness transpire.

The Transit Tracker system is a high-tech fix that reduces anxiety through cognitive channels: knowledge reduces uncertainty and this might in turn improve or align behaviours. It is important to realize that many such environmental solutions organized around the provision of information can be remarkably low budget and traditional. One might simply improve the provision of signage making it clear what the behavioural norms are in particular areas; for example, whether mobile phone use is considered acceptable or not in any given restaurant. Sometimes it is, sometimes it isn't. A sign can head off a problem even before the incivil act has taken place just by making policy transparent. Already such signage has done much to reduce the interactional problems associated with smoking in public places. Those potentially escalating disputes that do transpire – a cigarette has been lit in an ambivalent space such as a multi-storey car park – can perhaps be resolved one way or another simply by pointing to a plaque screwed to a wall that says 'smoking area' or 'smoke free zone'. It is interesting to note that the effectiveness of signage might be influenced by its civility as well as its visibility. The cognitive and moral are often fused in complex ways. For example, one experimental and observational study conducted in a real world hospital environment suggested that positively worded no-smoking signs were more effective than those which were simply negative in tone or grammar (Dawley, Morrison and Carrol 1981). Likewise, as Barry Schwartz pointed out long ago, the level of incivility in situations where queuing and waiting are involved can be dramatically reduced through the simplest forms of material culture. By contrast, the failure to provide adequate props and consequent information about queue order can lead to antisocial chaos:

Queue discipline is always tightest in those settings which provide the best ecological supports for it. These include queuing channels created by cords, such as are found in theatres, and painted lines or railings in other establishments ... Failure to provide a means for the dramatisation or registration of place gives rise to an anomic condition, for it precludes the application or enforcement of any allocation rule whatever ... Chaotic service systems present themselves in many contexts, ranging from crowded department store sales counters on bargain days to subways at rush hour ... being unable to tell exactly where to line up, or to ascertain who preceded whom in terms of order of arrival, each considers himself entitled to priority. The incontestable rationality of this individual assumption evolves often into the drama of collective irrationality: pushing, shoving, bickering, and a general disorder that delays everyone. (1975, p. 99)

If we have been enthusiastic about 'design' and the related 'diversion' strategies and are able to give a general thumbs up, we must also take pause. There is a small whiff of social engineering and the nanny state here. To be sure, people are making choices and are interacting merrily, but it would seem that the experts know best. One of the lessons of history has been that we should be suspicious of experts and their claims to authority, particularly when their strategies require small quantities of deception or epistemological advantage concerning the workings of the human mind. Choice exists, but it is also manipulated. Sometimes it is downright sneaky, bordering on the dishonest and patronizing. Consider an example. At intersections controlled by traffic lights, pedestrians will often push a button on a lamp-post in order to cross the road safely. Next they see an illuminated 'Wait' on the hand box or on the pole over the street. Eventually they get a 'Walk' signal or see the little green man light up. Then they cross. What they might not know is that in certain situations pushing the button achieves nothing at all to speed things up. This is the case when the pedestrian lights are synchronized to the motor traffic lights (*The Guardian,* Notes and Queries 2009). The pedestrian has been given the illusion of more control than they really have. They were able to summon the green man, true enough, but this was the limit of their control. Pushing the button did not mean they got him any sooner. Let's take this example one step further with a thought experiment. Imagine a crossing where the pedestrian pushes a button and then a light comes on saying 'Wait'. Imagine that there is nothing more going on. There is no more wiring. In fact, the green man appears *every time* one or both directions of traffic has a red light, even at two in the morning and regardless of whether or not any pedestrian is actually present or any button has been pushed. In this case our pedestrian has been disrespected and duped. One might argue that according to strict utilitarian principles this system is optimal. Objectively it reduces jaywalking fatalities by reassuring the pedestrian that they will get a little green man eventually; subjectively it allows them to feel important and valued. Still, the fact remains that someone decided that it was in the public's own best interest to be fooled.

We could say that the button and the 'Wait' light make a net contribution to civility. They are a 'design solution' that works by improving the calmness of pedestrians, making them think they have a say in the flows of the urban landscape, and also preventing disruptive or downright dangerous attempts to cross moving traffic. As we see it every person who presses that fake button is a patsy, just a step or two removed from the mugs on Candid Camera. Who would not prefer a more dignified and honest solution. Perhaps a sign saying: 'Automated

Pedestrian Crossing. Safe Crossing in 20, 19, 18 … Seconds'? Clearly not the City of New York: for the scenario we have just painted was not, in truth, a thought experiment (sorry, we tricked you for your own good so that you got the message. If you feel just a little angry at us for this conceit then you have understood the point of these two paragraphs at an intuitive level). Most Manhattan pedestrian and motor vehicle lights have been fully automated and computerized over the years. Pedestrians pressing buttons at odd moments were disrupting the synchronized flow of traffic. Still some 2,500 of the old boxes and buttons with associated 'press to cross' signage have been left in place, with the wiring disconnected. Only a few cynics have figured out that they achieve nothing by pressing the button, that these boxes are known in the trade as mechanical placebos or even as mechanical pacifiers (Luo 2004).

If the potential arrogance of social engineers and the 'we know best' tyranny of technocracy is one dystopian worry, it is not our only one. Engineered solutions to building civility often turn out to be bland, sterile or simulacral. One thinks again of Singapore, of the sort of neo-Tudor or neo-Georgian planned communities endorsed by Prince Charles, of the film *The Truman Show* and of Aldous Huxley's *Brave New World*. Any takers? It is notable that the most famous advocates of the new urbanism harped on and on about design and innovation, but for the most part chose to live in funky places like Greenwich Village that had emerged organically, not in the Legoland new towns and urban villages they inspired. Still, when applied in moderation the drawbacks to the situational and design approaches would seem to be less onerous than those of preachy civics lessons and parenting classes, scattered self-help or unenforceable laws. A few sensible interventions at hotspots and nodes for crowding, collisions and rushing might go a long way towards improving everyone's day. Only a virtuoso of dialectical reason or postmodern critical theory could object to a wider sidewalk, a nicer airport or a water fountain.

The paradoxes of incivility

The push of good design into city squares, streets, sidewalks, shops and transit hubs so that we have fewer Times Squares is one way we can reduce incivil encounter risks. Yet perhaps there is a paradox at play. We know that when new roads are built the incentive to use them improves. The new road might solve a traffic problem for a short while, but the reduced drive times simply lure more drivers onto the highway. Soon we are back where we started. Given time, perhaps, civility-enhancing built forms will produce again the problem they solve. Attractive places will attract people by changing incentive structures to use public space. Further, according to basic social psychology, people tend to attract people. Much as we might go to the restaurant that looks busy rather than the one that is empty when we are in a strange city, people come to civic spaces that look well used, popular and safe. Here they can people watch, or meet friends. They believe in the wisdom of crowds. So after we have improved our spaces the spectre of crowding emerges again, and with it the risks of collisions, overheard swearing, exposure to inappropriate body display or any of the other mundane incivilities we have captured in this book. One might argue that being a recluse and rarely venturing into public is the only path to safety.

This is a strategy for the eccentric privileged, and – here is our second paradox – even this might not bring satisfaction. The billionaire Howard Hughes holed up for many years in Las Vegas hotels, refusing all contact with the outside world as he watched repeated loops of *Ice Station Zebra* and urinated into empty bottles. He did not contribute to civil life. Nor did he stop complaining. Indeed, he became obsessed with small details and microscopic disruptions to his egocentric lifestyle; for example, stains on the clothes of those visiting him. Writing many years ago Emile Durkheim (2006 [1896]), whom we have discussed at various points in this book, explains this. He famously noted that definitions of deviance were flexible. In an orderly place like a monastery small infractions would be elevated to the status of great sins. Durkheim (1980 [1893]) argued that the cultural dynamics of society were such that deviance needed to be identified or even invented on a regular basis. By talking about deviance and punishing offenders, the rules of social life could be demonstrated for the rest of the community and life could go on. His analysis suggests that we will never be happy, that the most successful interventions of the kind discussed in this chapter will simply move the goalposts. Objective behaviours might change, but evaluations, emotions and subjective impressions must remain the same. If we need rudeness in order to define our personal or collective moral codes, then we are going to find it.

The historical work of Norbert Elias empirically confirms Durkheim's famous 'society of saints' hypothesis concerning the flexibility of the space between an action and its interpretation. Elias (1978 [1939]) demonstrates the obdurate persistence of emotions in the face of object-ive behavioural change. In the Middle Ages the threshold for disgust over bodily activity was set rather high. Amazingly, from our contem-porary, Western perspective, people found it quite normal to see others defecating in the street or spitting into the communal soup bowl. Today we are offended by merely spitting in the street. Routine actions have changed, yet the emotion of disgust endures. In our 'society of saints' we are still appalled, just at little things. As Lynne Truss neatly put it after her reading of Elias, 'while standards have been set ever higher, people have become all the more concerned that standards are drop-ping. Basically, people have been complaining about the state of man-ners since at least the fifteenth century' (2005, p. 51). The process in which the bar of expectations is dropped or raised need not, in fact, take centuries. When *Guardian* columnist Madeleine Bunting spoke to her teenage daughter about the incivil bus scene she had witnessed (we reported this a few pages ago): 'hardened by 18 months of second-ary school travel she smiled at my naivety. Being pushed, sworn at and squeezed onto overcrowded trains and buses is already routine to her' (Bunting 2008a). Put another way, the daughter's rudeness detection sensor had been set at a higher level than Bunting's own by virtue of her everyday experiences. As Georg Simmel (1997) pointed out over a cen-tury ago, urban life in particular contains a number of shocks. When these become too numerous our psychology adjusts. We stop noticing them or count them at little concern.[3]

To sum up: socio-psychological process demands that we will always detect a certain quantum of rudeness. Even if we set this social-theoretical ingenuity aside, there are also more prosaic and less counter-intuitive reasons why we are doomed to encounter the rude stranger. Let us quickly adumbrate these.

(1) Howard Hughes had billions of dollars. Objectively there is little chance for the rest of us of changing our ongoing routines. We

---

[3] Our research (Chapter 4) suggests that Simmel is not quite correct, at least insofar as rude stranger encounters are concerned. Respondents were often surprised and emotionally charged at the time of the event. They developed a blasé attitude only a little later due to coping (Chapter 6) and the half-life of emotions.

must all go to work, to the shops or to places of entertainment or education at some point in our lives. So we must encounter others, and some of these people are going to be understood as rude.

(2) We have suggested that to reduce risks and change behaviours through policy channels we must most likely spend money. Bigger sidewalks, new transportation hubs, better road junctions, more public spaces, talented actors and street artists, more buses, mood-shifting plantings and lighting. None of this comes cheap. Reducing rudeness is never likely to be far enough up the priority list to justify large expenditures. Less crime, better schools, lower taxes: these are what people care about just a little more.

(3) With the exception of some places like Japan where there is demographic decline, the world is experiencing increasing living densities and ongoing urbanization. Anecdotally at least the pace of life is increasing. People will be moving faster through crowded spaces. They will also likely be more self-absorbed and so less attentive to others.

(4) Volumes of international travel are increasing. Tourism and occupational or educational migration are all marked by upward secular trends. Travel brings people into places where they are unfamiliar with local norms. They are more likely to offend or give offence, often inadvertently. Let's break the list and talk about this. Consider personal space. As one commentator puts it, in the West:

we are accustomed to leaving about one body width in space between ourselves and others. This degree of space is a luxury and too large in China. Leave this much space in a queue and people will cut into the queue in front of you. When it is suggested they should go to the back of the line, they ask 'Why did you leave so much space? I thought you weren't part of the queue'. (Guppy 2008)

The possibilities for misunderstanding are endless. We can see this behind the proliferation of expat discussions on the Internet on topics such as 'Why are Parisians so rude?', or 'Why are Germans rude?' or 'Is Shanghai the rudest city on Earth?' These are often characterized by confessions of initial amazement at the level of rudeness, stories of specific rude encounters, then Bildungsroman-style accounts of learning to toughen up and fight for rights and respect. Yet it is hard to identify with the protagonists. Xenophobia, or worse, often seem near at hand. For example, one regrettably typical blogger writes from Shanghai:

I've been to quite a number of different countries, many third-world countries, and the Chinese are, by far, the rudest people I have ever encountered. I have now become a totally arrogant horrible **** to anyone that tries to beg from me, put travel-agents cards in my hand, passengers on the sub, taxi drivers and people who try to steal taxis from me. The other day in Xujiahui I was waiting for a taxi and this bitch just tried to take a taxi from under my nose. I literally had her over a railing threatening to kick the **** out of her. She wasn't that put out by the experience, because, given that we're in the rudest country in the world, my reaction probably wasn't that too out of the ordinary. I doubt if she's gained anything or learnt anything. (MayomingMaster 2005)

This is not very nice. Had the other woman known our blogger was waiting for a taxi? Who was incivil to whom?

Of course, what we have just written is somewhat politically correct. Rather than blaming ignorant foreigners we can tell a converse story. Perhaps knowledgeable locals exploit tourists who, lacking language capabilities and fearing embarrassment, don't complain. Further, the affluent foreigner might be perceived with resentment as a worthy victim. Nevertheless, the scenario holds: whether as victims or as perpetrators, outsiders are an engine of rude encounters.

(5) Finally we must speak to the ongoing ambiguity of social life. In many situations, even in our own home town, it is not really clear what we are supposed to do. Sometimes there is a 50/50 chance of doing the rude thing. A toddler waves at you from the back of a supermarket trolley. A parent is with them pushing the trolley. Is it rude to wave back? Perhaps it is. After all you don't have the parent's permission to interact with the child. Maybe they are being taught to be wary of paedophiles. Or is it rude *not* to wave back? Maybe. You might be seen as an antisocial misanthrope who is ignoring the friendly child. You have just disrupted the parent's plan to build social interaction skills in their offspring.

If we are fated to endure a Promethean eternity of public incivility, what can one do about it? Many years ago Sigmund Freud argued that we can never escape from our neuroses. There is no cure. Rather we come to understand them, and in the act of understanding regain some measure of control and happiness. When we explored coping behaviours earlier in this book we found something like this going on, not on the psychoanalyst's couch, but rather in the quiet mental life of the victim. People were trying to come to terms with what had happened, not to deny it or to wish things had been otherwise. Nor did they seek revenge.

Learning to comprehend our experiences of the rude stranger, to find reasons for these, and to put them into a narrative offers a kind of fleeting solace. This book has provided a set of social science resources for such a task. The next time something happens, you can think about the role of time and space, human movements and spatial patterns in the setting. You can identify the risk factors that were at play. You might develop some ideas as to why the rude stranger was also present, at that same time and place. You might even think about your own role in the event, or reflect back on your own complicity, or on your moral emotions, perhaps with a sense of shame. You might even discover that what seemed surprising to our commonsense self back there in the lifeworld was really not so unusual or disturbing after all. If in this book we have not offered much by way of an intervention or cure, we have offered tools for diagnosis. This, at least, is a start.

The main arguments of this chapter are:

- Efforts to control 'rude' behaviour might be a mask for illiberal politics. We need to be on guard for this.
- Strategies involving law enforcement do not look too promising for controlling low-level incivilities of the kind uncovered in this book.
- Methods such as diversion, distraction and innovative design look more promising but can be expensive, sneaky and result in boring environments.
- We will probably have to live with rudeness. Forever.

9 | *Twenty questions and answers*

We have tried to be as clear as possible in this book and to write scholarly material in a way that will appeal to a general audience. Still, books like this one can be wordy. Also the complex statistical tables can result in an overload of information, especially for general readers. Although we have included summary bullets at the end of each chapter, we would like to conclude with a more crisp and conversational outline of what we have discovered and what remains to be found out.

The following series of questions and answers replicates what we are often asked during both academic seminars and public talks. It offers a shortcut to the entire book. Scholars who require higher academic standards and a more serious tone, or those looking for extra information after reading an answer here must return to the book itself.

1. Why research the rude stranger?

Rudeness is a commonplace feature of everyday life. It impacts upon pretty much everyone. We should know about it. In the mass media and on the Internet we find a lot of chatter about this. Politicians often crusade for civility. Academic researchers looking at social capital, crime and everyday life have important things to say on these topics. Their ideas have substantially influenced policy and political agendas (Chapter 1).

2. Don't we already know a lot about rudeness?

No. We really have no idea at all. A lot of the time politicians, the mass media and social commentators simply recount anecdotes or make sweeping unsubstantiated statements on how the world is going to the dogs. Academic criminology has systematically investigated countable physical traces of incivility like graffiti and broken windows, but they have never been able to measure face-to-face encounters in depth. Symbolic interactionists have explored the process of 'interactions gone wrong' that involve people, but for the most part by elaborating typologies or developing concepts rather than measuring or benchmarking (Chapter 1).

3. Is there anything else that is problematic about the existing academic literature?

For policy reasons it seems to focus on a worst-case scenario involving threatening or quasi-criminal acts in bad areas. In so doing it might reproduce stereotypes. Further, there has been no comparative benchmark of ordinary or everyday incivility of the sort that impacts upon middle classes or simply average citizens – those living in diverse situations who never go near 'bad areas'. The focus on residential neighbourhoods seems to ignore the fact that people move around the city, for example, to work or shop (Chapter 1).

4. What did you do to find new information?

After some preliminary focus group work, we conducted a random national survey by telephone in Australia. This asked people for details of their most recent encounter with a rude stranger. We also collected information on demographic variables, on routine activities and general social attitudes. In a way the survey took the conventions of the crime victimization survey and applied them in a new context (Chapter 1).

5. Is Australia typical? Can you generalize?

Australia is a multicultural nation with a large proportion of persons born overseas. Many Australians come from non-English-speaking backgrounds, especially Asia, south Asia and southern and eastern Europe. It is anything but simply white and Anglo-Celtic. Although there are visible minorities including an indigenous Aboriginal population, it does not have really large concentrations of urban black poor. Our findings might have limited relevance to the Chicago Southside, to Brixton or to Baltimore. Still we argue that Australia is a typical developed nation. When we look at measures like household income, lifestyle, national pride or fear of crime it runs in the middle of the pack with places like the United Kingdom, Italy, Sweden or France, for example. We think our findings are far more applicable to most settings even in the United States than those from studies made in areas of concentrated disadvantage in that country. Of course, it is possible that people in other countries have differing thresholds, perceptions and standards for what is rude (e.g., body contact norms). We invite other researchers to pick up the torch and to locate interesting similarities and differences with our Australian data. We have provided the first systematic benchmark. Our more interesting findings are probably about locations, perpetrators, lifestyles, demographics, emotions and so forth. We think these findings will very likely hold good even if thresholds and bugbears vary cross-culturally.

6. How do you know what is rude?

We don't. We do not make judgements or set standards, in part because rudeness is so situational that to do so would be silly. There are also theoretical grounds for our interpretive stance which argues that what is 'rude' is what our respondents found to be rude. For example, a 'rude' act that nobody interprets as rude is like a tree falling in the forest that nobody hears. Rude encounters are first and foremost meaningful interpretations of experiences that people have (Chapter 1).

7. What do people do that is rude?

They do an amazing variety of things. When we clumped these together we found that much rudeness was related to blocked, bumped or impeded movement, or the invasion of personal space and lines of sight. Less common forms of rudeness involved bad language, poor body control and making unwanted noise (Chapter 2).

8. What causes rudeness? Where does it happen?

Rather than looking to personalities, we looked to situations. A lot of the time rudeness seemed to be generated by commonplace movements around the town or city. It takes place when people are trying to get somewhere more often than in a destination. Generally the rudeness did not seem to be deliberate, but rather to result from crowding, insensitivity and mixed trajectories and speeds. We see rude encounters as a near-inevitable result of circulating bodies following daily routines, especially in urban spaces. For this reason rude strangers are found wherever people are found – in respectable places rather than just in shady neighbourhoods. This finding confronts a lot of stereotypes in political and criminological thinking (Chapters 2 and 3).

9. Who is the rude stranger? Who is the victim?

Contra the stereotype of problematic young minority males, we found that rude strangers were just like everyone else. They were often seen as 'respectable' looking. Some two-thirds of rude strangers were male. These men were often middle-aged. But we don't want to push this too far. All social demographics were capable of generating rude strangers. Victims were also very mixed, but there was a slight tendency for women, the young, the better educated and the better off to encounter the rude stranger. To some extent this might reflect perceptions and thresholds – more refined people might be more prone to detect rudeness. But we also found that exposure to places with many strangers explained a good proportion of the differences across the demographic categories (except for gender). The likelihood of encountering a rude stranger partly reflects people's lifestyles and routines outside of the home (Chapters 2 and 5).

10. I don't believe you. Surely rude people are problematic individuals found in bad places picking on innocent passers by?

It may be that rude or antisocial people are lurking on skid row or in abandoned buildings waiting for middle-class victims. They will wait in vain. Nobody goes there. When we asked 'ordinary' people we found that rude encounters took place in their 'ordinary' daily routine. They found rude strangers in places they went often, places that were respectable and, in particular, during the middle of the day. When we looked at the minority of rude stranger encounters that took place where people went less often, we found these also generally involved respectable places and perpetrators. This is why many were surprised at the actions of the rude stranger. They were simply not expecting good people to behave badly in a nice place. These findings about the centrality of routine human movements were confirmed by other results. We showed there was a social similarity between victims and rude strangers. Further, at a more micro-level mixed movement speeds and baggage were typical features of an encounter (Chapter 3).

11. What exactly takes place in the interaction with the rude stranger?

We found quite a lot was going on. First, people could have varied emotional reactions – or none at all. This was surprising given the emphasis on 'fear' in the criminological and urban planning literatures, although it is consistent with work in the tradition of social theory on responses to norm breaching. We found surprise, anger and disgust were quite common emotions. These emotions often faded rapidly. Interactions with the rude stranger tended to be brief. Efforts to remonstrate, for example, were uncommon. Very few events escalated into ongoing conflicts. For the most part people just wanted to leave the situation or to let it drop. The emotion of anger best predicted ongoing interactions and efforts to sanction the rude stranger (Chapter 4).

12. What about afterwards?

Efforts at coping were quite common, especially among women. People usually wanted to 'move on' mentally or waited for their feelings to pass. Some others were more active, doing things like having exercise. Thoughts of revenge were not common. All this is consistent with the findings we have just discussed – people wanted to exit the event, to get on with life. Still, we did find some long-term changes in behaviour. Some people become hardened, others changed their routines to avoid certain places, but yet others resolved to be more civil. Here there was a mixed picture (Chapter 6).

13. You are talking in generalities. What can you say about specific experiences tied to gender, class or age?

To a large extent experiences of incivility are shared and cross over demographic boundaries. Put another way, we can identify fuzzy sets but not categorical differences. Women are more likely to be victims than men (Chapter 2), and this cannot be explained simply by the relative amount of time they spent in public places (Chapter 5). They are also more likely to experience fear (Chapter 5), to engage in coping activity and also to constrain their behaviour as a result of a rude encounter (Chapters 5 and 6). Put another way, the victimization of women seems more serious on close inspection. It is perhaps a social problem worthy of special attention. Younger people and the middle class also experience more incivility (Chapter 2). This seems to be a function of their time in public spaces (Chapter 5). Here there do not seem to be strong negative sequelae. While we are on the subject, we can also talk about men. This group seemed more prepared to remonstrate with the rude stranger.

14. What about events where people are deliberately rude versus those where the rudeness is accidental? Isn't there a qualitative difference?

We'd like to stress that the main drivers for both kinds of events seem to be routine activities. People have to be out and about in order to meet rude people, whether or not they have bad intent. Further, only about one in five events involved intentional rudeness. It's not that common. Also our general message that 'everyone is doing it' holds good. All social groups provided deliberately rude strangers. Still, our data did show some effects that support stereotypes. Teenagers, strangers in groups and rough-looking people were slightly more likely to be seen as deliberately rude (Chapter 2). Deliberately rude acts required more coping activity (Chapter 6) and were more likely to generate fear (Chapter 5).

15. Do interactions with rude strangers change people's general attitudes towards unknown others?

Let's backtrack a bit. First, we wanted to find out how people felt about the 'Other', including those in our sample who had not encountered a rude stranger in the prior month. We used common measures on social trust and on fear of crime to get a sense of this. Our analysis suggested that the majority opinion in social theory, urban sociology and cultural studies was wrong. People were neither particularly fearful, nor untrusting. Using regression analysis we compared those in our sample who had had a rude stranger encounter with those who had not. The rude stranger episode made a small difference for fear and trust, but much less than crime victimization. Aside from such experiences, factors associated with high levels of fear included being female, being younger, having been a crime victim and consuming lowbrow and crime related mass media. Low levels of trust were more often reported by the young, the less educated, consumers of lowbrow media, crime victims and among those spending less time in public settings (Chapter 7).

16. What can be done to reduce rudeness?

We looked at several options in the light of our findings. Legislation and enforcement don't seem very practicable. Much better seem to be attempts to change the mood of public settings through the use of street performers, music and entertaining didactic exercises. Further, we see real hope for initiatives to improve urban design or the built form of large enclosed public spaces, parks, plazas and sidewalks. What is important is to give people room to move at diverse speeds and also to eliminate minor hassles, for example, through the provision of better signage or free baggage trolleys. This perspective fits with our findings about the centrality of human movements in generating rude encounters. However, in some places, like Times Square in New York, this kind of design and building fix is going to be prohibitively expensive (Chapter 8).

17. Can we eliminate rudeness?

Probably not: it could be that there is a moving target. If behaviour improves we will all start to pick up on little things – a poorly knotted tie, for example. Marcel Proust was once in a totally silent room. He became annoyed by the ticking of a clock. Further, there are some worrying secular trends. Lives seem to be more hectic than ever. People are travelling more often to places where they are unfamiliar with local customs and conventions (for example, about reasonable personal space). The reworking of public space to reduce body congestion and 'pedlock' is always going to be lower on the priority list than other more urgent issues like education or crime (Chapter 8).

18. *Should we eliminate rudeness?*

We don't consider this issue at great length as it is a normative issue
that is somewhat outside our 'basic science' remit. But we do note that
the label of 'rude' has been used to put down minorities and those
engaged in social struggles and that 'rude' behaviour can be an effective tool of non-violent protest. 'Rude' people have also often been
creative outsiders. We also think some vigilance needs to be exercised
over social engineering solutions. These can be totalitarian, sneaky
and boring in some combination (Chapter 8).

19. *What could researchers do next?*

Chiefly, we would like to see this study replicated in whole or in part
in other countries. This would allow for a substantial increase in our
confidence over the evidentiary base. We could also begin to theorize
how diverse national or local cultures, or divergent forms of modernity might impact upon the distribution of rude strangers and rudeness
norms. It would be fascinating, for example, to run our survey in
Tokyo (ethnically homogeneous, 'Asian', leading edge), Rio de Janeiro
(developing world, 'Latin', strong gender norms), London (multicultural European world city) and South Central Los Angeles (poor,
minority, car-based culture). We also see some space for qualitative
work in which skilled interpreters really probe people on their experiences. A problem here will be recall. Also the fleeting events we found
most prevalent happen very fast, interpretation is instantaneous and
intuitive, and there is little to be said. Our pilot efforts at interview
and focus group work actually yielded less useful information than
the survey approach. Videotapes of real-world settings might offer
some dividends, but we fear there will be many hours of non-events
to each rude encounter. Coders would inevitably be imposing their
own definitions of rudeness on what they see. There is also the problem that the tapes will simply not pick up the more micro-level insults
and gestures. Finally, we are suspicious of many experiments due to
their non-naturalistic settings, contrived activities and over-reliance
on undergraduate students as experimental subjects, but if we think
creatively these might work quite well to tap into divergent interpretations of interactions and behaviours. One imagines actors could be
employed to engage in unpleasant behaviour in real-world settings.

We could then interview onlookers or victims, seeing, for example, if men and women read the situation differently. An issue here will be obtaining ethical clearance and legal permission to use representative public spaces such as mass transit. Further, we feel uncomfortable with the deception involved. The unwitting subjects might find the experimental behaviours frightening or stressful.

20. So overall, what have been the major achievements of this project?

We have opened up the world of everyday incivility in unprecedented depth. We have not only discovered a number of new facts, but also challenged some prevailing wisdom and offered an explanation for what is going on. To be sure, there have been other studies that have offered great historical insight, charted the experiences of particular groups experiencing particular indignities, developed brilliant concepts and theories, or explored in meticulous detail certain issues in certain places. Yet we believe a quantitative benchmarking effort directed towards generic experience should take place alongside such inquiry into more delimited or specialized issues. We hope our portrait of the banal, routine, low-key incivilities experienced in everyday life today will spur further efforts in this direction.

References

Airport International 2008. 'Music and Light Reduce Airport Passenger Stress', accessed online 5 January 2009 at: www.airport-int.com/news/2008/04/01/music-and-light-reduce-airport-passenger-stress.

Alexander, Jeffrey C. and Jacobs, Ronald N. 1998. 'Mass Communication, Ritual and Civil Society', in T. Liebes and J. Curran (eds.), *Media, Ritual and Identity*. London: Routledge, pp. 23–41.

Anderson, Benedict 1991. *Imagined Communities*. London: Verso.

Anderson, Elijah 1999. *The Code of the Street: Decency, Violence and the Moral Life of the Inner City*. New York: W. W. Norton.

2004. 'The Cosmopolitan Canopy', *Annals of the American Academy of Political and Social Science* 595(1): 14–31.

Anleu, Sharyn Roach, Martin, Bill and Zadoroznyi, Maria 2004. 'Editor's Introduction to the Special Issue: "Fear and Loathing in the New Century"', *Journal of Sociology* 40(4): 315–19.

Anon. 2001. 'How can I discourage strangers who want to touch my belly?', forum post at BabyCenter.com. Retrieved 8 May 2009 at: www.babycenter.com/400_how-can-i-discourage-strangers-who-want-to-touch-my-belly_500119_1001.bc.

2008. Answer to 'Have you ever had an experience with an extremely rude stranger?' *Yahoo Answers*. Retrieved 8 May 2009 at: http://answers.yahoo.com/question/index;_ylt=AlwYilpEoQZzUWRnSR5cdVsjzKIX;_ylv=3?qid=2008102123.

Are You Rude? 2008. Oprah.Com., accessed online 19 January 2009 at: www.cnn.com/2008/LIVING/personal/11/11/o.are.you.rude.test/index.html.

Armitage, John 1999. 'Paul Virilio: An Introduction', *Theory, Culture & Society* 16(5–6): 1–23.

Barber, Bernard 1983. *The Logic and Limits of Trust*. New Brunswick, NJ: Rutgers University Press.

Bauman, Zygmunt 2000. *Liquid Modernity*. Cambridge: Polity.

2003. *Liquid Love*. Cambridge: Polity.

Bean, Clive 2005. 'Is There a Crisis of Trust in Australia', in Shaun Wilson, Gabrielle Meagher, Rachel Gibson, David Denmark and

Mark Western (eds.), *Australian Social Attitudes: The First Report.* Sydney: University of New South Wales Press, pp. 122–40.

Beckett, Katherine and Godoy, Angelina 2010. 'A Tale of Two Cities', *Urban Studies* 47: 277–301.

Benjamin, Walter 1983. *Charles Baudelaire: A Lyric Poet in the Era of High Capitalism.* London: Verso.

Bettelheim, Bruno 1960. *The Informed Heart.* Glencoe, IL: Free Press.

Black, Donald 1970. 'The Production of Crime Rates', *American Sociological Review* 35: 733–48.

Blair, Tony 2006. 'Blair Respect Speech in Full', accessed online 10 January 2006 at: http://news.bbc.co.uk/2/hi/uk_news/politics/4600156.stm on 11/14/2006.

Booker, Jarrod 2009. 'Dame Kiri – the West's Top Hoon-scarer', *The New Zealand Herald*, accessed online 14 March 2009 at: www.nzherald. co.nz/nz/news/article.cfm?c_id=1&objectid=10560080.

Borooah, Vani K. and Carcach, Carlos A. 1997. 'Crime and Fear – Evidence from Australia', *British Journal of Criminology* 37(4): 635–57.

Box, Steven, Hale, Chris and Andrews, Glen 1988. 'Explaining Fear of Crime', *British Journal of Criminology* 28: 340–56.

Boyd, Elizabeth A., Berk, Richard A. and Hamner, Karl M. 1996. 'Motivated by Hatred or Prejudice: Categorization of Hate-motivated Crimes in Two Police Divisions', *Law and Society Review* 30: 819–50.

Boyle, Richard and Bonacich, Philip 1970. 'The Development of Trust and Mistrust in Mixed-Motive Games', *Sociometry* 33(2): 123–239.

Brodsky, Warren 2002. 'The Effects of Music Tempo on Simulated Driving Performance and Vehicular Control', *Transportation Research Part F* 4: 219–41.

Bunting, Madeleine 2008a. 'From Buses to Blogs, A Pathological Individualism is Poisoning Public Life', *The Guardian*, 28 January.

2008b. 'Sense and Incivility: Our Interaction With Strangers is Increasingly Edged with Aggression', *The Guardian*, 1 February.

Caballero, Maria Christina 2004. 'Academic Turns City into a Social Experiment', *Harvard University Gazette*, 11 March.

Caldwell, Mark 1999. *A Short History of Rudeness: Manners, Morals and Misbehaviour.* London: Picador.

Cantor, David and Lynch, James P. 2000. 'Self-report Surveys as Measures of Crime and Criminal Victimization', *Measurement and Analysis of Crime and Justice, Criminal Justice 2000*, 4: 85–138.

Carter, Stephen L 1998. *Civility: Manners, Morals and the Etiquette of Democracy.* New York: Basic Books.

Cartner-Morley, Jess 2009. 'Life at a Snail's Pace', *The Guardian*, 15 April, section G2, p. 4.

Chivers, Mark 2008. 'How Airports Deal with Problem Passengers', *Aviation.com*, accessed online 9 January 2009 at: www.msnbc.msn.com/id/25147767/wid/17621070.

Clarke, Ronald V. 1997. 'Introduction', *Situational Crime Prevention: Successful Case Studies* (2nd edn.). Guilderland, NY: Harrow and Heston.

Clotfelter, Charles T. 1983. 'Tax Evasion and Tax Rates: An Analysis of Individual Returns', *The Review of Economics and Statistics* 65(3): 363–73.

Cobbina, Jennifer E., Miller, Jody and Brunson, Rod K. 2008. 'Gender, Neighborhood Danger, and Risk-Avoidance Strategies Among Urban African-American Youths', *Criminology* 46: 673–710.

Cohen, Lawrence E. and Felson, Marcus 1979. 'Social Change and Crime Rate Trends: A Routine Activity Approach', *American Sociological Review* 44: 588–608.

Cohen, Nick 2004. 'Turning Right to Wrong', *The Observer*, 1 August 2004.

Collins, Randall 2000. 'Situational Stratification', *Sociological Theory* 18(1): 17–43.

  2004. *Interaction Ritual Chains*. Princeton University Press.

  2008. *Violence*. Princeton University Press.

Cornish, Derek B. and Clarke, Ronald V. (eds.) 1986. *The Reasoning Criminal: Rational Choice Perspectives on Offending*. New York: Springer-Verlag.

Cowlishaw, Gillian 1988. *Black, White or Brindle: Race in Rural Australia*. Melbourne: Cambridge University Press.

Craik, Kenneth H. and Appleyard, Donald 1980. 'Streets of San Francisco: Brunswick's Lens Model Applied to Urban Inference and Assessment', *Journal of Social Issues* 3: 72–85.

Crawford, Charles 2006. 'Car Stereos, Culture, and Criminalization', *Crime Media Culture* 2: 85–92.

CrazyHappy 2008. 'Mature Content – 8 Rude Stranger Cards', accessed at: www.etsy.com/view_listing.php?listing_id=18196130, 28 January 2009.

Dale, David 2006. *Who Are We? A Miscellany of the New Australia*. Sydney: Allen & Unwin.

Dant, Tim 2004. 'The Driver-Car', *Theory, Culture & Society* 21(4–5): 61–79.

David 2007. 'What to do with Rude People', retrieved online 27 January 2009 at: www.equalityloudoun.org/?p=590.

Dawley, Harold H., Morrison, John and Carrol, Sudie 1981. 'The Effect of Differently Worded No-Smoking Signs on Smoking Behaviour', *Substance Use and Misuse* 16(8): 1467–71.

Day, Kristen 2000. 'The Ethic of Care and Women's Experience of Public Space', *Journal of Environmental Psychology* 20: 103–24.

Dayan, Daniel and Katz, Elihu 1992. *Media Events: The Live Broadcasting of History*. Cambridge, MA: Harvard University Press.

Design Council 2003. *Think Thief*. London: Design Council.

Dowler, Kenneth 2003. 'Media Consumption and Public Attitudes toward Crime and Justice', *Journal of Criminal Justice and Popular Culture* 10(2): 109–26.

Durkheim, Emile 1980 [1893]. *The Division of Labor in Society*. Glencoe, IL: Free Press.

　　2006 [1896]. *On Suicide*. London: Penguin.

Dziekan, Katrin and Kottenhoff, Karl 2006. 'Dynamic At-Stop Real-Time Information Displays for Public Transport: Effects on Customers', *Transportation Research Part A: Policy and Practice* 6: 489–501.

Elias, Norbert 1978 [1939]. *The Civilizing Process Vol. 1: The History of Manners*. Oxford: Basil Blackwell.

Ellis, Bret Easton 2005. *Lunar Park*. London: Picador.

Federal Highway Administration 1999. 'Sidewalk Design Guidelines and Existing Practices', retrieved at: www.fhwa.dot.gov/environment/sidewalks/chap4a.htm, 12 January 2009.

Felson, Marcus 2007. 'Situational Crime Prevention', in S. G. Shoham, O. Beck and M. Kett (eds.), *International Handbook of Penology and Criminal Justice*. Boca Raton, FL: CRC Press, pp. 295–320.

Furedi, Frank 1998. *Culture of Fear*. London: Cassell.

Gardner, Carol Brooks 1995. *Passing By: Gender and Public Harassment*. Berkeley, CA: University of California Press.

Garfinkel, Harold 1967. *Studies in Ethnomethodology*. Englewood Cliffs, NJ: Prentice Hall.

Garofalo, James 1979. 'Victimization and the Fear of Crime', *Journal of Research in Crime and Delinquency* 16: 80–97.

Garofalo, James and Laub, John 1978. 'The Fear of Crime: Broadening Our Perspective', *Victimology: An International Journal* 3: 242–53.

Gendleman, Irina 2006. 'The Romantic and Dangerous Stranger', *M/C Journal* 9(3).

Geoghegan, Tom 2008. 'What Makes a Good Airport?', *BBC News Magazine*, accessed online 5 January 2009 at: http://news.bbc.co.uk/2/hi/uk_news/magazine/7290432.stm.

Gerbner, George, Gross, Larry, Morgan, Michael and Signorelli, Nancy 1980. 'The Mainstreaming of America: Violence Profile Number 11', *Journal of Communication* 30(3): 10–29.

Giddens, Anthony 1984. *The Constitution of Society*. Cambridge: Polity Press.

Goffman, Erving 1963. *Behaviour in Public Places.* New York: Free Press.

   1967. *Interaction Ritual.* Chicago, IL: Aldine.

   1971. *Relations in Public.* London: Allen Lane.

Goldstein, Herman 1990. *Problem-Oriented Policing.* New York: McGraw-Hill.

Gottfredson, Michael R. and Hirschi, Travis 1990. *A General Theory of Crime.* Palo Alto, CA: Stanford University Press.

Guppy, Daryl 2008. 'Why is Your Foot Under my Foot?', *China In Touch: Australia–China Business Council Northern Territory Branch Newsletter,* 11 June, p. 3. Retrieved online 28 January 2009 at: www.acbc.com.au/deploycontrol/files/upload/newsletter_NT_080611.pdf.

Habermas, Jürgen 1984. *The Theory of Communicative Action.* Boston, MA: Beacon, Vol. 1.

   1989. *The Structural Transformation of the Public Sphere.* Cambridge, MA: MIT Press.

Harcourt, Bernard E. 2001. *The Illusion of Order: The False Promise of Broken Windows Policing.* Cambridge, MA: Harvard University Press.

Hawkins, Mary 2007. 'Stop Wishing Bad Things Would Happen to Rude Strangers', Retrieved online 12 January 2009 at: www.43things.com/things/view/1425997/stop-wishing-bad-things-would-happen-to-rude-strangers.

Heath, Linda 1984. 'Impact of Newspaper Crime Reports on Fear of Crime: Multi-methodological Investigation', *Journal of Personality and Social Psychology* 47: 263–76.

Hindelang, Michael S., Gottfredson, Michael and Garofalo, James 1978. *Victims of Personal Crime.* Cambridge, MA: Ballinger.

Hindman, Baker M. 1953. 'The Emotional Problems of Negro High School Youth Which Are Related to Segregation and Discrimination in a Southern Urban Community', *Journal of Educational Sociology* 27(3): 115–27.

Hirschman, Albert O. 1970. *Exit, Voice and Loyalty.* Cambridge, MA: Harvard University Press.

Hobsbawm, Eric 1991. *The Age of Extremes: A History of the World, 1914–1991.* London: Vintage.

Home Office 2006. *Perceptions and Experience of Anti-social Behaviour: Findings from the 2004/2005 British Crime Survey.* London: HMSO.

Jacobs, Jane 1961. *The Death and Life of Great American Cities.* New York: Random House.

Jain 2007. 'Don't Hate Me Because I Drive a Hummer', retrieved online 9 February 2008 at: www.associatedcontent.com/article/331749/dont_hate_me_because_i_drive_a_hummer.html?cat=27.

Jennings, M. Kent and Stoker, Laura 2004. 'Social Trust and Civic Engagement Across Time and Generations', *Acta Politica* 39(4): 342–79.

Johnson, Holly 2005. *Crime Victimization in Australia: Key Results of the 2004 International Crime Victimization Survey*. Canberra: Australian Government/Australian Institute of Criminology.

Katz, Charles M., Webb, Vincent J. and Armstrong, Todd A. 2003. 'Fear of Gangs: A Test of Alternative Theoretical Models', *Justice Quarterly* 20: 95–130.

Katz, Elihu and Lazarsfeld, Paul 1955. *Personal Influence*. New York: Free Press.

Katz, Jack 1988. *The Seductions of Crime*. New York: Basic Books.

1999. *How Emotions Work*. Chicago, IL: University of Chicago Press.

King, Gary, Tomz, Michael and Wittenberg, Jason 2000. 'Making the Most of Statistical Analyses: Improving Interpretation and Presentation', *American Journal of Political Science* 44: 341–55.

Kitsuse, John I. and Cicourel, Aaron V. 1963. 'A Note on the Uses of Official Statistics', *Social Problems* 11: 131–9.

Lane, Jodi and Meeker, James W. 2003. 'Ethnicity, Information Sources and Fear of Crime', *Deviant Behaviour* 24(1): 1–26.

Lasley, James 1998. '"Designing Out" Gang Homicides and Street Assaults', *National Institute of Justice Research in Brief*, November 1998. See http://popcenter.org/library/scp/pdf/104-Lasley.pdf.

Lee, Gang Heong, Cappella, Joseph N. and Southwell, Brian 2003. 'The Effects of News and Entertainment on Interpersonal Trust: Political Talk Radio, Newspapers and Television', *Mass Communication and Society* 6(4): 413–34.

Levi, Primo 1996. *Survival in Auschwitz*. London: Touchstone Books.

Levitt, Steven D. 2005. 'Making Profits from Incivility on the Roads', *New York Times* 18 November.

Levy, David 2008. 'Fire-Eaters and Stilt-Walkers booked for Christmas ... to stop drunks from fighting', *Daily Mail*, 17 December 2008.

Liska, Allen E. and Baccaglini, William 1990. 'Feeling Safe by Comparison: Crime in the Newspapers', *Social Problems* 37: 360–74.

Livingstone, Sonia and Markham, Tim 2008. 'The Contribution of Media Consumption to Civic Participation', *British Journal of Sociology* 59(2): 351–71.

Lofland, Lyn 1973. *A World of Strangers*. New York: Basic Books.

Long, J. Scott, and Freese, Jeremy 2006. *Regression Models for Categorical Dependent Variables Using Stata*, 2nd edn. College Station, TX: Stata Press.

Luo, Michael 2004. 'For Exercise in Futility, Push Button', *New York Times*, Region, 27 February.

Loukaitou-Sideris, Anastasia 1999. 'Hot Spots of Bus Stop Crime: The Importance of Environmental Attributes', *Journal of the American Planning Association* 65(4): 395–411.

Markowitz, Fred E., Bellair, Paul E., Liska, Allen E. and Liu, Jianhong 2001. 'Extending Social Disorganization Theory: Modelling the Relationships Between Cohesion, Disorder, and Fear,' *Criminology* 39: 293–320.

MayomingMaster 2005. 'Post in Reply to Question: Do you find you are more rude here?', accessed online 29 January 2009 at: www.shanghaiexpat.com/MDForum-viewtopic-t-36503.phtml.

Merry, Sally Engle 1981. *Urban Danger: Life in a Neighborhood of Strangers*. Philadelphia, PA: Temple University Press.

Messner, Steven F. and Tardiff, Kenneth 1985. 'The Social Ecology of Urban Homicide: An Application of the "Routine Activities" Approach', *Criminology* 23: 241–67.

Miethe, Terrence 1995. 'Fear and Withdrawal from Urban Life', *Annals of the American Academy of Political and Social Science* 539 (May): 14–27.

Miethe, Terrence D., Stafford, Mark C. and Long, J. Scott 1987. 'Social Differentiation in Criminal Victimization: A Test of Routine Activities/Lifestyle Theories', *American Sociological Review* 52: 184–94.

Millie, Andrew 2008. 'Anti-Social Behaviour, Behavioural Expectations and Urban Aesthetic', *British Journal of Criminology* 48(3): 379–94.

Milliman, Ronald E. 1982. 'Using Background Music to Affect the Behaviour of Supermarket Shoppers', *The Journal of Marketing* 46: 86–91.

Montezuma, Ricardo 2005. 'The Transformation of Bogota, Colombia, 1995–2000', *Global Urban Development Magazine* 1(1): 1–10.

Moy, Patricia and Scheufele, Dietram 2000. 'Media Effects on Social and Political Trust', *Journalism and Mass Communications Quarterly* 77(4): 744–59.

Mullins, Pat, Natalier, Kristin, Smith, Philip and Smeaton, Belinda 1999. 'Cities and Consumption Spaces', *Urban Affairs Review* 35(1): 44–71.

Mutz, Diana and Reeves, Byron 2004. 'Videomalaise Revisited: Effects of Television Incivility on Political Trust', *Journalism and Mass Communication Educator* Spring: 59/1.

Muzzatti, Stephen L. and Featherstone, Richard 2007. 'Crosshairs on Our Backs: The Culture of Fear and the Production of the D.C. Sniper Story', *Contemporary Justice Review* 10(1): 43–66.

Newman, Oscar 1972. *Defensible Space: Crime Prevention through Urban Design*. New York: Macmillan.

Norris, Pippa 1996. 'Does Television Erode Social Capital? A Reply to Putnam', *PS: Political Science and Politics* 29: 474–80.

Notes and Queries 2009. *The Guardian*, 15 April, section G2, p. 15.

Oregon Regional Intelligent Transportation Systems (ITS). 2003. Integration Program: Final Phase III Report: Transit Tracker Information Displays. Accessed online 5 March 2009 at: www.itsdocs.fhwa.dot.gov/JPODOCS/REPTS_TE/13938.html#_Toc54771535.

Paxton, Pamela 2007. 'Association Membership and Generalized Trust: A Multi-level Model Across 31 Countries', *Social Forces* 86(1): 47–76.

Phillips, Scott and Cooney, Mark 2005. 'Aiding Peace, Abetting Violence: Third Parties and the Management of Conflict', *American Sociological Review* 70: 334–54.

Phillips, Timothy 2006. 'Uncivil Relations with Strangers: How Individual People Reflect on a Commonplace Experience in Everyday Life', *Australian Journal of Social Issues* 41: 395–411.

Phillips, Timothy and Smith, Philip 2003. 'Everyday Incivility: Towards a Benchmark', *The Sociological Review* 51(1): 85–108.

2006a. 'Rethinking Urban Incivility Research: Strangers; Bodies and Circulations', *Urban Studies* 43(5–6): 879–901.

2006b. 'Collective Belonging and Mass Media Consumption: Unravelling How Technological Medium and Cultural Genre Shape the National Imaginings of Australians', *The Sociological Review* 54(4): 817–45.

Porath, Christine L. and Erez, Amir 2009. 'Overlooked but not Untouched: How Rudeness Reduces Onlooker's Performance on Routine and Creative Tasks', *Organizational Behaviour and Human Decision Process* 109: 29–44.

Pratt, John 2008. 'Scandinavian Exceptionalism in an Era of Penal Excess Part II: Does Scandinavian Exceptionalism have a Future?', *British Journal of Sociology* 48(3): 275–92.

Public Agenda 2002. *Aggravating Circumstances: A Status Report on Rudeness in America*. New York: Public Agenda.

2003. 'Push Comes to Shove: Passengers and Travel Workers Call Rudeness a Real Problem', *Public Agenda Press Release*, 18 December, New York.

Putnam, Robert 1995. 'Tuning In, Tuning Out: The Strange Disappearance of Social Capital in America', *PS: Political Science and Politics* 28: 664–83.

2000. *Bowling Alone*. New York: Simon & Schuster.

Reggio, Godfrey 1982. *Koyaanisqatsi*. IRE Productions.

Sacco, Vincent F., and Kennedy, Leslie W. 2002. *The Criminal Event: Perspectives in Space and Time*, 2nd edn. Belmont, CA: Wadsworth/ Thompson.

Safe, Mike 2000. 'All the Rage', *The Australian Magazine*, 29–30 January, pp. 18–23.

Salmi, Venla, Smoleg, Mirka and Kivivuori, Janne 2007. 'Crime Victimization, Exposure to Crime News and Social Trust among Adolescents', *Young* 15(3): 255–72.

Sampson, R., Morenoff, J. D. and Gannon-Rowley, T. 2002. 'Assessing Neighbourhood Effects: Social Process and New Directions in Research', *Annual Review of Sociology* 28: 443–78.

Sampson, R. and Raudenbush, S. W. 1999. 'Systematic Social Observation of Public Spaces: A New Look at Disorder in Urban Neighbourhoods', *American Journal of Sociology* 105(3): 603–51.

Sartre, Jean Paul 1987 [1944]. *Huis Clos*. London: Routledge.

Scheufele, Peter M. 2000. 'Effects of Progressive Relaxation and Classical Music on Measurements of Attention, Relaxation, and Stress Responses', *Journal of Behavioural Medicine* 23: 207–28.

Schwartz, Barry 1975. *Queuing and Waiting*. University of Chicago Press.

Schwartz, Richard D. and Orleans, Sonya 1967. 'On Legal Sanctions', *University of Chicago Law Review* 34: 274–300.

Scott, Michael S. 2001. 'Disorderly Youth in Public Places', *Center for Problem Oriented Policing*, accessed online 19 January 2009 at: www. popcenter.org/problems/disorderly_youth/1.

Sennett, Richard 1992. *The Fall of Public Man*. Oxford: Norton.

Shearing, Clifford D. and Stenning, Phillip C. 1984. 'From the Panopticon to Disney World', in A. Doob and E. Greenspan (eds.), *Perspectives in Criminal Law*. Toronto: Canada Law Book Inc.

Simmel, Georg 1997. 'The Metropolis and Mental Life', in D. Frisby and M. Featherstone (eds.), *Simmel on Culture*. London: Sage, pp. 174–85.

Singapore Expats 2007. Posts in reply to thread 'Expats, Do you think Singapore is that boring place?', accessed 16 May 2009 at: www. singaporeexpats.com/forum/ftopic44901.html&sid=de29c19b824e 0037d6b59b481f27d5b4.

Singer, Simon I. 1981. 'Homogeneous Victim–Offender Populations: A Review and Some Research Implications', *Journal of Criminal Law and Criminology* 72: 779–88.

Skogan, Wesley G. 1990. *Disorder and Decline*. New York: Free Press.

Skogan, Wesley G. and Hartnett, Susan 1997. *Community Policing, Chicago Style*. New York: Oxford University Press.

Skogan, Wesley G. and Maxfield, Michael G. 1981. *Coping with Crime: Individual and Neighborhood Reactions*. Beverley Hills, CA: Sage.

Smith, Philip and Phillips, Timothy 2004. 'Emotional and Behavioural Responses to Everyday Incivility: Challenging the Fear/Avoidance Paradigm', *Journal of Sociology* 40(4): 378–99.

South, Scott J. and Messner, Steven F. 1986. 'Structural Determinants of Intergroup Association: Interracial Marriage and Crime', *American Journal of Sociology* 91: 1409–30.

Spiegel Online. 2006. 'Germany's Fairy Tale Come True', 6 June, retrieved online 25 March 2009 at: www.spiegel.de/international/spiegel/0,1518,422401,00.html.

Spierenberg, Pieter 1984. *The Spectacle of Suffering*. Cambridge University Press.

Spitzer, Eliot 1999. *The New York City Police Department's 'Stop and Frisk' Practices: A Report to the People of the State of New York from the Office of the Attorney General*. New York: Office of Attorney General.

Sykes, Gresham 1958. *Society of Captives*. Princeton University Press.

Taylor, Ralph B. 2000. 'The Incivilities Thesis: Theory, Measurement and Policy', in R. H. Langworth (ed.), *Measuring What Matters*. Washington, DC: National Institute of Justice/Office of Community Oriented Policing Services, pp. 65–8.

Taylor, Ralph B. and Hale, Margaret 1986. 'Testing Alternative Models of Fear of Crime', *Journal of Criminal Law and Criminology* 77: 151–89.

Thaler, Richard H. and Sunstein, Cass R. 2008. *Nudge: Improving Decisions about Health, Wealth and Happiness*. New Haven, CT: Yale University Press.

The Quiet Zone 2002. 'Preserve the Peace', Winter, 2–7.

Thompson, S. C. 1981. 'Will it Hurt Less if I Can Control It? A Complex Answer to a Simple Question', *Psychological Bulletin* 90: 89–101.

Times Square Alliance 2005. 'Problems and Possibilities: Re-imagining the Pedestrian Environment in Times Square', retrieved online 12 January 2009, at: http://timessquarenyc.org/facts/documents/Problems_and_Possibilities_sm.pdf.

Totten, Jim and Karol, Kristofer 2008. 'Brighton OKs Annoyance Ordinance', *Daily Press and Argus*, 21 December 2008.

Truss, Lynne 2005 *Talk to the Hand: The Utter Bloody Rudeness of the World Today*. New York: Gotham.

Tyler, Tom R. 1990. *Why People Obey the Law*. New Haven, CT: Yale University Press.

Uggen, Christopher, and Blackstone, Amy 2004. 'Sexual Harassment as a Gendered Expression of Power', *American Sociological Review* 69: 64–92.

Updegraff, John A., Cohen Silver, Roxanne and Holman, E. Alison 2008. 'Searching for and Finding Meaning in Collective Trauma: Results From a National Longitudinal Study of the 9/11 Terrorist Attacks', *Journal of Personality and Social Psychology* 95(3): 709–22.

Urry, John 2000. 'Mobile Sociology', *British Journal of Sociology* 51(1): 185–203.

2004. 'The System of Automobility', *Theory, Culture and Society* 21(4–5): 25–39.

van Dijk, Jan, van Kesteren, John and Smit, Paul 2007. *Criminal Victimization in International Perspective*. The Hague: Wetenschappelijk Onderzoeken Documentatiecentrum, accessed online 8 March 2009 at: http://rechten.uvt.nl/icvs/pdffiles/ICVS2004_05.pdf.

Village Voice 2008. 'Best Reason to be Rude to a Stranger', accessed online 28 January 2009 at: www.villagevoice.com/bestof/2008/award/best-reason-to-be-rude-to-a-stranger-691042.

Virilio, Paul 1986. *Speed and Politics*. New York: Semiotext(e).

Vitale, Alex S. 2008. *City of Disorder: How the Quality of Life Campaign Transformed New York Politics*. New York University Press.

Walby, Sylvia and Myhill, Andrew 2001. 'New Survey Methodologies in Researching Violence Against Women', *British Journal of Criminology* 41(3): 502–22.

Warr, M. 1994. 'Public Perceptions and Reactions to Violent Offending Victimization', in A. Reiss and J. Roth (eds.), *Consequences and Control*. Washington DC: National Academies Press, pp. 1–66.

Western Australia Planning Commission 2006. '*Designing out Crime Planning Guidelines*', Perth, Australia.

Wilson, James Q. and Kelling, George L. 1982. 'Broken Windows', *Atlantic Monthly* 211: 29–38. Also available online at: www.theatlantic.com/doc/198203/broken-windows.

Winner, Michael 1974. *Deathwish*. Dino de Laurentis Pictures.

Wober, J. M. 1979. 'Comments and Letters: Televised Violence and Viewer Perceptions of Reality', *Public Opinion Quarterly* 43(2): 271–73.

Woodward, Ian 1998. 'The Shopping Mall, Postmodern Space and Architectural Practice. Theorising the Postmodern Spatial Turn Through the Planning Discourse of Mall Architects', *Architectural Theory Review* 3(2): 46–58.

2003. 'Divergent Narratives in the Imagining of the Home Among Middle Class Consumers', *Journal of Sociology* 39(4): 391–412.

Woodward, Ian and Emmison, Michael 2001. 'From Aesthetic Principles to Collective Sentiments: The Logics of Everyday Judgements of Taste', *Poetics* 29(6): 295–316.

Wright, Edmond 2005. *Narrative, Perception, Language and Faith*. London: Palgrave Macmillan.

Yardley, William 2007. 'No Cutting in Line for Puget Sound Ferries, Under Penalty of Law', *New York Times*, 11 April.

Index